HEALING
FROM THE WAR

HEALING
FROM THE WAR

TRAUMA AND TRANSFORMATION
AFTER VIETNAM

☆

Arthur Egendorf

Boston
HOUGHTON MIFFLIN COMPANY
1985

Copyright © 1985 by Arthur Egendorf

Library of Congress Cataloging in Publication Data
Egendorf, Arthur.
Healing from the war.
Bibliography: p.
1. Vietnamese Conflict, 1961–1975 — United States.
2. Vietnamese Conflict, 1961–1975 — Psychological
aspects. 3. Veterans — United States. I. Title.
DS558.E34   1985   959.704'33'73   85-11801
ISBN 0-395-37701-3

Printed in the United States of America

P 10 9 8 7 6 5 4 3 2 1

The author gratefully acknowledges permission to reprint previously
published materials:
From *The Cat's Cradle* by Kurt Vonnegut, Jr. Copyright © 1963 by Kurt Vonnegut, Jr.
Reprinted by permission of Delacorte Press/Seymour Lawrence.
Excerpts from Homer's *The Odyssey* translated by Robert Fitzgerald.
Copyright © 1961 by Robert Fitzgerald. Reprinted by permission
of Doubleday & Company, Inc.
From *Dispatches* by Michael Herr. Copyright © 1977 by Michael Herr.
Reprinted by permission of Alfred A. Knopf, Inc., a division of Random House, Inc.
From *This Is It and Other Essays on Zen and Spiritual Experience* by Alan W. Watts.
Copyright © 1958, 1960 by Alan W. Watts. Reprinted by permission of Pantheon Books,
a division of Random House, Inc.
From *Opus Posthumous* by Wallace Stevens, edited by Samuel French Morse.
Copyright © 1957 by Wallace Stevens. Reprinted by permission of Alfred A. Knopf, Inc.,
a divison of Random House, Inc.
From *The Odyssey: A Modern Sequel* by Nikos Kazantzakis. Copyright © 1958
by Simon and Schuster, Inc. Reprinted by permission of Simon and Schuster, Inc.
From *The Saviors of God: Spiritual Exercises* by Nikos Kazantzakis.
Copyright © 1960 by Simon and Schuster, Inc. Reprinted by
permission of Simon and Schuster, Inc.
From *The Warriors: Reflections on Men in Battle* by J. Glenn Gray (Harper & Row),
copyright © 1959 by J. Glenn Gray.
Reprinted by permission of Ursula A. Gray.

Contents

Preface ix

Introduction 1

1. Coming Back 15

2. Retracing Steps 45

3. Getting Involved 75

4. Digging Inside 109

5. Reaching Bottom 137

6. Turning It Around 171

7. Mastering Everyday Life 207

8. Transforming Warriors 247

Appendix:
Suggestions for Healing Action 283

Acknowledgments 297

Notes 299

Index 317

We are healed from suffering only by experiencing it
to the full.

MARCEL PROUST

All the clever thoughts have long since been thought.
What matters is to think them anew.

GOETHE

Author's Note

The names and identifying characteristics of my therapy clients, lovers, and friends have been altered, with the exception of those who have granted permission to be quoted directly.

Preface

Healing is the way we restore ourselves. To help spread healing from the suffering of war, this book consists of vignettes I hope will inspire others. The focus is mainly on veterans, people I know from doing research and psychotherapy with them. I refer to one veteran in particular because he's the one I know best, myself.

Healing is also an art, whose mastery comes through practice and rigorous dialogue with fellow practitioners — all those who would heal themselves and help others do the same. To contribute to this dialogue, that is, to aid others in tapping their own sources of healing, I also include in each chapter reflections on the healing work I've done.

This book, then, is a duet played by two facets of myself, by the seeker of healing and by the one who offers healing. The writing shifts between story and reflection, which allows you to read one or both according to your own taste and interest.

The structure of the book is intended to convey a crucial point. Rather than think of healing as a process, I see it occur in special moments, discontinuously, and not in a smooth flow. Appreciating this point enables people to recognize that any and every moment can be a profound opportunity for their lives. And so, in accord with the nature of healing, each chapter focuses on a different instant and consists of a series of episodes, personal and reflective, strung together like an extended meditation.

The moral of the stories and the theme of the reflections are the same: With a little help from our friends, we can heal ourselves, even from war.

To those who serve

Introduction

WHAT DOES IT MEAN to heal from war? What does it take? These are the questions this book addresses, but without offering solutions in any ordinary sense. Answers don't heal; people do. We open ourselves to healing by asking repeatedly the kinds of questions that raise it as a possibility. And so healing unfolds as a personal quest, the kind of deep inquiry that we devote our lives to. The purpose of this book is to invite you to ask key questions for yourself, to make the quest your own.

Why healing? Because the suffering goes on, and not just among veterans. Americans at home fought one another over the war in Vietnam, often with more venom than was unleashed by our soldiers in battle. Both the domestic battles and the fighting in Vietnam left deep gashes that haven't yet closed.

Almost 120,000 American mothers and fathers have known the pain of losing a son to an early, violent death in Vietnam, a pain familiar to many more sisters, brothers, wives, lovers, friends, and children. Wounds of another sort came home with the hundreds of thousands of Americans who were physically disabled. Most of these men returned to family and friends who were glad to have them, regardless of the shape they were in, but who have had to bear their share of the agony in the years since. For the wounded, and for the families of those killed or disabled, the worst pain of all was the doubt raised about the value and worth of the cause for which they suffered.

The ripple effects extend even further. After coordinating and participating in veteran rap groups from 1970 to 1974, I helped organize a group of sociologists, psychiatrists, and psychologists to investigate the extent of psychological problems among the men of the Vietnam generation. From 1977 to 1979, we conducted face to face interviews, lasting three to five hours, with each of fourteen hundred men who had grown up during the war years. We chose equal numbers of veterans and their nonveteran peers, contacted through telephoning people at random in the urban and suburban sections of Atlanta, Los Angeles, Chicago, and New York, and in rural areas near these cities.

Our work culminated in the congressionally mandated report of 1981, *Legacies of Vietnam*.[1] Certain of our findings have been quoted widely in the national media. For instance, we found that a substantial minority of combat vets across the country reported symptoms severe enough to be called a disorder. Many more, about half of all Vietnam veterans, were still suffering from less acute forms of distress — almost two million men struggling to avoid unsettling emotions, blaming their pain on others, or diminishing themselves through self-punishment and self-pity.[2]

After studying hundreds of our interviews I was struck by a fact that is usually overlooked. Every troubled veteran comes into daily contact with many other people — family, friends, co-workers, and children — whose lives become infected with the unresolved pain. Since the suffering is most acute among the readily identified minority of men who actually fought, public and professional attention focuses on "postcombat" trauma. But the difficulty experienced by troubled vets is only a fraction of the long-term cost to American society. The toll includes the life-squelching bitterness, resentment, and resignation among the lovers, spouses, friends, and relatives who feel stuck with veterans whose suffering doesn't stop.

Troubling vestiges of the war are also present among people who had no direct contact with Vietnam or with people who served there. Compared with the toll on veterans and their families, the burdens that linger among people who didn't fight are so much less dramatic that almost nobody mentions them. In absolute numbers, however, there are many more men who didn't serve, men who "got off" through the lottery or by making fateful decisions during the war years that rendered them ineligible. A few refused military service outright, acting on deep and abiding conviction. But many others who objected to the war and to national policies used their objections as reason to compromise themselves. Many falsely portrayed themselves as sick, crazy, or otherwise infirm to avoid unpleasant and dangerous duties.

In recent years, a few of these men have said publicly that they drew on fashion, fear, and youthful prankishness to take what seemed the easy way out.[3] Their confessions are helpful, but full healing calls for something more. During the years of protest, millions of the most gifted men and women of the largest American generation in history saw greater virtue in proclaiming, "Hell no! I won't go!" then in vowing, "Yes! Count on me!" Years later, many of these people still talk cynically about their lives and the world, as if committed to the ideal of no commitment. Over and over in our interviews, men who came of age during the war years complained about unsatisfying relationships, unfulfilling jobs, lackluster national leaders, and the loss of idealism. To many, these disappointments justify their inaction in the public sphere, and so they focus on narrow interests and neglect the needs of the communities where they live and work. They are resigned to a sense of impotence about themselves and to deep resentment toward those whose beliefs differ from their own. A healing question for them to ask is what it would take to increase their options, so that saying "Yes!" to serving others could become a self-respecting choice.

Another large minority of Americans are still embittered not because they questioned the war and our national integrity but because we lost. They believe that we let ourselves get pushed around, or that we were sold out at home. Although these people may cheer our recent military actions abroad and the revival of patriotism at home, cheerfulness is not the same as healing. Ask them about Vietnam and their unresolved resentment comes through. Many of these people have avoided confronting our failures in the war and the humbling experience of learning something new by maintaining an antagonistic posture. For them the war still rages.

To the extent that people fail to embrace healing, old hurts rather than good judgment govern behavior. This principle applies to our leaders as much as to the rest of us. One form the old hurt can take is neoisolationism, the tendency of national policy makers to try to avoid the mistakes of Vietnam by objecting to involvements anywhere else. The idea is that since our intervention went wrong in

Vietnam, we shouldn't intervene anywhere again, for any reason.

Another, more fashionable impulse is to equate national strength with military might. A large constituency applauds the most inflated peacetime military budget in history — as if we could redeem our loss of national stature by flexing technological muscle. Our more sophisticated strategists recognize this as pure defensiveness, which is inherently self-defeating. But as a people we have not yet regained the capacity to distinguish between living the principles of freedom and trying to impose our ways on others through threat or use of force. Our nation has acted in recent years with the pettiness and pugnacity of a threatened bully, rather than with our more traditional generosity and breadth of spirit.

Healing is the way to renew our quest for greatness as a people. Only through healing can we reverse the trend of the past decade, when every Third World trouble spot rekindled the fires of Vietnam-era controversy here at home. American foreign policy experts complain that our difficulties abroad stem from another of the so-called casualties of Vietnam, the loss of a bipartisan consensus on how to conduct relations with other countries.[4] The simple but seldom-noted truth is that there will be no consensus so long as we fail to create one. A consensus has to develop authentically, and for this to happen we must nurture a sense of common purpose.

It is the American spirit, therefore, that most needs to heal — a job open to anyone willing to take it on. Healing of this scale calls us to ask ourselves anew: What does it mean to be an American? What are we contributing to a world in which instant communication is ushering in a global age? What are we giving to a humanity threatened by ecological disaster and nuclear holocaust? And what are we bringing to an international arena in which the demands of newly independent nations call for an unprecedented degree of wisdom from established powers?

These questions make more sense after we ask the more fundamental question: What does it mean to be human? Asking this question is a powerful act, for it opens the possibility that each of us can contribute to humanity by the way we respond, by the way we go about our lives. By asking this question of ourselves we become better prepared to ask it of each other, and when we clarify together what we offer to the world, rather than what we expect from it, then we will appreciate anew our contribution as a people.

And so healing from the war, a vast collective task, begins with and comes back to you and me. It is our challenge, or it is nobody's. I convey what I know about it here by writing about myself and other veterans, recognizing as I do that stories about veterans often serve as parables.

Unfortunately for the cause of healing, we have so far been rather shortsighted in speaking about the veteran experience. We talk about vets in pain, or about those who have made it, in much the same divisive tone as we express our dovish and hawkish sympathies. To one point of view, troubled veterans prove how awful the war was, whereas successful veterans confirm for others that the cause was noble and that those who still complain simply lack the moral and patriotic fiber to succeed.[5]

Something in the veteran experience speaks profoundly to our widespread need for healing. But we won't hear the message until we study more closely the reality that ex-soldiers have lived through, to discern what we have missed until now.

If you look, it's not hard to find veterans who are engaged in healing. I met one of them eight years ago while visiting a VA hospital. His name was Jim, an ex-Marine from the Bronx recovering from his latest breakdown, back for another of the hospital visits that began a year after he returned from Vietnam. I introduced myself as a fellow vet, now a psychologist, who wanted to interview him for a study that would help Vietnam vets.

"You want to help me?" he asked. "For six years I've been in and out of this hospital and I've heard enough of shrink talk. I want to know how you made it. That's how to help me. Tell me how did you get it together?"

I responded by making him an offer. If he would let me interview him, he could ask me anything he wanted. He accepted and spent ten hours telling me his story. Before the war he was the kind of youngster teachers like. He behaved well in class and worked part-time after school. During his teens he had seen a psychiatrist for "nerves," but generally had held his own. In 1969, when he was eighteen, Jim was drafted and goaded into "volunteering" for the Marines, then sent to combat duty in Vietnam. He saw action in I Corps, in the north of South Vietnam.

Ever since he came back, his mother and his wife had been trying to tell him that something was wrong. For the first year all he did was stay in the apartment, smoke dope, and listen to music. Then one day while looking out the window he saw a junkie trying to steal the radio from his car. Jim grabbed a baseball bat, ran after him, and started pounding the guy so fiercely it took three people to tear him away. After that he knew he was out of control and went for help.

Seven years after coming back, Jim described his burdens this way: "Before I went, I worked for six years. I was the best assistant manager Martin's Bargain Store ever had. I can't work now. They messed up my head. How the hell are you supposed to concentrate after all I've been through? Reality sucks. It's not what you know, it's who you know. That's why a nineteen-year-old acidhead or college guy gets out of it. Who do I know? My shrink from before the war said I was fine. Now the VA says I was always cockoo and my problem's got nothing to do with the war. My wife is scared of me. My family thinks I'm nuts. We were supposed to be over there fighting for freedom, killing people who never did us any harm. What are you supposed to do after that?"

I listened, particularly to what was left unsaid. He had just started to find some direction in life when the war crashed in. Then it was "pussy," as his drill instructors called him, and thirteen months of being constantly threatened with death, and seeing a dozen guys he knew pulverized into heaps of bloody flesh. Others made fun of him, mocking a grunt from New York who resented the practice of calling Vietnamese "slopes" or "dinks" or "gooks." And when the time came to go home and he looked forward to leaving the mess behind, he found that things didn't work as he expected. After coming back he wasn't anybody's hero, the afterimages of shattering brutality stayed fixed in his mind, and the business-as-usual reality at home had no room for what he carried inside.

For Jim and many like him, it was not them but the world that was crazy. What was keeping all of it from blowing up, just like the people and places he had seen "wasted"? Presidents give the orders and people die. It's like a primitive ritual with human sacrifices to bloodthirsty gods. Jim was sure about only one thing: The people pulling the strings didn't care what happened to him.

"How'd you get it together? That's what I want to know," he kept asking. Our backgrounds were different, but the war gave us a common bond. Jim was a ghetto kid who didn't finish high school before entering the service, whereas I had gone to private school, Harvard,

and then Europe for a year of postgraduate study before my draft board notified me. Unlike him, I never saw a psychotherapist while growing up and was never seriously upset until after I came back, and then never so bad that I couldn't go to school and hold a job, too. All the same, he knew. "Something got to you too, huh?"

He tested me to see if I'd open up with him. "People like you go into psychology to straighten themselves out, right?" Yes, I told him, he was right about that. After years of taking pills and hearing therapists interpret his past and try to modify his behavior, Jim wanted to "relate." It was the same hunger that led a dozen of us to form the veteran rap groups that began meeting in New York City in 1970. In these groups we had asked each other and the therapists who volunteered to assist us in gaining the same openness Jim now wanted.

After a few meetings Jim asked to be a regular client. At the beginning he couldn't take much — he would miss appointments and "forget" to return my phone calls. Eventually, though, we met more regularly, and he began to thrive on the questions I raised.

What had gotten to him? What was so troubling? What made him so vulnerable? What was he going to do about it now? How was he going to handle his life? I didn't intend for him to answer my questions the way elementary pupils answer their teacher's drill. Rather, the idea was for him to use the questions to orient himself, to direct his energies where the questioning pointed. It was time for Jim to stop telling the same story over and over and to begin living out a new one.

The more we worked together, the more he saw opportunities to make himself useful — a gesture that would help his wife, an odd job to pick up some cash, a game he could play with his kids. He studied himself enough to distinguish his sensitive reactions from his deluded flights of fancy. And when he was ready, he acknowledged that his suffering would never make sense on its own. It would only be valuable if he took it as a lesson, something he could use to remind himself that how he handles his life is up to him.

After a few months of groundwork, Jim was out of the VA for good. Then he got off tranquilizers and stayed away from pot. In the next year, he and his wife stopped fighting and started talking, and soon after that he was holding a job for the first time since he left the Marines. Two years after we began meeting he bought his own house and was holding down two jobs. Instead of complaining about his two kids, *which is all he had done when we first met, he'd brag about them.*

The time came when he raised a more ambitious question. Given his suffering and what he'd learned, what purpose would he devote himself to? "People, I want to do something for people," he'd say. One of his dreams was to save enough money to start a summer camp for ghetto kids. In the meantime, he began seeing the people in his daily life as the ones to serve.

Jim still has bad days and times when his kids get to him, but he no longer doubts that his life is workable, which gives him a certainty that makes him proud. He's especially happy about the way men who live on his street now listen to him. "They figure I must know something after all I've been through. They ask me how they can straighten themselves out." He volunteers at the local Outreach office for veterans, run by the Veterans Administration. "If a high school dropout ex-cuckoo like me can do it, anybody can."

"How did you do it?" was the question Jim kept asking. I knew he wouldn't be satisfied with some formula or set of rules. He wanted me to open up, to make it safe for him to open up to himself and to me. And so I told him about myself, but not to give him know-how. I simply related bits of my story as they became relevant. For example, I told him how sensitive I was when I came back. At first, little things would get to me. I'd be overwhelmed by seeing a dead dog lying on a highway, or the picture of a mourning woman in a magazine, or newspaper listings of the soldiers just killed. Strangers halfway around the world, especially dead ones, seemed closer to me than anyone had ever been except my family and one or two lovers.

I also told him about how I threw myself into issues connected with the war. Before Vietnam I had read newspapers casually. In the months and first years after coming back I would tear into the pages to see what new horrors I needed to absorb and to find out which people in high places I would cheer that day and which ones I would scream at during the hours I spent raging in my head. I was more deeply moved by tenderness than at any time in my life, and I was also more easily angered. I'd write scathing letters to editors, congressmen, and the President. I'd blurt out slogans to old friends and family, who didn't know how to talk with me anymore.

I didn't tell Jim only about matters that weighed me down. I made sure to tell him some things that were hard to admit to myself at first, things I needed guts to say, but once said would leave me feeling lighter. I told him it wasn't just the pain that had surprised me; I had also begun to catch glimmers of some secret joy. I was happy I had made it through the war when others didn't, which was hard to acknowledge. But something else delighted me even more. Strangely, I was glad to feel so much hurt, as if having allowed something to tear me open meant that one day I would give birth to something I might treasure.

Jim would compare himself to me and decide that I was so much better off that I had to know something that made life easy. So I also let him know about my awkwardness — the many times I flip-flopped back and forth, from wallowing in my distress to trying to hide from it. But I also told him I learned more from my mistakes and weaknesses than from anything else. In fact, my about-faces, in which neither wallowing in the pain nor turning my back on it satisfied me, eventually led me to the realization that I was searching for a third way. I couldn't say what it was at first, but I figured somebody had to know or there wouldn't be such people as counselors and therapists. They must know, I thought, and so, hungering to find out what they knew and daring to think I'd know too once I joined their ranks, I took a job as a crisis counselor.

Jim grasped the irony of my story. Contrary to what he had initially thought, I wasn't useful to him because of any information I had. What I had to offer lay in my willingness to admit that I don't have anything in particular to tell people until I hear them talk. I'm willing to be with them without answers, so that I can assist them with their own search. I told Jim that I'm as surprised as anyone when this works. The moment someone trusts me enough to tell me his troubles a change takes place in me. I suddenly have more wisdom for them than I usually have for myself. I listen, make comments, and, without having to think or plan in advance, ask questions they find helpful.

In the end, what Jim accomplished by being with me wasn't new information to pass along, something he could go out and tell someone else. He developed an approach to life that transformed his experience of the war from a burden to an opportunity for healing. The shift happened as a result of our being together and by our pursuing a joint quest that fostered trust, respect, appreciation, and the openness that is healing in itself.

Most crucial is the openness. I've noticed this not only with Jim but with hundreds of others I've worked with since, and with dozens of therapists I've trained. In this book I intend to convey what I mean by openness, in such a way that healing from war dawns as a possibility for you.

Usually people think of healing as a process to go through: start with a wound or an affliction, and bit by bit it mends. Healing as I mean it here, however, is not something to be undergone so much as a way to be, a way that emerges by reaching beyond whatever is piecemeal and fragmentary and finding a unitary and all-encompassing ground.[6] Concretely this means that healing unfolds through engaging our experience as a whole, rather than analyzing things in bits and pieces or specifying causes, effects, and categories. In healing, we pass up analytical talk or interesting commentary, as when we ask ourselves: What was that experience like? What does it mean? And what will I carry away from it?[7]

The nature of healing, then, is holistic, which you can readily observe by looking back on the healing that has already taken place. Look thoroughly and you'll see that the whole of your life has participated in bringing it about, just as your whole life is enhanced with each step you take.

Healing occurs most prominently at the breakthrough points we associate with the shifts in perspective that come with "aha!" experiences, insights, or openings to new possibilities for living. Since each of these instants occurs at a different point in personal and shared history, people think that the *sequence* of these experiences is fundamental and that healing is an ongoing, continuous flow. But if you observe closely, you'll notice the discontinuity; each healing breakthrough occurs as a distinct moment. And yet, each such moment returns us to the core phenomenon. What draws us, over and over, is not some particular next step in a process so much as the ultimate source of healing — the opening within ourselves that comes as the ecstatic release that moves us on our way. Healing as a way of being means returning repeatedly to this fundamental ground, thereby multiplying our perspectives, enriching our appreciation, and widening our access to what is essential.

Regardless of what we think and say about breakthrough points, the experience each time is quite singular. It is a sense of expansiveness and relief. The feeling in our bodies may or may not come with a clear thought; but whether it does or not, and no matter what the thought is, an underlying intuition occurs as well. It is the at least implicit dawning of possibility, which we hadn't noticed a moment before. With this emerging sense we can say that each healing moment brings openness, which hints, when it doesn't announce outright, that the challenges in front of us are workable.

In using this experience as our reference, we can see that healing occurs through opening ourselves to possibilities implicit in life as it is and not by struggling to get through, beyond, or to the other side of whatever distresses us. To view healing in this way frees us from the widespread assumption that humans grow by striving to get ahead. As we recognize that new possibilities spring from embracing things as they are, we no longer need to fight with others or ourselves to get to some imagined "better place." And we no longer need to condemn others or ourselves for not being there already. Healing, as a way to be, is the supreme antidote to war and to inner battles as well.

I don't deny that movement and change are constants in our lives, or that human aspiration will always be with us. But by conducting ourselves in a healing way, we can fulfill our aspirations, not by goading ourselves and others to change our environment, each other, and ourselves, but by allowing change to unfold from a more fundamental striving. Once committed to healing, we no longer reach for some new vantage point beyond where we are now, but for the openness that is the ground from which any new creation arises.

Rather than offering step-by-step instructions or lists of "stages," this book is a series of invitations, for you to be healing for yourself. Each of the eight chapters opens a distinct perspective on healing from war that I draw out in autobiographical, psychological, historical, mythical, and philosophical terms. My purpose is not to "do" these disciplines but to be healing — using these various terms to flesh out what it means to heal from war.

One of the points I make in several ways is that healing, engaged in fully, transforms our relationship with horror. What is horror, exactly? What horrifies us most? Trauma and stress are the usual answers given with regard to veterans. But as I try to show in chapters 1 through 5, terms like these don't reveal the essence of it. Many of us experienced horror over the war in Vietnam when we concluded that no political or ideological rationale could justify violence on that scale. The horror grew for those of us who acknowledged our personal complicity in the wrongs. The pain was most intense for those who saw that we had gone to war out of personal blindness — that we gave ourselves to violence to retaliate against past hurts, and that we craved glory to dispel doubts about our worth.

Creating ways to understand our personal role in the horror reduces its pain. After searching for individual motives we may turn to metaphysical insights. Some of us, for example, realized how we had been tempted by the delusion that swept up generations of soldiers before us — that by going to war we had enacted the lusty fantasy of buying immortality by shedding other people's blood. Even this interpretation, however, does not make the pain go away altogether. Nothing we say about the horror we've perpetrated or witnessed can tame it completely.

In chapters 5 and 6 I note that understanding alone is insufficient to relieve suffering. For now it is enough to assert that at the core of the worst horror — in war or elsewhere — is the stark confrontation with nothingness, with the utter absence of anything to stand on or provide security for us or for the world we call home.

The most thorough kind of healing emerges when we embrace the pain of facing nothingness. Ultimately what we confront at that point is ourselves, and how limitlessly and unendingly we are able to care. If war has spurred us to such self-revelation, we may acknowledge its horrors as potential crucibles for the soul. Surely people needn't go to war to learn about caring. And going to war is no guarantee that anyone will put the experience to good use. It is by no means the best or most efficient way for people to wake up. But for those who do, healing ultimately comes through claiming the extraordinary sensibility that can blossom after surviving the worst.

Healing culminates in a renewed vision of what is possible — for us and for our world. In the light of this vision, our individual healing shifts from being the center of attention to an instance of a much more encompassing possibility: healing from war for all of humanity.

Delivering humanity from war is an ancient dream that has particular relevance for us now, for what was once only a prophet's hope has become a practical necessity. Many of the most pragmatic futurists foresee in the next century a worldwide community in which warfare is obsolete.[8] Clearly, this world community can emerge only from a cultural transformation as far-reaching as those that transcended cannibalism and slavery.

The healing that a soldier knows can shed special light on what this transformation requires. Anybody whose chest ever swelled under a starched uniform or who felt goose bumps marching past the flag knows the energy and spirit that have fueled every great campaign in history. It is the warrior within and among us that we call upon to do the impossible, to serve life when life itself depends on it. And world healing points to the greatest campaign ever: creating a world culture in which warfare is outmoded. Skeptics call it preposterous; proponents know that it calls for a warrior's devotion.

And so it is not just the warrior in us that cries out for healing, but healing that summons the warrior. Healing from war is no tenderhearted pursuit. It is a way to serve that begins when we say "Yes! Count on me!" and thereby court risks of the most fateful disasters, as the soldier does when charging into battle. It is a call for transformed warriorship, in which the virtues of courage, commitment, and care are dedicated to a cause beyond war — a commitment inspired not by blind faith, glory, or physical daring, but by the vision that comes with opening our hearts.

Such visions alone don't alter the stark realities we face. The antagonisms among nuclear superpowers and among scores of militarist cliques and their violent challengers make our time the most dangerous in history. For a generation, the best military minds have declared that nuclear weapons have already made warfare outmoded. And yet the spread of "liberation wars" and the proliferation of nuclear weaponry increase the risk that accident, miscalculation, or maniacal whimsy could ignite all of life in the last human holocaust. This is the historic context in which the Vietnam War took place and why it loomed so menacing. And it is this same context that healing must ultimately address.

Very few people have direct influence on the decision makers in the White House, the Kremlin, and in the command posts on either side of the dozens of "hot" conflicts now unfolding around the world.

For most of us the greatest power we exert on the course of humanity is in how we choose to live our lives. That is the one vote that nobody can take away from us and that registers unmistakably wherever we go and whatever we do. To live our everyday lives out of a vision of human possibility does not require action in the usual sense, but a widened way of being, a presence in which the possibilities we envisage are embodied in whatever we say and do — not someday in the future, but here, now.

At the end of his book about Vietnam veterans written more than a decade ago, Robert Lifton asked, "The warrior in us will hardly disappear, but are we not capable of mobilizing that 'warrior'-self on behalf of the special illumination made possible by our dreadful and strangely hopeful historical moment?"[9] A question like this can be answered only with deeds that lift our spirits, acts such as those I report in the later chapters of this book. Once we know where to look, we find many signs that point the way to transforming warriors.

As I write, soldiers are dying in the Middle East and in Central America, where U.S. policy is strained in ways that are familiar to those who knew our situation in Indochina. Young men and women are also fighting in regions of Europe, Africa, and South Asia, while in Indochina the orgy of blood and pain enters its fifth decade. Those who survive these conflicts will be marked in ways we cannot foresee, yet I am certain that many will eventually find their way to asking what it takes to heal from their war.

In the meantime, Americans have not finished with Vietnam. This book is for those who served, for the people around them who want to help, and for the men and women who lived through the war at home and who know that the suffering is not over. It is a tribute to Jim and to the many like him who let me have a hand in their lives, my way of saying thanks.

COMING BACK

The soldier must form a soldier's habits, learn to be proud as a soldier, learn to live, eat, sleep, dress, bathe as a soldier, adjust his sex life to the soldier's necessities. He is thereby unfit for civilian life.

WILLARD WALLER[1]

THE SOLDIER'S JOURNEY back from war is an old story. Almost three thousand years ago, Greek poets sang about a great warrior-hero named Odysseus. He was the most cunning of the Greek generals at the siege of Troy, the one who infiltrated the fortress city by hiding soldiers inside a wooden horse. For this "wiliest of men," the way home took twenty years. Before his journey was over, he lost all his comrades, matched wits with dangerous goddesses, battled one-eyed monsters and vengeful storm kings, and suffered a passage through hell. Today we regard such myths as metaphors for a person's inner journey, meaning, at least in one sense, that not much has changed in several millennia. As many veterans put it, after Vietnam the biggest hassle was the one in their head.

What makes coming back so hard? Many say they didn't know what they had been through until after they had left, as if coming home makes whatever they've left behind far more vivid than it was up close. Some people seem to walk away from misery, pain, killing, and death with no aftereffects, but veterans who haven't had it so easy are skeptical. "Wait and see," they say, implying that there's more to the journey than the physical return. "It'll come back to them," they say.

What do they mean? What's the "it"? The war? Memories? What is this "coming back"?

When I came back from the war, I didn't expect my year in Vietnam to be more than just another experience, a slice of cheese in a thick life sandwich, as I had said once with a swagger. On April 11, 1969, I flew back to the States, to Oakland from Tan Son Nhut. To get some breath-

ing room, I spent a couple of nights in San Francisco before going home to Philadelphia. I slept for two days. When I got up, I noticed little things, like the free shampoo in the hotel, free shoe polish, and even a souvenir shoe-polishing cloth with the hotel name on it. God-damn decadent, I thought. I'd just been through something, and having it soft so suddenly was hard to take.

My parents met me at the airport in Philadelphia. After walking from the plane, I kissed my mother's cheek and shook my father's hand. "What are your plans now, son?" he asked. Finish my last year in the Army, then go back to Europe and continue studying international economics, I said. I didn't know what else to say. They didn't know what else to ask.

A few nights later I had dinner with Maggie and Hank, the parents of Spee, my best friend through high school and college. Since high school, Maggie and Hank's house had been my home away from home. She was always warm to me, and when I was in high school, I thought of Hank as the ideal father. He was brawny, funny, and would drink and talk dirty in front of us.

During the meal, a few of the other guests were discussing a new book, Portnoy's Complaint, *about a Jewish guy who beat off a lot and hated his mother. Nobody was talking about it as literature. The point of the conversation was one I had heard many times, beginning with the Rosenbergs' spy trial eighteen years before. "Don't you think this gets a bad name for the Jews?" Sitting across from Maggie and Hank, all I could think was halfway around the world guys are dying so these people can talk about whether some book gets Jews a bad name.*

Hank could tell I was getting annoyed. He leaned over the table and asked, "How was the stuff over there?"

I forced a smile.

"Lost your sense of humor in the war, boy?" he asked, ribbing me.

"You'd lose yours too if you saw what we're doing with your tax money." Hank owned a string of pawn shops and had lots of banker friends. He wasn't big on social programs or high taxes. During World War II he had been in the Army Air Force in North Africa and still had a "rough and ready" attitude. He had sent Spee to the same Quaker school where I had gone, and where some of the teachers were conscientious objectors. Maggie and Hank would sometimes invite the teachers to dinner, and Hank would spar with them, making fun of

their liberal politics. It was good natured sport, and back then I had enjoyed watching. This time, I wasn't a spectator.

"We're spending billions over there. Your taxes are buying beer, bombs, misery for millions, and promotions for the career guys in the Army. And yes, there are lots of construction contracts for civilian companies to build more prisons, roads for our trucks and tanks, and villas for the Vietnamese who're growing wealthy on graft from us. Funny, huh Hank? In Saigon there's no such thing as an honest powerful politician. You're either one or the other. It's no wonder we keep winning battles and losing the war. If I were a young Vietnamese, after what I've seen, I know which side I'd be on, and it wouldn't be the one we're propping up."

Everyone stopped talking. Hank stayed cool. He grinned and said, "I liked you better before you went over there and got radicalized." Me? A radical? Is he serious? As far as I knew, all I really wanted was to save my ass without compromising too much or letting too many people know that's all I cared about. But even I couldn't ignore the guys still over there, or the Vietnamese and what we were doing to them.

Strangely, it was becoming more vivid as a memory. Vietnamese friends had said goodbye to me stoically, having watched waves of young men come and go before me. Only one broke the polite facade when I told her I was leaving: "You scared! You afraid VC! Go home! I no want you here!" It was easier to dismiss her words than the truth behind them. I was glad to leave, and believed with more conviction than I had ever noticed in myself that the rest of our troops should leave too. My Vietnamese friend was right. I was definitely afraid — of what would happen if we stayed and of what would happen if we left. I also knew who would suffer most when we were no longer there to protect them and shore up their way of life — my friends and acquaintances, the educated and privileged, the relatively few Vietnamese who were similar in temperament and taste to the people I was eating dinner with.

People don't share history so much as interpretations of history. Before I went to Vietnam I knew most of the facts. At that time I took what I knew as the truth. Coming back, the same facts had a radically different meaning.

☆

In the nineteenth century, the French conquered and colonized Vietnam. During World War II, after the Nazi defeat of the French in 1940, Vietnam fell under Japanese control. American intelligence agents established ties with an underground Vietnamese resistance movement led by Ho Chi Minh, who was eager for the United States to help him fight the Japanese and free Vietnam from all colonial domination. President Roosevelt declared his support for Ho's plan. When the war ended, however, Roosevelt was dead, and the emerging rivalry with the Soviet Union brought a change in U.S. policy.

Determined to build a strong Western European alliance, the United States was concerned about France. Weakened by its defeat in World War II, and governed by former anti-Nazi resistance fighters, France was determined to regain its old colony. The United States decided to support the French fight against Vietnamese independence. In this way, our ally Ho Chi Minh became our enemy.

From the late 1940s until their defeat in 1954, the French military in Vietnam received arms and supplies from the United States. Ho received aid primarily from the Soviet Union and China. A peace treaty, signed in Geneva in 1954, called for national elections to unify the North, under Ho's control, and the South, under the control of Bao Dai, a ruler picked by the French. But the treaty was violated in 1956 when Bao's successor, Ngo Dinh Diem, refused to carry out the election plan, and President Eisenhower supported him. Both leaders believed that the North maintained unfair control in the South through its political and paramilitary cadres. In the following years, the North stepped up its infiltration of the South.

In 1963 President Diem's regime was on the brink of collapse from its failure to respond effectively to Buddhist protests against his government's harsh rule. U.S. aides in Saigon gave American support to a group of generals, who overthrew and killed Diem in a coup d'état. U.S. forces took a major role starting in 1964 with the first American bombings of the North, intending to discourage further infiltration of northern forces into the South.[2]

By 1973 most of our forces had withdrawn, although the official end didn't come until 1975, when Saigon fell to North Vietnamese troops. During the decade of active U.S. involvement, about 4 million American men and about 5000 women served there at one time or another.[3] On the U.S. side, 58,000 died, 300,000 were wounded, and about 1000 are still missing. On the Vietnamese side, our government estimates that close to 1 million died, about 2 million were wounded, and 6 million became homeless in the South alone.[4] For the entire country, the present Vietnamese government estimates that 15 million people were directly affected by the U.S. intervention, if the dead, wounded, crippled, and refugees throughout the country are included.[5]

Westerners do not have access to reliable accountings of the arms and munitions shipped by China, Russia, and the other Soviet-bloc nations to Ho and his successors. As for ourselves, we spent $150 billion on the war, dropping seven times more bomb tonnage on that country than the quantity unleashed by all the powers involved in World War II, and poured and sprayed 30 million gallons of herbicides, such as Agent Orange, to kill plants and trees used as cover.[6] According to the present Vietnamese government, bombing and shelling has left major damage in all of the principal towns and villages of the North and in two-thirds of those in the South. They estimate that major sectors of what was once prime farmland won't be fit to plant for another half century.[7]

The U.S.-Vietnamese peace treaty negotiated in 1973 called for an accounting of the Americans missing in action, respect by the North for the cease fire line, economic aid by the United States, and renewed diplomatic relations. A decade later, none of these terms has been met fully, and each side continues to blame the other for the violations and inflexibility.

It was the longest war in American history, the most divisive national experience since our Civil War and the only major international conflict we lost since 1812. It was the first war broadcast live on TV and a major formative experience for the most populous generation in U.S. history. Future historians will likely cite it as a watershed in twentieth-century American life.

Our government, and a succession of South Vietnamese regimes, called it an antiguerrilla war to stop communist subversion. The North Vietnamese government, and now the people of a single Vietnamese state, call it their war of national liberation. Since the late 1960s, most Americans have called it a mistake.[8]

After that first dinner, I knew something wasn't right with me, and that it wasn't just political. I felt a deep emptiness that had begun as a gnawing in my gut as I was leaving Saigon. I was sick that day, and not from anything I ate or drank. I had expected to be brimming with joy but kept running to the bathroom instead. Scared shitless, the guys would say. I couldn't figure it. Half a million GIs were literally dying to get out of that place and I was afraid to leave.

I had proclaimed the past year as the healthiest of my life. Maybe it was the steady tropical climate, but the challenge of staying alert may have helped, too. I recalled reading somewhere that physical and emotional illness in London decreased dramatically during the blitz. Under conditions of real threat, people find strength to overcome ordinary infirmities. Maybe the same thing happened to me in fifty-two weeks of being near enough to the war to feel the danger, but not so close as to suffer ill effects.

When the gnawing started, I tried to brush it off. No big deal. So I'm having a reaction, so what? I had learned not be bothered by things like that, or by too much else. I remembered what one of the career intelligence agents in Vietnam had said to me. "You're good in this business 'cause you're not easy to get to know, and even harder to get to. I like that."

I wanted to be tough inside. The week before I left Saigon I said goodbye to a nurse who had been my lover. "You seem to be going without batting an eyelash. Do you have ice water in your veins?" she asked. I knew she was fishing for me to tell her I'd miss her. No dice. What she didn't know was that I took her question as a compliment, that I could keep my emotions under control. As for the gnawing in my gut, I half suspected it was some deep questioning of whether I had the courage to face up to what was coming next.

The emptiness came with me wherever I went. The day after my homecoming dinner I went to see Linda, my girlfriend from before the war. She had written to me regularly. I was glad for that, but driving to her house I felt more obligation than desire. I didn't feel close, not to her or anyone else, even though in the six months before Vietnam I had felt romantic toward her.

Now things were different. I was both more aloof and hungrier to be involved than ever before. Sitting next to Linda, I felt her scent draw me to her again. We were together that night and for many nights afterward. I wanted her to hold me. Tenderness and touching relieved me, but didn't make the gnawing go away. I kept yearning for something more. I'd ask her what she thought about the war, about the bombing of North Vietnam. Did she think the protests would stop it? Didn't she want to march? These weren't issues that concerned her. She looked worried that I was so troubled, but didn't share my thoughts. We'd go out for an evening and my head would ache. I began to suspect that I needed to get something out, and I couldn't do it with her. Something was in the way.

Women have always played a crucial role in the drama of soldiers' homecoming. Odysseus, the hero of Homer's *Odyssey*, has as his mentor Athena, a daughter of Zeus and goddess of wisdom. As the poem begins, another goddess, Kalypso, holds the great warrior with her seductive powers, offering him immortality in return for his companionship. Wisdom, in the person of Athena, instructs him to refuse the tempting offer. He chooses to remain mortal and vulnerable, and sets off for his homeland to rejoin his wife Penelope. Before he reaches that goal, he goes through life-threatening trials and adventures, including a series of encounters with witches, sirens, and a maiden princess.

These confrontations, seductions, and intricate dealings with feminine forces offer rich material for psychological interpretation. They portray what Jungians see as the ceaseless human struggle to reconcile inner opposites — light and dark, hard and soft, masculine and feminine. A man who subdues his feelings and feminine qualities and hardens himself to danger and suffering faces a particularly acute challenge: overcoming his inner one-sidedness. And no encounter throws the imbalance into sharper relief than meeting a woman who offers tenderness and sensitivity, for one of the truisms of modern psychology is that we cannot receive from others what we cannot tolerate in ourselves.

Although sound, the psychologist's generalizations may miss the raw truth of actual lives. After World War I, Ernest Hemingway wrote a story called "Soldier's Home," which conveyed the veteran's sense of women back home:

Vaguely he wanted a girl but he did not want to have to work to get her. . . . He did not want to tell any more lies. It wasn't worth it. . . . Now he would like a girl if she had come to him and not wanted to talk. But here at home it was all too complicated. He knew he could never get through it all again. It was not worth the trouble. That was the thing about French girls and German girls. There was not all this talking. You couldn't talk much and you did not need to talk. It was simple and you were friends. He thought about France and then he began to think about Germany. . . . He did not want to come home. Still, he had come home.[9]

Concerned more about love than sex, Erich Maria Remarque wrote about the soldier's return in his book *The Long Road Back:*

If someone actually did love me . . . even though the ecstasy of some blue, silver night should gather about us, endless, self-forgetting in darkness, would not the vision of the fat whore come between us at the last moment? Would not the voices of the drill sergeants suddenly shout their obscenities? Would not the memory, scraps of talk, army jokes, at once riddle and destroy every decent emotion? In ourselves even now we are still chaste, but our imagination has been debauched without our being aware of it; before we knew anything of love at all we were already being lined up and examined for sexual diseases. . . . Though the time was when the woman was not a whore, yet it did not come back; though I believed it might still be otherwise, and though she embraced me and I trembled with desire, yet it did not return. . . . Afterwards, I was always wretched.[10]

After every war, many men experience these contrary inner pulls. On one side is the estrangement from women that comes from feeling gruff, brutish, and marked by foul deeds, military prejudice against tenderness, and the habit of taking sex for release, like alcohol and cigarettes. On the other side is an even stronger and unaccustomed hunger that leads many ex-soldiers to seek the comfort, companionship, and physical closeness that women provide. Many women, in turn, are especially attracted to men who've become vulnerable through life-wrenching experiences. This mutual attraction accounts for the hasty unions known as wartime marriages, and adds to the heightened romance and lustiness that come with war.

After Vietnam it was the same story, but with something new. Until late in the war, people in the antiwar movement looked down on soldiers for their part in it, and activist women regarded veterans with suspicion. Working out relationships became even harder in the face of challenges posed by the women's liberation movement.

☆

Not long after I was back, I received a letter from a woman I had known in Saigon, a Chinese physician who had traveled extensively in Europe. She was on her way to the States to marry an American she had met in Hong Kong. On the last leg of her trip, flying home from France, she met a young woman from Philadelphia she thought I'd like. "You're from the same city, and you're both interested in travel and music," she wrote. I called the woman. One weekend she and I met for coffee. Newsweek had just run a special issue on the new women's liberation movement. This woman could have been on the cover — she was serious, thoughtful, very intense, and wore no makeup. I told her where I had been and what I was looking forward to. She seemed interested. We agreed I'd call and arrange another time to meet.

Each time I phoned she said she was busy. I started to get the idea she was avoiding me and I didn't understand why. I thought we had hit it off okay on our first meeting and didn't want to drop it, so I wrote her a note asking what was up. She wrote back that she hadn't been fully honest with me, that she had a boyfriend already, but that wasn't all. She said she couldn't go out with me again in any case. "You've been to Vietnam and there's no horror in your voice."

I fumed about that note for days. Finally I wrote a response. "If people like me didn't go there, people like you wouldn't ever know what's really going on."

For guys from small towns in middle America, coming back might not have been so jolting, but ask most vets what it was like and they'll tell you about a run-in with somebody who didn't have the faintest idea what was going on over there. Maybe it was some pro-war hardhat or an antiwar student. In either version, the vet lost out.

One story veterans tell so often that it's part of the folklore goes like this: "I went to the American Legion hall and some dude, class of forty-six, a vet from World War Two, says, 'We won our war. How come you didn't win yours?' " Almost any guy who was over there can rattle it off. Another piece goes, "I got off the plane in Oakland and some hippie spit on me, calling me 'baby killer.' "

If you listen and then ask, "What hurt the most?" the vet won't point to the war, but to something someone said back home. Gunfire from a stranger, as long as it misses, is easier to brush off than a cutting comment from someone you love. After about 1968 you couldn't be a veteran and not meet somebody whose viewpoint was opposed to yours and who mattered enough for the things they said to hurt.

Nobody says it, but the feeling that you got a raw deal is nothing new for veterans. In Homer's epic, Odysseus returns to discover that his house has been taken over by a horde of young men who are eating his food, drinking his wine, and demanding that his wife choose one of them as her new husband. The great general has to sneak about, disguised as a beggar, to rally old friends in a bloody uprising before he can regain his home. Commenting in 1944 on more recent experiences, Willard Waller, a historian who had served in World War I, characterized America's treatment of its former soldiers since 1776 as "too little, too late."[11] World War II may have been an exception, but with Vietnam we returned to our customary pattern.

The Vietnam vet story is a variation on the ancient theme. By 1970 newspaper and magazine articles appeared with titles like, "The Vietnam Veteran: Silent Perplexed, Unnoticed."[12] We were different, they said, tragic victims of a war that went bad, in a time of cultural change and conflict between blacks and whites, men and women, old and young, hawks and doves. *No Victory Parades* was an early study by Murray Polner, a historian who interviewed two hundred veterans whose opinions spanned the political spectrum. "Not one," he concluded, "was entirely free from doubt about our involvement in Vietnam. Every personality had been affected to some extent."[13] Coming back one by one, "they fade into the American backdrop," was the way the story went. No prominent Vietnam veterans were running for office. No powerful leaders were lobbying for their interests, and they were a minimal presence on the nation's campuses.

The "troubled vet" image took hold long before there was solid evidence to document the war's impact. It seemed to strike a chord with the public. I noticed that military officers and others who defended the war would voice support for vets almost as readily as housewives and antiwar activists. The reasons varied: antiwar liberals saw vets as the victims of an immoral war, and prowar conservatives viewed vets as patriots who were wrongfully lumped to-

gether with a war everyone wanted to forget. Either way, the conclusion was the same — it's wrong to blame policies set in Washington on nineteen-year-olds who went to war respecting the law and
their fathers' example.

Many people have tried to explain this sympathy for veterans by
suggesting conspiracies of the left or right. "The doves want to make
it hard for us to defend our country again," some said. Others claimed
that "The hawks don't want it to go too bad for the vets or they'll
have trouble raising an army the next time they want to fight." As I
see it, populism, more than liberal or conservative sentiment, legit-
imized the "troubled vet" image. Anyone could root for the good
guys who did their duty and didn't get a fair shake. These feelings
were stirred by the media, which followed a long rhetorical tradition. Whether it's *Uncle Tom's Cabin*, the book that mobilized northern abolitionists before the Civil War, or *The Grapes of Wrath*, or the
plays of Clifford Odets, which aroused sympathy for the poor during the 1930s, the device is the same. The way to move the public is
to tell about ordinary people who endure extraordinary suffering.

The image took hold quickly. According to a Louis Harris poll
published in 1971, the plight of returning veterans had already become "a serious burden on the conscience of the American public."[14]

*After staying with my parents for a few weeks, I went to Washington to
report for my next assignment. There I saw my buddy Spee and his
girlfriend Suzette, whom I had visited on weekends before I went to
Vietnam. In the late 1960s Georgetown was very different from the stately
section I had first visited with my sixth-grade class a decade and a half
before. It had a carnival air from the succession of peace demonstrations, wildly dressed people on the streets, and new shops selling out-
landish clothes and paraphernalia of the drug culture, such as psyche-
delic neckties, beads, hash pipes, and rolling papers, and irreverent
posters protesting the draft with slogans like "Girls say yes to boys who
say no."*

*After I returned from the war, the mood had changed again. This
time, though, I knew the difference was in me. The first night in Washington I went for a drive with Suzette. I wanted just to look around, to
see the place again, and to take advantage of the evening calm to get*

my bearings in the city I'd be living in for the next year. As we approached the Capitol, I stared at the white rotunda, illuminated against the night sky. Then I asked her to stop the car. The sight touched me like a bugler playing taps. This is what it was all for, I thought, looking at the white dome. I was relieved to be back — safe and whole. Even more, I felt an old pride for the aspirations of a people dedicated to self-government, and a sharp pain for having lost that pride in the war. I got out of the car and started to cry.

This was totally unexpected. I never cried like that in front of anyone. I had gone away still playing it cool and detached. But here, in front of the Capitol, I suddenly realized that I wasn't going through the motions anymore. This country had a problem and I had a stake in it. And I didn't know where this would take me.

The following day I reported for my next assignment. The U.S. Army Field Activities Command was an elite intelligence outfit, with responsibilities for collecting information from all over the world. I was to work with the Pacific Area Command, with a few operations in Thailand, the Philippines, and Japan. My job was to read reports from the agents in those areas and draft responses for my boss, Major Huggins. He had been raised on a farm in Iowa. When he was thirteen, Huggins made the mistake of waking up his father on a day the old man should've been left to sleep it off. His father threw a pitchfork at the boy, who left the farm and never went back. After high school he enlisted to see the world. Since then he had fought in Korea, parachuted behind enemy lines to help the French at Dien Bien Phu, and later went on secret operations into Cuba.

Huggins loved action. He also loved raunchy jokes. A few days after we met he asked for a cup of coffee. "How do you like it?" I asked. He looked delighted that I gave him such an opening. "Like I like my women: hot, strong, and black."

He briefed me on our operations. One of them involved an American priest in the Philippines who was supposed to be keeping his ears open for local talk of revolution. Another was built around a retired Army sergeant in Bangkok posing as an American businessman hoping to find people who could sneak into Cambodia and find out something interesting. In Japan, we had another retired Army officer running a school in Tokyo and trying to seduce a young Japanese secretary, who came to him to learn English. This last one got to me. The woman was working for a company that handled teletype communications with communist China for a group of agricultural producers. The idea was that if only our man could seduce her, maybe she would give him copies of the telecommunications. Great idea. We might get to spy on some farmers. Wonderful. Some young Japanese girl gets manipulated by a bunch of U.S. spies so we can brief the general that we've got an in with the "Chicoms." Data on hog and grain shipments — what a way to fight for freedom!

It didn't take long for Huggins to pick up what I thought of all this. It was the same absurdity I had known in Saigon. I had spent the year undercover with three agents working for me, Frenchmen, former paratroopers in the Algerian war who had become soldiers of fortune. I was their case officer. My job was to train, brief, and dispatch them on reconnaissance missions into Cambodia, and then debrief them and write up intelligence reports after they returned. If this was espionage, it made James Bond's heroics look like wild fantasy, and Graham Greene's absurdities look mild. We never came up with much information worth reporting. And as I found out later in Washington, there's little chance that even valuable information is ever put to good use. How can you trust anything a spy tells you? If you hear something from someone who lies, cheats, and steals for a living wouldn't you be just as likely to think the opposite of whatever he tells you is true?

I would throw all this up to Huggins. He'd handle me just fine: "You miss the point, Art. Spying's like war. It's just a game. If you don't appreciate it, why play?"

Sympathy for the Vietnam veteran has now joined motherhood and apple pie as a hallmark of true Americanism. In opinion polls taken since 1970, and at family gatherings and cocktail parties across the country, people readily express their sorrow for the raw deal received by the average Vietnam vet. Almost nobody, however, seems to realize that this "average vet" is fictitious. Like other fictions, it has its uses, but talk about the average vet obscures the variety and individuality of the millions who served. Furthermore, focusing attention so exclusively on the average vet hides the broader truth of who needs to heal.

Veterans differ along the traditional political lines of left, right, and middle of the road. There are antiwar vets and prowar vets, combat vets (or grunts) and REMFs (Rear Echelon Mother Fuckers). Some served early in the war and felt close to the Vietnamese. Some served at the very end, when most of the enlisted men were smoking dope and cigarettes laced with opium or heroin. The Marines spent the bulk of their time in the field, leading the life of the grunt. Most Air Force and Navy men had comfortable barracks, and so did many of the men in the Army.

Veterans also vary in education and life style. Some are college graduates who've married and have kids and fulfilling careers, whereas others have stayed single, rootless, and live hand to mouth. About 20 percent live in obviously disadvantaged conditions, and another 5 to 10 percent seem to be flourishing, while the vast majority fall somewhere in between. *Soldier of Fortune* magazine was started by Vietnam veterans who warm to war stories and recruiting ads for mercenaries in Africa, while the VA's Outreach program was founded and staffed by vets who talk about "post-traumatic stress disorder" and the need to "work through the war."

You can find blacks, whites, Hispanics, Asian Americans, and native Americans who served in Vietnam. No reliable numbers are available on many other subgroups, but we know that some guys are still strung out on dope, a notable minority are in prison, a few still make the news with frightful crimes, and more than we'd like to admit are in the back wards of mental hospitals. Vets fall into just about every occupational category, including laborers, tradesmen, executives, physicians, professors, lawyers, poets, filmmakers, plumbers, actors, and the guy next door, who never seemed like the kind who went there until you hear from his wife that he made a special trip to Washington to see the memorial.

If you ignore most of these differences and count heads on strictly defined measures of adjustment, statistical estimates become possible. Of the approximately four million who went to Vietnam, one in five had serious difficulties after coming home.[15] The proportion is higher, about one in three, for those who were heavily involved in combat.[16] The absolute numbers are staggering — hundreds of thousands of young men who survived military screening, rigorous training, and service in a war zone now live on the frayed edges of society. The estimates are higher still if, instead of looking for gross mental illness, you focus on the more limited difficulties stemming from unresolved war experiences, such as bad dreams, guilt, anger, and emotional withdrawal. Sorting through an unbiased sample of interviews with veterans from across the country for a report to Congress, I found about half whom I would recommend for counseling or therapy, which means that about two million men out there could use a hand.[17]

The public readily expresses sympathy for the fictional "average vet," but this sentiment is more a symbolic expression than a commitment veterans can bank on. For example, the concern has not given rise to many concrete acts on behalf of those in greatest need. Priorities in this area are reflected in the history of the program designed to enable the Veterans Administration to reach out to Vietnam veterans. First proposed by congressional committees in 1970, Operation Outreach was not voted on and funded by both the House and Senate until 1979, a decade late for most of those who had served in Vietnam and returned home. Its passage was not due to widespread public support but to a handful of Vietnam veterans who by that time had either been elected to Congress or had risen to influential positions in the Veterans Administration and traditional veterans' lobbies. A second program, the Vietnam Veterans Leadership Program, introduced in 1981, was likewise created by a small group of veterans rather than as a response to widespread public demand.

In the same vein, the Vietnam Veterans Memorial in Washington, dedicated in November 1982, was conceived and built only after still another handful of Vietnam veterans led the way. Afterward, the public responded energetically, with thousands of visitors flocking to it each day. Why? It wasn't the sheer numbers of dead that drew them. Fifty-eight thousand deaths are more than enough for anyone to mourn, but such a toll doesn't necessarily evoke great outpourings of concern. In the United States during the war years, more people — sixty-seven thousand — died from shootings with handguns without drawing much national attention. And for the past two decades, about fifty thousand Americans have died on the nation's highways *every year*, almost as many as were killed throughout the entire war, a fact we generally ignore.[18]

The meaning of this public sympathy for veterans is seldom appreciated. People in this country have been moved not so much because veterans have suffered, but because of what that suffering came to represent.

I realized this soon after I came back. Each time someone has said to me, "Vietnam? You were there? That must have been rough!" I've noticed that sympathy for veterans stems from what people *think* we went through. People I've met casually and others I've interviewed through my research speak so readily about the legendary trials of the "average vet" that they are clearly expressing something other than concern for an individual's actual experience. Talk about veterans serves a widespread need to symbolize what happened to this country during the war years. The Vietnam Veterans Memorial has become the focus for national mourning because the Vietnam veteran has become a popular metaphor for the nation's postwar conflicts.

To put it even more plainly, sympathy for veterans is a veiled confession of a need to heal by those who voice it. For the first decade after the troops came home, sympathizing with the vets became the way Americans expressed sorrow for themselves and for the greatest casualty we suffered — the blow to national pride and our common sense of purpose. But this sympathy has its drawbacks. Not only does it obscure the toll on those who didn't serve — lost pride in citizenship, disrespect for public institutions, and unwillingness to take part in collective projects — but it has made matters worse for veterans by creating an indulgent mood that many vets have found hard to resist. If glory and respect are not forthcoming, sympathy is a lot more comforting than being ignored.

From research we know that a minority of veterans still need special assistance, and a majority are still struggling to work through their war experiences, mostly on their own. Sympathy for the "average vet" doesn't provide support for either group. Even worse, it lulls people who weren't there into thinking that they are expressing the right sentiments, instead of asking themselves the useful questions: "What has been the impact of this war on *my* life?" and "What do I need to heal?"

Spee had been my best friend through high school and college. He was a year older, more successful in school, and more sociable. I looked up to him, and he was often protective of me, as long as I didn't embarrass him too much. Our way wasn't to speak intimately but to pick up on each other's signals, so it was a feeling I got, rather than any-

thing he said, that made me think he was increasingly embarrassed by me in the months after I came back.

Spee lived in a house in Georgetown, and his friends were graduates from Harvard and Yale who had draft-deferrable jobs in the Pentagon. He was there as an Army captain, having done ROTC at Harvard and received a degree in the kind of engineering that is always in demand at the Pentagon. Although I never knew for sure, I suspected his friends had used political pull to get high-level civilian jobs while they waited out their years of eligibility for the draft.

His acceptance by them was a coup on Spee's part, since it was rare for a guy who had not belonged to one of the high-class clubs at Harvard to be close friends with prep school graduates who had. As one of Spee's nonclubby friends, I felt his subtle cues for me to be diplomatic. But I said what I thought anyway — that the war stunk, that our whole government would be tainted by it, and that all of us would be paying the price for years to come. Remarks like that didn't fit with cocktail party etiquette. Spee and I drifted apart.

Such talk was nothing strange to my roommate Rick and his buddy Chris. They had met in intelligence school and served in the same unit in Vietnam. Both were unusually clean-cut and well behaved, and impressed their commanding officer to the point that he rewarded them with a recommendation to this elite assignment in Washington to finish out their enlistment. Rick had been an all-star athlete and business major at a small midwestern college and was now engaged to Bobbitt, his girlfriend of many years. Chris was raised in southern California by his mother, who had left the Midwest in search of spiritual truth, and had pledged herself and her son to a sect that seemed to be a cross between Christian Science and Hare Krishna, with a strong flavor of California health food. As polite and well-behaved as they were, Rick and Chris had lost all illusion that Americans were the good guys in Vietnam.

Rick reminded me of Midwesterners I had known in college. Occasionally, he and I would go for a run or a swim together. He was neat, dependable, and though there were sometimes awkward silences, it was a breeze to do things with him — from our weekly shopping at the Army commissary to getting out of the apartment on time to make work by 7:30 A.M. We were worlds apart culturally, but similar in that we had been raised to respect the country and do our duty. After six months of intelligence school and a year in Vietnam, both of us had changed to the point where old national pieties had become a cruel joke.

Chris was different. Soft spoken, gentle to a degree I had never known in a close friend, he grew up with people for whom suspicion of government was an article of faith. His sect was so devoted to the curative power of prayer that he had never seen a dentist before the Army inducted him. I never understood why he didn't file as a conscientious objector, but I was sure that when he enlisted for intelligence duty, being trained as a spy was the furthest thing from his mind.

Chris lived in another apartment near Rick and me. The three of us would drive to work together every morning and come home in Rick's car in the afternoon. Many mornings Chris would tell us his dreams. A prominent figure in them was the leader of his cult, back in California. He grew up believing she was faithful in her marriage but was dreaming regularly that she was not.

Chris was about to be married to a young woman who had also grown up in the cult, and he was having some fears about making that commitment. Listening to him I recalled my readings of Freud, and told him his conflicts were coming out at night. I said it sounded like a crisis of faith, that he had been out in the world and could no longer hold his old beliefs in the way he had before. I suggested he read a book about Martin Luther and his crisis of faith by a well-known psychologist, Erik Erikson.

It was my first bit of counseling, and I learned something important. I gave clearer advice to other people than I often gave to myself. In fact, what I said to Chris was just as true for me. I began to see myself as having a crisis of faith. I had believed in a progressive, benign ideal about my country and assumed that those in charge would take care of things so that people like me wouldn't have to worry. Now all that seemed terribly naive. Before the war, I had studied multinational corporations at Harvard and in Europe, believing that they were helping to weld a global economic order that would benefit all humankind. Inside the intelligence bureaucracy, I discovered that thousands of U.S. companies were secretly cooperating with the CIA. Government records were being falsified to hide all this — not from the Russians, who knew all too well what we were up to, but from people like me, who'd be horrified to learn of our government's manipulations. I couldn't see how we could advance the principles of an open society if we compro-

mised ourselves so much and kept using other people's misdeeds as our excuse.

After recommending Erikson to Chris, I picked up one of his books myself, *Identity: Youth and Crisis.* It was a first for me. Although Erikson taught at Harvard while I was there, I never took his courses, thinking they were over my head. Out of curiosity, I had read some of Freud in high school, and briefly considered majoring in psychology before giving up that option as too weird and much less practical than economics.

In the book, Erikson wrote about the traumatized veterans he saw when he first began practicing psychoanalysis in this country during World War II.[19] I didn't have any of the extreme symptoms he described — the panic reaction, severe nightmares, insomnia, and the rest. Rick, Chris, and I had had it easy by comparison. But one theme was very familiar. Erikson reported these men's complaint that they didn't know "who they were" anymore. That was it. For us, too, old moorings were shaken and once trusted leaders appeared faithless, as in Chris's dream. I couldn't connect with old friends, meetings with women were strained, and my future was more uncertain than ever. Though I had planned a career in economics, I could no longer imagine working for a corporation. I knew I'd be prone to speak out, just as I did at Spee's parties. I was no longer a button-down type. For the first time in my life, I held opinions too passionately to keep myself in check.

Erikson noted the exaggerated tendency among his veteran patients to blame circumstances "for their failures as soldiers and as men." I didn't see how I was doing that, but something in the comment stuck. He also noted a cultural tendency among Americans, a "deliberate tentativeness" that leads us to insist that if the next step in our lives is not wholly up to us, we will feel terribly thwarted. "In this country, the migrant does not want to be told to move on nor the sedentary man to stay where he is," wrote Erikson. I was reminded of the old saying, "You can always tell a Harvard man, but you can't tell him much."

Erikson put his finger on a big part of the hurt, that the one thing Americans fear more than almost anything else is being taken for a sucker, "one who lets himself be sidetracked and stalled while oth-

ers are free to pursue what could have been his chance and his girl."
That was part of the separation between Spee and me. For a time I
had been bitter, feeling like a sucker for spending three years doing
idiot work while he was advancing his career.

Erikson's brand of psychology was an unexpected comfort. His
writings made it legitimate for me to be as I was. When I'd see pictures in the morning paper of Vietnamese women weeping over their
dead husbands and children, I'd break into tears, as I had the first
night in Washington in front of the Capitol. I couldn't keep myself
from sharing in the pain. Erikson was saying that if you're young
and just going out in the world and find yourself rudely awakened
by seeing that it's not what you thought, it doesn't mean you're sick
or crazy. It may even be a good sign — that you're on the way to
something useful, not only for yourself but for others as well.

He emphasized the turning points, or "developmental crises," that
occur naturally even in normal lives. Through the heightened sensitivity that comes at those moments, people can develop a personal
relationship with larger, or collective, human concerns. This is often
fortunate for them and for society, since people who are touched in
this way often forge long-term commitments, an "identity," through
which they make it their business to take care of matters that stretch
beyond their most immediate concerns.

A new possibility was dawning for me. I was used to thinking of
myself as a scheming, self-centered person who couldn't afford to
let other people know what I was really up to. I had chosen economics as a profession because it was practical, and intelligence because
I believed it would be fairly safe. The new possibility was that I
might choose to do something after the Army that really mattered
to me, even though I had no idea what it would be.

What matters? Before I went to Vietnam, Indochina didn't matter to
me. One of my college professors had said that Americans should
simply leave that part of the world and return it "to the obscurity it
so richly deserves." That's how I felt, until I went there.

Thailand, Malaya, Laos, Cambodia, and Vietnam are located on a
peninsula that juts southward from the landmass of China. The
western portion bears the traces of successive waves of cultural expansion from India over the past three thousand years. Cambodia,

Laos, Malaya, and Thailand show greater affinity in language, script, dress, and architecture with the Indian culture to the west. In this respect, Vietnam is distinct. In language and cultural heritage, the Vietnamese are more like the Chinese to the north.

These countries have a long history of cultural and political domination by powers beyond their borders. In the last three hundred years, the Portuguese, and then the British and French, vied for colonial supremacy in this part of the world. All that remains of indigenous culture through the continual waves of military and cultural invasion are the primitive tribes living in the remote mountainous regions.

In studying and living in Vietnam and Thailand — I had to make several "business trips" to Bangkok to rendezvous with my agents — I was most struck by the discrepancy between the standards of living of the Western-oriented elite and the masses. True, the United States had friends in those countries, but the picture was uncomfortably close to what I had regularly dismissed as paranoid, anti-U.S. propaganda. Our friends were the unusually privileged few who could afford to travel outside their country, give their children Western educations, and send the profits from local enterprise to foreign banks. In temperament and background, I had most in common with local elites. But I understood as never before the venom of liberationist leaders. Our friends lived in air-conditioned villas. The masses were often illiterate peasants, living next to dunghills.

The U.S. policies in the area were justified on grounds that local revolutions were supported by our adversaries, China and Russia. To protect our standing in the world and to protect the local peoples from undemocratic, Marxist-inspired tyrants, we could not allow such revolutions to prevail. Inside the intelligence bureaucracy, I saw ample evidence that insurgent movements were not committed to a Western notion of democracy. The record was clear: The leaders of modern Marxist revolutions do not honor our concerns for individual rights and for the importance of self-government.

But a new question began to burn in me. On what grounds do these differences justify killing patriots in foreign countries who don't think the way we do? I knew the usual answer: "We've got to stop them there before they reach our doorstep!" But peasant armies didn't seem to pose the greatest danger to us. My country, the land of the free, had ended up playing the role of dogmatic oppressor. And this seemed to me a far greater loss than if centrist, communist regimes took power elsewhere.

My mother ran the family business, a memorial park for blacks, which her father had started during the Depression. He had been a rabbi's son, but was too touched by the spirit of American enterprise to follow the traditional ways. He left school before the eighth grade and went to make his fortune, first as a milk man and then as a broker of stocks and bonds. His life changed when the black maid who worked for my mother's family died in childbirth. My grandfather went to the cemetery to supervise the burial, and was appalled by the sight of crooked, randomly placed gravestones overgrown with weeds. He vowed to "give those people a decent place to be buried in." And he did. When he died, my mother took over and buried his ashes there.

After coming back I felt uncomfortable around my mother in a way I never had before. Face to face with her, I'd feel knotted up, torn, wanting to explode, convinced she would never understand. Strange thoughts would come to me. She had worked at the cemetery to put me through school and college, and although I wanted to be grateful, I was sick at what her work had done. Money and the privileges it bought had murderous power — they make the difference between who lives and who dies. My life had been bought by the advantages that separated me from the grunts. And the means that purchased it were now tainted with the blood of the guys who died on our side, and the many others who died on theirs.

For months I ruminated about this, and one day when I was alone with her, I just blurted it out. I told her I wasn't clean, that I might never have pulled a trigger, but the blood was still on my hands. What made it worse was that I got off easy only because black people's deaths paid my way. I now had three blood debts — black, white, and yellow — and I wanted her to sell the cemetery, to get it back into the hands of people it belonged to. It wasn't ours. The stock my grandfather had given me, not a great fortune but the one piece of property registered in my name, wasn't mine, couldn't be mine. I would give it to the park, to pay off expenses so that she could sell the business.

My mother had never seen me like this. I was crying, talking about blood and guilt, telling her what to do with her life in a way I never had. She was speechless. The harder I tried, the more I could see I wasn't convincing, but only turning her off inside.

At my office the next day, Major Huggins knew I was upset. I told him that I had to save my family's honor, that black deaths paid for me to get off easy while poor whites and still more blacks and Asian people died, that I had to divest myself of properties that carried such a taint. I needed time off to see a lawyer, for advice about selling the stock, and to draw up a will to make certain I wouldn't have my ashes in that cemetery. Huggins looked concerned.

"They shouldn't send guys like you over there," he said. "They should save it for callous bastards like me." Of course he gave me the time.

I felt bad that I had fallen apart, but I felt even worse that I didn't get through to my mother. So I wrote both my parents about the stock, hoping that a letter would help explain.

Dear Ma and Pa,

I'm not giving back the stock out of spite or vengeance. But they stand for something I can't accept anymore. I've sensed for a long time that I would have many things to sort out after these years in the Army. I never anticipated, however, that this last year would begin the process with such turmoil. But begin it did. I'm glad.

I agree with you, Dad, that a person has to be able to look themselves in the mirror in the morning. But I don't agree with how much you pride yourself on keeping quiet. The object for me is not to remain silent or avoid commitment.

Mom, I cried out to you that there isn't an honest bone in my body. Not yet anyway. Many things have been garbled for me, basically because I refused to sort them out. There have been good things too. The main one is that I'm willing to find out the truth now.

Many people who grew up during the late 1960s tell similar stories of being uprooted and coming to see the world in a new light. One of the events that left its mark on that time was the first moon landing. Rick, Chris, and I joined a few others to watch on TV as Neil Armstrong said, "That's one small step for a man, one giant leap for mankind."

Afterward, reports from the war came on the news, a sign that the old world was still very much with us. Sitting around the TV set, we noted the difference between the moon landing and the war

in Vietnam. Halfway around the world, many were getting themselves killed and it didn't matter, whereas all Armstrong had to do
was take one step and a new period in history began.

That year and the year before, many events occurred that seemed
to mark the end of much that was familiar and the beginning of
something unknown. A few weeks before I left for Vietnam I was in
Washington when the news broke: Martin Luther King, Jr., was shot,
setting off a wave of riots, protests, and mourning. Later that year
Robert Kennedy was killed. The yearning he voiced for greater justice in the world seemed to echo the political uprisings and social
movements that were erupting — in Czechoslovakia, France, Japan, Mexico, China, and many places in between.

In college I learned in anthropology that the similar Stone Age
implements discovered in Europe, Africa, and Asia suggested sur-
prisingly rapid communication among even the most primitive pre-
historic cultures. While traveling through Asia, it occurred to me
that Confucius and Buddha lived and spread their teachings during
the same century as Socrates. The great temple of Burobudor in Indonesia, the Kamakura Buddha in Japan, Angkor Wat in Cambodia,
and temples of the Incas in Peru were erected about the same time
as some of the most majestic Gothic spires in Europe. Evidently, the
most startling developments in the world don't appear to have any
simple cause, but rather erupt all over in a synchronous way.[20]

More than likely, the years 1968–1969 will be seen as a watershed
in human history, with similar stirrings around the globe. The moon
landing, brought live to viewers worldwide through satellite communications and computers, was just one of the signs that an unprecedented shift was at hand. No other single event revealed so
clearly the possibility of a global human family. The very idea challenges the ancient assumption of the inevitability of war, and many
of us who had been to war took the challenge personally.

*One evening I was alone and turned on the TV to see a special broad-
cast. "Ladies and gentlemen, the President of the United States." His
face came on, looking straight into the camera. He was trying so hard
to be sincere, he looked phony before he began. "If this guy were one
of my spies I'd order a polygraph on him," I said to myself. I had gone
from mild suspicion to firm conviction that I'd never trust this man
Richard Nixon.*

At that moment, he said, U.S. forces in Vietnam were engaged in a special operation to destroy the central headquarters of the North Vietnamese army and Vietcong in the border region of Cambodia. This was necessary to protect our troops from the infiltration of communist personnel and materiel into South Vietnam. He said this was a defensive operation, necessary to guarantee the safety of Americans.

I pulled off my shoe and flung it at the TV. "You lying bastard!" I screamed. He was talking about something I knew firsthand. In Vietnam I was in charge of agents who went on spy missions into Cambodia. After returning to Washington, I continued to read intelligence reports and background documents about that country. No doubt that North Vietnamese and Vietcong forces used the border region as a sanctuary. The Cambodian government was too weak to drive them out. But the Vietcong "headquarters" wasn't a fixed establishment like ours. They moved much more quickly than we did, which meant we would probably destroy more of Cambodia than of the enemy we were chasing.

Even worse, we would only be pushing the people we opposed farther into the Cambodian interior. There was no telling what would happen to the delicate political and social balance in Cambodia itself. It was especially dangerous since Nixon was not planning to take charge of the situation in Cambodia as a whole, but only invade the border regions.

Our invasion of Cambodia would not limit the war, as Nixon claimed, but widen it. More dying, more pain, and more destruction, tearing at me as if the events in that distant country had strings attached to my guts. I didn't care about military justifications. The issue for me was that you can butcher people only when you feel no kinship with them. Apologists for our war policies held themselves aloof from the people whose homes we were destroying, whose suffering we intensified, and whose daughters we drove into prostitution to feed their families. Our leaders didn't hear the bludgeoning roar of our bombs or witness the corpses. But these things were no longer abstract for me.

Joseph Campbell, a scholar of the world's myths and legends, has written about the timeless themes that appear like common threads in the traditional lore of all cultures.[21] Many myths tell of a great journey. Toward the end, the hero faces the challenge of delivering the fruits of his difficult passage to the ordinary world at home.

Some who journey may not accept the challenge and choose to remain in exile, like the veterans who decline to speak by saying, "You
can't know unless you were there, so I can't tell you." Others may
not be able to return on their own and need to be rescued, as were
many of us who went to others for help. Always, however, the goal
is to bring the essence of the dark beyond into the light or, as Campbell put it:

> How [to] teach again . . . what has been taught correctly and incorrectly,
> learned a thousand thousand times, throughout the millenniums of man-
> kind's prudent folly? How [to] render back into light-world language the
> speech-defying pronouncements of the dark? How [to] represent on a
> two-dimensional image a multi-dimensional meaning? How [to] translate
> into terms of "yes" and "no" revelations that shatter into meaningless-
> ness every attempt to define the pairs of opposites? How [to] communi-
> cate to people who insist on the exclusive evidence of their senses the
> message of the all-generating void?[22]

According to the *I Ching*, the ancient book of Chinese wisdom,
the return is a turning point that comes after a time of decay or
wearing down. It is a powerful light, once banished, now restored.
It is a moment that "calls for decision and is an act of self-mastery.
. . . It is made easier if a man is in good company. If he can bring
himself to put aside pride and follow the example of good men,
good fortune results."[23]

Coming back to ourselves means raising timeless questions about
the meaning of life and our place in the world. The only way we can
address such questions, of course, is in the terms of life as we know
it. And so, when we question deeply we not only engage in an age-
less human inquiry. We bring back the experiences that in retrospect
seem crucial for having introduced us into the world. What we come
back to, therefore, is not a preestablished place, but a confrontation
with the life we've lived so far, something that occurs only as we
bring ourselves to it.

Coming back has another meaning as well. It is a matter of being
at home with oneself, which is in contrast with the "removed" look
in people's eyes. When the daze leaves their faces, we can say they
have "come back." Returning, in this sense, means "being all there,"
and no longer estranged.

Coming back, then, is not limited to a single point in veterans' lives. As a facet of healing, it is an ever-present possibility. In fact the antidote to recurring dreams, memories, random associations, and the more intrusive recollections called flashbacks is precisely this inward move to come back, to ground oneself more fully by engaging one's experience and by discovering what it is to be at home with oneself.

As an ever-present possibility, coming back, like each of the chapter-length perspectives on healing I describe in this book, is therefore not merely a stage in a process. We can call it that, but it is also one entry to the whole of healing. This may appear paradoxical until we notice that a flash of insight occurs in the context of an ongoing life yet reaches beyond it. A truly liberating realization always transcends what went before, and in bringing us to grasp what was formerly beyond our reach, the creative leap arises ecstatically, like a momentary contact with a timeless dimension where everything is already together and whole. By providing us an opening onto this all-encompassing realm, coming back to ourselves, once we know the way, remains an ever-available source of renewal.

Coming back to ourselves may sometimes bring a moment of relaxation, allowing us to settle in and take it easy. But the more we've been estranged, the more disruptive it is to return. And so, coming back from war is rarely gentle. It poses the challenge of creating some way to be at home inwardly without deserting all that one has left behind: hopes, dreams, innocence, and the dead.

Living in Washington with time to spare for cultural activities was a welcome change from two years of full-time training and war. Rick, Chris, and I went regularly to see films shown at the National Gallery. One was a series by Japanese directors. My favorite was The Harp of Burma, *originally a tale written for children.*

The story takes place in Burma at the very end of World War II. The truce has just been signed, but the news has not yet reached a platoon of Japanese soldiers holding out in a cave. The British tell the Japanese company commander, who has already surrendered, that if the rest of his troops don't lay down their arms within twenty-four hours, the British will assault the cave with artillery. The company commander asks for a volunteer to go up to the cave and tell the others that the war is over. *The most courageous soldier steps forward, a man always ready to undertake dangerous missions, known for the beautiful way he sings and plays a hand-held harp.*

When the man arrives at the cave, the soldiers hit and spit on him for talking of surrender. After beating him unconscious, they throw him into the back of the cave. Then the shelling comes. Everyone is killed except the harp player. He starts out to find his company, passing dead bodies wherever he goes. When he reaches the compound where his buddies are waiting in a British POW camp for their return to Japan, he turns around and goes back out into the fields. Everywhere he goes he buries the bodies he finds — Japanese bodies, British bodies, Burmese bodies. Soon after that he begins wearing the robes of a Buddhist monk. From time to time he returns to the compound and stands silently outside the fence in his robes. At first the men in his unit think he is a peculiar Burmese. Later on they suspect that it is their long-lost comrade, but they never speak to him directly. The company goes home, and he stays to clean up the wreckage from his war.

Until then I had managed to hide my crying from Rick and Chris. This time I didn't try. The tears came, and we had to wait for everyone to leave the theater before I would get up. I took that movie as a sign of what I would do. I would help clear up the wreckage from my war.

☆ 2 ☆

RETRACING STEPS

I am afraid to forget. I fear that we human creatures do not
forget cleanly, as the animals presumably do. What protrudes
and does not fit in our pasts rises to haunt us and make us
spiritually unwell in the present.

J. GLENN GRAY[1]

WHAT DO YOU DO with an experience that touches your core? Bury it? Run from it? Stalk it like an enemy? Charge into it with full force? Surrender to it? Some vets try a variety of approaches, keeping silent about it at one time, talking to anyone who'll listen at another. Those intent on healing keep coming back to one question in particular: "What happened over there?" In asking this, they are struggling to come to grips with what took place, to mourn and hopefully move on. The ones who were touched most deeply search to make contact once again with whatever pierced their shell.

In Homer's epic, it takes divine intervention to free Odysseus from the jealous hold of Kalypso, the exquisite goddess who kept him estranged from the world on her faraway island. She consents to let him go only when commanded by Zeus, the king of the gods. But even aid from the gods doesn't keep Odysseus from further anguish. He sets out on a raft and is battered by a fierce storm unleashed by the god of earthquakes and the oceans. Stranded far from land after his raft has been ripped apart, Odysseus wishes he had died in battle with his fellow soldiers:

> Would God I, too, had died there — met my end
> that time the Trojans made so many casts at me
> when I stood by Akhilleus after death.
> I should have had a soldier's burial
> and praise from the Akhaians — not this choking
> waiting for me at sea, unmarked and lonely.[2]

Psychotherapists in the analytic tradition view the mythic struggle at sea as a symbol of the inner struggles of the unconscious. Popular phrases such as "You've got to keep your head above water" and "It's either sink or swim," apply not only to mundane tasks but to the inner challenge of confronting the "deep waters" of stormy emotion, which survivors of unusual suffering know as rage, grief, and guilt. Odysseus' wish that he had died in battle, rather than face the storms of his return home, has a metaphorical equivalent among veterans who say, "I don't want to dig it all up again." or "What good does it do to talk about it? It's over, done, forgotten, so let sleeping dogs lie." Many refuse to retrace their steps to a painful past, and dismiss the effort as senseless. As some ask, "Why suffer twice for the same experience?"

Despite the discomfort, the way of healing is nonetheless clear, both from ancient myth and modern psychology. In a talk before fellow physicians in 1904, Freud described his psychotherapeutic method as a way to have patients engage the relevant aspects of their lives that they prefer to ignore.[3] He noted that it is natural for these efforts to meet resistance, since people experience pain in confronting explicitly what they have either forgotten or haven't yet noticed. Much of healing work brings people to accept through understanding what they formerly avoided out of fear.

In Homer's poem, Odysseus manages with the aid of a sea goddess to make his way to shore. Athena, goddess of wisdom, then intervenes by having him meet Nausikaa, the beautiful maiden daughter of the local king. Brought by the princess into her father's town, Odysseus is welcomed as an honored guest, though nobody knows his name. The king orders a feast to celebrate the stranger's arrival, after which a minstrel entertains the gathering with an epic song of the Greek siege of Troy. On hearing of his bloody battles and fallen comrades, Odysseus starts to cry and tries to hide his tears from the others. Someone hears him, stops the singing, and asks Odysseus who he is and why he is weeping. It's at this point, only after he has reached safe ground and sits among gracious hosts, that he recounts his travels and suffering.

One of the morals of the ancient tale of the warrior's return is that mourning doesn't begin in the middle of heated action, but only later, in a situation that allows events to be savored that passed too quickly to grasp the first time around. And usually it takes someone being there, listening with care.

*Months after coming back, I was in Philadelphia on a weekend leave
and looked up an old girlfriend from high school days. By coincidence,
Liza was there visiting her parents for two days. Now a New Yorker and
an aspiring writer, she spoke with an infectious energy and asked many
questions that got me to talk. She had a way of listening with appreciation, rather than with awe or judgment, which let me say things I had
never told anyone before.*

*"What was someone like you doing in Vietnam?" she wondered, as
many others have asked since. I interpreted the question to mean, "Since
you're sensitive, and the kind of person who is appalled by the war,
why did you go? Why didn't you find some way to avoid it, like so many
others of your age and background?" The answer is that I didn't think
of myself as sensitive before I went. I didn't expect to be appalled. I
didn't like the idea of going, but I accepted the principle of serving
when called. I ended up enlisting in the Army, but only after being
notified that I'd be drafted shortly.*

*In telling the story to Liza, I took pains to say things I usually kept to
myself. So I told her how, knowing the risks, I had left myself vulnerable to the draft. After college I had gone to Europe for a summer and
decided to stay for the year. I registered in a succession of schools and
studied international economics, languages, and music. But my secret
hope, which I never told anyone, was to be touched in some way that
would reveal what I should do with my life.*

*After eight months in Paris I went to a small German village near
Augsburg. I wrote my parents the practical-sounding explanation that
I might as well learn German after having learned French. My grandmother wrote back, "How could you go to such a place?" She hated
the Germans for what they did to our people. I tried to explain how
important it was for me to experience that country for myself, to see
what I would feel after I had lived there and learned the language. To
Liza, I said it simply: I had to go where my people once thrived and
then were slaughtered, to live for a time as a Jew in Germany before I
could feel like a man in this world.*

*While I was in Europe, most of the men I knew were getting married,
going to school, or taking special jobs to avoid the draft. A few had
protested actively, burning their draft cards and risking jail. Those alternatives didn't sit well with me. I was neither a protester nor someone content to foreclose my options to avoid the war. There was some-*

thing I had to do, and although I couldn't say what it was, I knew it involved taking some chances.

Following the rules of the Selective Service at the time, I reported each change in my address, knowing as I did that my letters were like waving signs at them saying, "Here's a young man who isn't settled and ripe for plucking." The prospect of being drafted did not, in fact, horrify me. I figured I'd have been one of the first to pick up a gun if called a generation before, so it couldn't be too bad. When the draft notice finally came, I enlisted, which meant going in for three years rather than the two required of draftees. In return for the extra year, I could select my "specialty."

I chose the Army's Area Studies program, which was described in the brochures as leading to jobs that required one to work with civilians, study and analyze foreign cultures, and "gather information." I expected to be assigned to a desk job in Washington. Only after signing the contract and completing two months of Basic Training did I find out that Area Studies is the cover name for espionage. I was to be trained as a spy.

In Vietnam my job was to plan spy missions for my agents, who would go into Cambodia, talk to people, take pictures, and come back to tell me what they learned. The most time-consuming part of the work was dreaming up and writing plans, selling them first to one echelon and then to the one above and the one above that. Since everybody in the intelligence business is a professional liar, we had to work extra hard to convince superiors that the agents we recruited were real and that something would come of the operations we proposed. Once approval came, we had to train the agents, dispatch them on their missions, and then debrief them in detail when they returned. And then came our great reward. We got to write still more reports about everything the agents told us, precious little of which made any difference to anyone.

My agents were Frenchmen, a few years older than I, who had served with the elite paratrooper corps when the French fought to keep Algeria as a colony in the early 1960s. When de Gaulle declared an end to the war and gave the country to the Algerians, right-wing generals bolted and recruited men from the elite units into the Secret Army Organization, which terrorized Algerian and French leftists for several years. My agents had joined and become underground terrorists before being captured, imprisoned, and later given amnesty. They had since *become soldiers of fortune. Working with them, I learned to get along with people whose politics I disagreed with. I came to love their raw guts, and the way they stuck by each other and whomever they were loyal to. I also found out through their example how confused and rootless men can become after a lost colonial war.*

At first Liza was captivated by my story. But after a while she stopped listening for tales of adventure and heard what I had not yet managed to put into words. "You feel guilty, don't you?" Her question stunned me. After years of lying and deceiving, neither trusting nor being fully trustworthy with anyone — including my colleagues in espionage — I was finally telling the truth to someone who mattered to me. Before talking with her about it, I used to think that I could do anything; I didn't believe I had a conscience. By bringing the pain into focus, her words showed me something new about myself. Feeling it came as a relief.

When someone asks, "What can I do to help a vet I know?" I usually say, "Listen to him. The people who helped me the most gave me a chance to speak." But I'm never satisfied giving this answer, because so few people know what it means. Many think of listening as sympathizing, or "believing what he says." It doesn't. Listening is attending with the sense that you're hearing what is important, at this moment, for this person to say. When people speak genuinely about their experience, what they say conveys a truth about their personal sense of things at a particular time. But a helpful listener doesn't have to believe or do anything about it. What's crucial is to hear it.

Clarity about the nature of listening is one of the enduring contributions of American psychologist Carl Rogers.[4] Throughout his career Rogers has emphasized the importance of providing people with settings where they can speak openly and completely without being dismissed, ridiculed, or silenced in any way. Rogers has insisted that listening "with unqualified positive regard" lies at the core of psychotherapy. In the 1940s, when he first proposed this term, and for years afterward, "unqualified positive regard" was a more acceptable phrase than the traditional word for what Rogers meant, which is the acceptance called love.

In recent decades, Rogers and his students have been teaching listening not only to therapists but to a wide range of helping professionals. His techniques have been incorporated into "Parent Effectiveness Training," "Teacher Effectiveness Training," and countless curricula for training executives, salespeople, customer service representatives, and schoolchildren who are asked to listen to each other in class. The key point taught in all these trainings is to grasp the heart of what another person wants to say. This takes practice. Most of the time we say we're listening we're actually doing something else — such as telling ourselves silently that we already know what the other person is saying, or waiting for the other to finish so that we can make a point that to us is far more important.

How does listening help? When people have something they very much want others to hear, they carry it around until they feel they've gotten it across. Much of the psychic pain that weighs on people comes from their having resigned themselves to the idea that they either can't say what matters, or if they did, nobody would take it in. Among veterans, the situation is complicated by the nature of what they have to say. Many have "horror stories" they think nobody could hear without condemning them. It is precisely such stories that need most to be heard.

Saying the worst can be healing, but not because talking takes something from "inside" and puts it on the "outside." This is the popular but mistaken idea, one that is based on thinking about people as if they were machines. In fact, trying to "get out" your anger or sadness or guilt rarely leads to more than temporary relief, as people who go around "spilling their guts" soon find out. Nor is it the mere transfer of information from someone who has been there to someone who has not that brings about the cure.

By saying the worst you free yourself from having to live up to an image you think is necessary for others to like you. Saying the worst to someone who cares enough to listen never sounds as bad to him or her as you're afraid it will, for the very saying of it dignifies your listener as someone you trust, and reveals you as one who cares about the truth. Speaking truthfully to someone you trust brings about a relationship between you and your listener that casts even the worst deeds in a redeeming light.

From 1965 until late 1969, when a lottery replaced the draft, conscription swelled the military ranks by taking millions of men directly and inducing an even greater number to enlist. In the end, more than half of those who served during the war years chose to enlist; the option advertised on recruiting posters was Choice, Not Chance. Several years after the war was over, my research colleagues and I asked vets why they enlisted. From tabulating the answers, we found a majority of 55 percent who said they were looking to get away — from boredom, unemployment, problems at home, a lack of direction, drug use, a woman who wanted them to get married before they were ready, or a jail sentence. About 21 percent cited the advantages of military service: GI benefits, job training, time to grow up, travel and adventure. Sixteen percent said their family and friends encouraged them, and an even smaller group, 8 percent, said that they were bound to be called anyway, so they simply signed up on their own.[5]

If you listen past these pat explanations, you'll hear a more intricate variety of motives, expectations, fears, and hopes. Some went for the thrill, others because they didn't want to be left behind. Some were afraid of being on their own and looked to army life to give them something to do, to put a roof over their heads and food on the table. For some it was a way to "earn their spurs" — to become a man, to look good in a uniform and make heads turn when they walked around back home. Many simply wanted to get away for no reason they could say. A few went because they worshiped the flag.

Based on what vets now recall about the time they went in, their attitudes toward the military differ according to the years when they served. The later they were inducted, the more negative they were, a trend that parallels the waning public support for U.S. policies in Vietnam. Sixty-four percent of Vietnam veterans who went in during the years 1961 to 1965 felt "positive" about the military, whereas only 16 percent of those who entered between 1972 to 1974 felt that way.[6] It's more common to hear guys who served earlier say, "I wanted to go. I was very pro-American at the time, really wanted to get in there and fight." Of those who served later, more hold a contrasting view. "I thought it was more or less an illegal maneuver, for the government to draft me without me being able to say no, especially to an illegal war."

Regardless of when or how they went, the overwhelming majority look back on going to war as a reasonable thing to do. Even draftees talk this way, like the one who said, "If I had my druthers

I wouldn't have went at all, but since I was drafted, I figured I'd go ahead and do my time." Another said, "I wasn't about to rush out and join, but if they called me, okay, it wasn't a bad thing to do."

With rare exceptions, the enlistees recall thinking it would work out well for them personally. "I figured if I have to go, might as well make the best of it," is a common statement. One vet claimed, "It was killing two birds with one stone — get it over with now and get an education for jobs later, and anyway, it would be an experience, the big experience." Others talk about the hope they had that the military would help them. "I didn't do so good at school, I was only working part-time, I was lost, and figured it might set me straight."

Whether they were drafted or enlisted, virtually all vets now speak of going in as if it were an everyday thing to do, for the rupture of going away soon paled in comparison with what came later.

Like many vets, and many people who watched the war at home, I didn't want to get personally or emotionally involved at the outset. Even if I had to go, I wanted to go as a spectator. During the early months, it was easy to keep this inner distance by making fun of the Army. Basic training was rigorous enough, something like eighteen hours of football practice each day for two months. But being in better physical shape than most of the other recruits, I took it in stride, and found the classroom work was absurd, pitched to slow learning eighth-graders.

My way of coping was to excel. Soon after training began I became a squad leader, responsible for ten other men. A few days later the company commander was watching us march and singled me out. "Egendorf!" he snapped. "You've got fine military bearing. Get out there at the head of the company. Show 'em how to keep cadence." I knew my friends at Harvard would laugh, but I felt tingles of pride being out in front.

Intelligence school, supposedly for the cream of the cream, often was a joke. A few of us made a game out of asking the instructors questions they couldn't answer. In between classes, my best buddy Clinton would egg me on. He spoke French too. "De l'audace! Toujours de l'audace!" he'd blurt out. It was a cultivated way of saying, "Balls! Give 'em balls!" We were each other's best audience, and got a kick out of being outrageous. A Tennessee boy who had gone to a military academy, Clinton pulled strings to get into the Army because he couldn't imagine not serving and had trouble passing the physical. Intelligence school was teaching him a new skepticism.

Clinton could always get me to double-up with laughter by telling me the story about a prayer meeting he attended as a boy. The preacher was thumping against foreign languages in the schools. "The sermon rose to a fever pitch, and the preacher delivered his punch line: 'Read the Bible! There you see it! Why, if the English language is good enough for Jesus Christ, it's good enough for me!' " Clinton would then say with a redneck twang, "Why naturally after such good training I'd join up one day to kill commies for Christ."

We made light of everything. Go to war in this Army? Die for the silliness they were trying to feed to the cream of the cream? The absurdity would've hurt too much if we hadn't kept laughing. Then came the end of our six-month training. Instructors handed each of us a mimeographed sheet so we could evaluate the school. I threw mine away and stayed up half the night writing a twenty-page critique. Twelve hours after handing it in I was called in to the office of Colonel Gaines B. Hawkins, head of the school. Ready to hear the worst, I was stunned when he said, "Private! This is the best damned thing I've seen written about this place since I've been here. I'm promoting you to sergeant. And if you want a special job at MACV headquarters over there in Saigon, I'll let 'em know you're coming." I thanked him for the rank but declined the job. If I was going all the way to Vietnam, I couldn't see spending the time in an office. "Sir, I'd rather be in the field, doing what I'm trained for."

I never felt what some men call their love of the corps. The Army wasn't for me, but I often felt profound respect for individual soldiers. Colonel Hawkins was one of them.

After intelligence school I was sent to Vietnam, arriving in Saigon eight weeks after the 1968 Tet Offensive. As one of my first official acts, I reported to the personnel sergeant for my new unit. He asked me what cover name I would be using for the year. Spies need to have false identification, so that if you're captured by the enemy, the identification you carry can't be traced to the U.S. Army. I knew I'd be working with local French people, former colonists who had ideas about race and politics that led many of them to collaborate with the Nazis during World War II. So I told the sergeant, "Make the name Levy." He looked stunned. "You want a Jewish name?" I nodded, figuring that if I had to lie about who I was, it might as well be the truth.

It was fun to be Artie Levy, though occasionally very scary. During my first few weeks I could hear the cracking of gunfire in the streets throughout the day and night. I was cautious poking my head out the door and doubly cautious whenever I walked out of the building where our intelligence unit lived and worked. People I met were still talking about the famous Vietcong Tet Offensive and about the intelligence people who had been killed and wounded. Units like ours were over-run during those hellish weeks, when even the U.S. Embassy in Saigon was under siege.

Within a few weeks, I grew accustomed to the sniper fire. It was the rockets that were hardest to get used to. In the distance they sounded interesting, the same kind of deep rumble that goes through you when you listen to a super stereo or kettle drums. It nudges a place behind your stomach. When closer, the ka-ploom is more menacing. The thing hits, and it's so loud and sudden that you're dizzy for a long moment afterward.

The rockets fell mainly at night. The VC used the cover of dark to set up and launch them. They didn't care exactly where the rockets landed, as long as it was somewhere near the center of the city. The purpose was to display force, frighten people, and show that the Americans couldn't stop them. From that standpoint, it was a good tactic. When a rocket would land near us at 3 A.M., the explosion was almost enough to blow us out of bed. It made it hard to get back to sleep, and difficult to avoid feeling a little frazzled the next day.

For a couple of months, I lived with a team of eight other "case officers," the official name for spy handlers, in a villa the Army rented from a Vietnamese gentleman named Monsieur Mui. He was among the wave of well-born and well-educated northerners who had come south to preserve their lives and property when the communists took over North Vietnam in 1954. When I had arrived, times were hard for people like Mui. They depended on the Americans as their last hope. Economic necessity forced the Mui family to move out of their villa so they could rent it to us, leaving them to occupy what had been the servants' quarters. They treated us graciously, saying often that they owed us their lives.

One night I jumped out of bed so quickly that I was on my feet *before realizing I was awake. My ears hurt, my heart was pounding fast, and my body was shaking. I had literally been blown out of bed. Collecting myself, I wondered if the VC had exploded our front door and were rushing in to kill or torture us. I crawled to the office where we kept the rifles and then to the balcony to peer out at the street below. No attackers. I ran to the back of the house and saw the Muis scurrying around the courtyard. A rocket had fallen on our house, sending shrapnel through the hallway a few feet from where I slept. Miraculously, nobody was hurt. But the rocket permanently destroyed my illusion that Saigon was safe. It was about that time that I decided the war was no joke.*

In World War II the ratio of noncombatants to combatants was ten to one. In other words, for every rifleman who shot and got shot at, ten soldiers worked on supplies, personnel, intelligence, medical support, engineering, and mounds of miscellaneous paperwork. The war in Vietnam rewrote the book. A Harris survey in 1980 concluded that about a third of the Vietnam vets they interviewed qualified as "heavy combat" types, and another third fit the "moderate combat exposure" group. Seventy-seven percent of a national sample of veterans said they saw Americans killed or wounded in Vietnam. Forty-three percent said they killed or thought they killed someone over there. Twenty-three percent were wounded.[7]

What was it like? Maybe you can find a grunt who'll tell you. But most just whip out the smooth version designed for public consumption, keeping to themselves anything other than the stories that are easiest to say and hear. Very, very few ever say it precisely enough to evoke the reality with words alone. One of the exceptions, a correspondent named Michael Herr, spent ten years digesting his experiences before publishing his descriptions in *Dispatches*.

"Quakin' and Shakin'," they called it, great balls of fire, Contact. Then it was you and the ground: kiss it, eat it, fuck it, plow it with your whole body, get as close to it as you can without being in it yet or of it, guess who's flying around about an inch above your head? Pucker and submit, it's the ground. Under Fire would take you out of your head and your body too, the space you'd seen a second ago between subject and object wasn't there anymore, it banged shut in a fast wash of adrenaline. Amazing, unbelievable, guys who'd played a lot of hard sports said they'd never felt anything like it, the sudden drop and rocket rush of the hit, the reserves of adrenaline you could make available to yourself, pumping it up and putting it out until you were lost floating in it, not afraid, almost open to clear orgasmic death-by-drowning in it, actually relaxed. Unless of course, you'd shit your pants or were screaming or praying or giving anything at all to the hundred-channel panic that blew word salad all around you and sometimes clean through you. Maybe you couldn't love the war and hate it inside the same instant, but sometimes those feelings alternated so rapidly that they spun together in a strobic wheel rolling all the way up until you were literally High on War, like it said on all the helmet covers. Coming off a jag like that could really make a mess out of you.[8]

Herr's words paint the colors of the war and catch the rhythm and beat of the grunts "rapping it down" and listening to acid rock of the late 1960s. "Far out" and "mindblown" and "mother fuckin' " good sounds, like fellow vet Jimi Hendrix's, "playing his guitar the way a grunt tears into pussy." And making no bones about saying it the way he saw it, Herr echoes the post-Vietnam credo that is widespread throughout a generation: Combat blows your mind. The belief is that anybody who gets near it is marked for life. This is now the reasonable, humane, and sensitive view. Herr, the firsthand witness, earned the right to say it of himself.

In early December I came back from my first operation with the Marines. I'd lain scrunched up for hours in a flimsy bunker that was falling apart even faster than I was, listening to it going on, the moaning and whining and the dull repetitions of whump whump and dit dit dit, listening to a boy who'd somehow broken his thumb sobbing and gagging. . . . [T]he heavy shooting stopped but not the thing: at the lz [landing zone] waiting for choppers to Phu Bai one last shell came in, landing in the middle of a pile of full body bags, making a mess that no one wanted to clean up, "a real shit detail." It was after midnight when I finally got back to Saigon, riding in from Tan Son Nhut in an open jeep with some sniper-obsessed MP's. . . . I put my fatigues out in the hall room and closed the door on them, I may have even locked it. I had the I Corps DT's, livers, spleens, brains, a blue-black swollen thumb moved around and flashed to me, they were playing over the walls of the shower where I spent a half-hour, they were on the bedsheets, but I wasn't afraid of them, I was laughing at them, what could they do to me? I filled a water glass with Armagnac and rolled a joint. . . . When I turned off the lights and got into bed . . . all I saw was blood and bone fragment.[9]

Combat is what takes the toll on veterans — that's the prevailing view and the common interpretation of a growing body of research. The major studies comparing Vietnam vets who were heavily involved in combat with those who weren't have produced similar findings. On the average, the guys with the most exposure are more likely, even a decade later, still to be thinking about the death and dying they saw. They're more alienated, report more signs of stress, drink more heavily, are more likely to get arrested and to say that the war screwed up their lives.

Why? What is it about combat? Almost nobody asks the questions because the answer seems so obvious. In the current professional jargon, combat is "a recognizable stressor," defined as "a psychologically traumatic event that is generally outside the range of usual human experience."[10] But those who study postwar reactions closely find sooner or later that "combat," like the "average vet," is a convenient fiction at best. Not only do the actual events vary enormously from one firefight to another, but the impact of the events doesn't follow an observer's predictions so much as each individual's view of what was going on.

Grinker and Spiegel, two American psychiatrists who wrote the definitive study of psychiatric problems among World War II veterans, make the point this way:

> Combat experiences . . . cannot be measured or averaged because they are not objective, even though they seem so real at the moment. What is traumatic to one may be innocuous to another. One [man] . . . may crack up after the death of his buddy and yet be unafraid of [the] . . . enemy, while with another the reverse may be the case.[11]

Taken by themselves, the correlations between combat exposure and later difficulties are therefore misleading. They are commonly interpreted as evidence that "combat does it," to counter the skeptical and less generous view that veterans with problems are "bad apples" who would've been rotten whether they went to war or somewhere else. Neither view, however, advances healing. Saying that "combat does it" leaves out the people involved, and saying that "the bad apples are the ones who complain" turns people's suffering into something for which they, or their pasts, are to blame, like a moral failure.

Healing occurs by strengthening the person at the core of the suffering. And to accomplish healing we need to appreciate the role that people play in their suffering as well as in their potential cure. None of us has much control over the settings in which we find ourselves, particularly in the midst of a war. But each of us is ultimately the one who assigns meaning to those settings and draws the implications from whatever we experience there. Healing calls for us to acknowledge, respectfully, that the pain known to combat veterans has everything to do with the posture they've taken toward their experiences. And when a combat vet continues to feel pain for years afterward, it is not the events of his past that weigh on him, but his revulsion — over the things he did or failed to do, or over things he saw, heard, or thought about.

Attributing veterans' pain to revulsion alerts us to the intense personal significance of these responses. That most people would be revolted by what takes place in combat is no reason to ignore the crucial part people play in responding to what they see and do. To speak of the revulsion at the heart of postcombat responses avoids the tendency of ordinary psychodiagnosis to stigmatize people, as if they suffer from some affliction imposed by circumstances. Troubled veterans don't "have" anything, strictly speaking. Nobody ever saw or measured a "stress disorder," but only the complaints that researchers agree to call the traces of it. From a healing point of view people are always implicated in their own distress, and if we fail to take note of that, we do no service to them or to the truth.

What troubled me wasn't the gore. If I had been immersed in swamps and firefights and bloodied bodies it surely would've been different. But unlike most, I had enough time and comfort to think. And as many former grunts will say, what made the war bearable for them was precisely that there was no time to think. My problem, as some would say later on, was that I tried at times to make sense out of it all. And that made me vulnerable in a strange way; strange because I had to lie to virtually everyone I met about my name, my business, what I was doing, the purpose of my conversations with them. Somehow my need to know the truth about the war grew the more I falsified everything else.

Part of my job was to keep my eyes open for potential spies, so I'd talk to anyone. I was particularly impressed by a Frenchman I met early in my tour who had lived in Indochina for forty years and was teaching school in Saigon. He knew the country well. I was struck by how soft his eyes were and by the unusual calm in his voice. His words were the kind that only thoughtful people use. We talked about the war — it was standard espionage procedure to feel people out about their ideological allegiances. He regretted the situation, he said, because he knew the Americans wanted to help. The truth, he said, was that the situation was untenable. "Given the people you've put in power and the way you're bombing and burning to try keeping them there, the insurgents will keep looking like the true patriots to people in the countryside."

I wondered whether this man had been swayed by rebel propaganda. Was he trying to erode American morale? Or was he another French communist or communist sympathizer? The questions never left my mind, but the more he spoke, and the more I noticed his calm and reasoned tone, the more I realized that he didn't care whether I believed him or not. Then it dawned on me that he would be able to stay on in the city he loved only if we Americans stayed too. Whether it was for these reasons or not, his words touched me as no antiwar rhetoric ever had.

I never tried to recruit him. I was certain he would decline if I had tried. He seemed too balanced to want to be involved in the silly games of spying. In any event, he had won me over to his view: The war was already lost, and the only thing to do was to live out our time in it with as little loss of self-respect as possible.

Many call the war a tragic mistake. Some insist it was a crime. Others say "a noble cause." But nobody claims it was an accident. It grew from the same approach to international affairs and from the same alignment of domestic economic, social, and political forces that have kept the United States continuously mobilized for war for the past four and a half decades.

Since 1940 we have fought one world war (1941–1945), a land war in Korea (1950–1952), and have been involved through military or CIA and paramilitary forces in many countries. A list of only the more prominent engagements includes Greece (1948), Iran (1953), Guatemala (1954), Indonesia (1958), Lebanon (1958), Laos (1960–1975), Cuba (1961), Congo (1964), British Guiana (1964), Dominican Republic (1965), Vietnam (1950–1975), Cambodia (1969–1975), Chile

(1970–1973), Iran (1979), and Lebanon (1982–1984). Our troops are still involved in El Salvador (since 1981), Nicaragua (since 1981), and Grenada (since 1983).[12]

Since the day we entered World War II Americans have believed it is our duty to enforce order throughout the world. We began in 1941 by leading the fight against Nazi and militarist Japanese aggression. Within two years after the defeat of Germany and Japan, the definition of this world responsibility shifted to the defense of the free world, a role we developed in the Cold War against the Soviets. Opposition to communism and the need to counter Soviet influence became the main justification for U.S. military activities in the following decades.

In the early 1960s Norman Podhoretz, the writer and magazine editor, agreed with critics that Vietnam was the "wrong war, at the wrong time, in the wrong place." Later he became a strong supporter of the principle for which we fought: the containment of communism.[13] Yet even Podhoretz, who vigorously defends that policy, questions the way it was implemented in Vietnam. In *Why We Were in Vietnam* he argued strenuously against the view that it was an immoral war. He pointed out that U.S. policy was restrained — in not giving the military a freer hand, in not bombing the major harbors and dikes in the North, and in holding civilian casualties to about the same percentage as in World War II. After accusing the antiwar movement of contributing to the horrors of repression in Vietnam that followed the American defeat, Podhoretz nonetheless concluded that the war was wrong, "because in any event the issue in Vietnam was fundamentally 'political' and could not be resolved by military means."

But how did we happen to pursue a political struggle by military force? What brought us to employ such inappropriate means? Such questions will be debated for a long time to come. The view I find most plausible was articulated more than a decade ago by Richard J. Barnet, an official in the Kennedy administration who became a critic of the war. Barnet wrote that since the beginning of World War II the major institutions formulating U.S. foreign policy have developed a momentum that prejudices the options of top decision makers in favor of military solutions.[14]

We began in 1940–41 by building the Pentagon, the largest building in the world (its shape, one art historian has noted, is the ancient sign used for black magic).[15] After 1945 vast institutional changes that had been devised to fight Germany, Italy, and Japan became permanent features of American life. Before World War II, the United States had major military bases only in Guam, Hawaii, the Philippines, and several other minor overseas installations. In 1945, at the end of the World War II, U.S. forces controlled 434 bases around the world, and by 1969, at the height of the Vietnam War, 1,222,000 U.S. troops were stationed in 399 major overseas military bases and 1930 minor installations.[16]

Before World War II, officially sponsored espionage was rare in the United States. During the Hoover Administration (1929–1933), Secretary of War Henry L. Stimson rejected a proposed national intelligence agency by saying, "Gentlemen do not read each other's mail." During World War II, the Office of Strategic Services was organized under Major General William J. Donovan, who recruited and trained over thirty thousand spies, spy handlers, intelligence analysts, and other support personnel. *Even before the rivalry with the Soviet Union emerged as a dominant factor in the postwar period*, Donovan had laid plans, according to his assistant, Robert H. Alcorn,

> . . . for the future of espionage in our country's way of life. . . . We were everywhere already, he argued, and it was only wisdom and good policy to dig in, quietly and officially, for the long pull. Overseas branches of large corporations, the expanding business picture, the rebuilding of war areas, Government programs for economic, social and health aid to foreign lands, all these were made to order for the infiltration of espionage agents.[17]

Before World War II, the American business community and the military were, with rare exceptions, at odds. Some of the most prominent business leaders, such as Andrew Carnegie and Henry Ford, stood for the internationalist and pacifist solution of peace through world trade. If businessmen looked down on military action as a crude and outmoded approach to human problems, military leaders saw businessmen as a leisure class that was insufficiently patriotic and unwilling to serve anything other than its own greed. But by the end of the 1950s, our only modern President who had served previously as an Army general, Dwight Eisenhower, saw fit to warn the American people of the mounting influence of a "military-industrial complex." Large sectors of U.S. manufacturing had come to thrive on defense contracts, and the careers of thousands of Pentagon officials had become dependent on purchases and management of the increasingly sophisticated and expensive weaponry provided by modern technology. A vast institutionalized constituency had developed that favored a militarized approach to foreign policy problems.

The crucial turn had taken place during World War II, when the federal government pressed U.S. business into the war effort and paid handsomely for its cooperation. During the years 1941 to 1945, the gross national product more than doubled, and business leaders, such as Charles Wilson, president of General Electric and later secretary of defense under Eisenhower, were calling for a "permanent war economy." [18]

In a similar fashion, new sources of federal funding that opened during World War II brought researchers based in the universities into various activities to support the war. And price-wage policies that required close coordination with and cooperation from labor leaders converted an essentially oppositionist labor movement into another part of the national war machine.

To manage these changes, the executive branch of government gave rise to expanded bureaucracies, mostly under the departments of State and Defense. As administrative authority became more centralized, the power of Congress waned. In the 1930s military spending was a low priority in Congress, which came close to blocking the Selective Service Act a few months before Pearl Harbor, and almost passed an act in 1938 that would have forbidden the President to send troops abroad without a national referendum. In contrast, all of the "brush fire wars" fought by the United States since 1945 have been initiated and conducted by the chief executive without a declaration of war by Congress, as required under the Constitution.

In broad terms, a great war gave rise to the social machinery to fight it and that machinery in turn acquired a momentum all its own. According to Lewis Mumford, a renowned cultural anthropologist and historian of technology, this pattern has occurred repeatedly throughout history. [19] What he calls the megamachine, the centralized bureaucratized state, both stems from and gives rise to war.

Thus, a society geared for war is not likely to formulate constructive alternatives to military responses, even when some of its best military minds counsel against the use of force, as ours did even before the large-scale landing of U.S. troops in Vietnam.

Many vets changed during the war. People ask, "What did it?" and expect to hear a story that explains how it happened. But the expectation is misplaced. The change is never explained by the sequence of events. All you get from the story is that a man goes into a situation looking at the world one way, and, then, after his whole view comes apart for reasons he can never fully explain, he emerges seeing things another way. You hear about killing and being shot at and observing horrors. But since war is filled with such events, the question inevitably is how this particular incident gave rise to so profound a change. From a healing perspective, the ultimate answer is that regardless of what helped set the stage, it is always the person at the center of the experience who shapes and colors what takes place. And the times and places we call turning points in our lives can no more be explained or justified than the elements an artist chooses for a work of art.

Early in my tour I had an experience that I later came to recognize as the night my life changed. My spy team hadn't moved into our villa yet, and I was still living in the large hotel that was headquarters for Army intelligence in the Chinese section of Saigon. It was after dinner, and I was on my way up to the roof to get some air when I heard one of the career sergeants curse and cheer, "Hot shit! Look at them flares." The night was lit all around the city and the sergeant major was celebrating his vicarious triumph. "Damn if that's not kicking ass!" Helicopter gunships were darting in and out of the darkness, spewing fire. Flares came first, then rockets, then tracers from their mini guns — super machine guns that pumped sixty bullets a second on whatever lay below. (Fffooomm, not rat-a-tat-tat-tat-tat.) Four other career sergeants and a warrant officer were chuckling along with the sergeant major. "Just like goddamn Fourth of fucking July, and it's weeks away! Give it to 'em. Shit." They were swigging beer, poking each other in the ribs, and taking turns calling attention to each new series of bursts in the sky and explosions on the ground.

It was a good vantage point for watching the night, the roof of the tallest building for a mile or more on all sides. Next door was the sec-

ond tallest building, the largest whorehouse in this section of the city. We could look down and see the girls milling around on the rooftop below. The men in our unit used to think of it as their own private harem until a few months before I arrived in Vietnam, when it was declared off-limits. The Tet Offensive hit our section of the city badly, much too close for comfort, so regular contact with people in the surrounding area was cut off for security reasons.

The sergeant major and the others looked me over, barely acknowledging my presence with a nod. I didn't hang out with them. I didn't drink much, and preferred to spend my nights reading or practicing the piano at a Vietnamese friend's house. Bill Robertson, another first-term enlisted man like myself, was on the roof when I arrived. Robertson came from Alabama, hated the Army, and was seething most of the time. All he could talk about was how much money he was going to make when he got home. He'd say it to me in a cutting tone, because he saw me as more cooperative with the Army he hated than he was. I would wise off, teasing the career officers and sergeants by claiming to have infiltrated U.S. intelligence for the international communist-Jewish conspiracy. But I did it without getting them angry. Robertson couldn't keep from enraging his superiors. He had already told a few sergeants to fuck themselves and was near to being transferred out of our unit to an infantry battalion.

I was standing next to Robertson, leaning on the railing that enclosed the roof. We could see the lights of downtown Saigon, the posh diplomatic district, and the long line of neon lights on Tu Do Street — named for the Vietnamese word for freedom — where bars and massage parlors, called "steam and cream" or "turkey jerks" by the GIs, occupied virtually every storefront for two blocks. Behind our building was half a square mile of dark. There were no lights, buildings, or people, only cinder, charred beams, and gnarled tin that had once served as roofing for cluttered acres of huts and shanties. A few weeks before my arrival, several squads of Vietcong snipers had infiltrated that area. To flush them out an entire section of Saigon's Chinatown had been decimated by the kinds of attacks we were watching on the horizon at that moment.

The girls on top of the next building caught my eye. Their waist-length hair was waving in the breeze in the same rhythm as the flaps on their ao dias, the traditional Vietnamese dress slit on each side from *waist to ankle, revealing long silk pants underneath. One of the girls looked up at Robertson and me and giggled. My face flushed and heat came into my body. Whores like her delighted me, the same effect they had on many soldiers. Unlike the Vietnamese women you'd pass on the streets, the joy girls didn't act aloof and shy. Seeing her look my way embarrassed me, but also opened me up. Why should women have such power to arouse desire? I resented the way they could penetrate my reticence. But I was also grateful, because some of the rare moments of tenderness I had over there came with such women.*

While thinking about lovemaking, I heard the sergeant major blurt out a fresh tribute to a salvo on the horizon. "Goddamn, that's a gorgeous sight!" I looked where he was pointing and could see the faint outline of the jumbled huts bursting into flames less than a mile away. Blazing tracers rained from the gunships in a stream that fed the fires below. An explosion blew a few roofs to the ground, and walls fell soon after. I watched, amazed, as an entire neighborhood went up in flames. I'd never seen such a sight, and felt an urge to draw closer when a choking, nauseated gasp came high into my throat. In a flash I saw beyond the flames, to the people being incinerated like trash.

"How can they laugh?" I hissed to Robertson, gesturing toward the sergeants. "People are under those flames!"

"What do you care?" asked Robertson. "You're not going to do anything about it!"

I didn't answer him. But I knew then that something had touched me, and that I'd never be the same.

Veterans' psychological complaints now have an official name. The media and the public have followed the lead of the mental health professions in adopting the terms "delayed stress" and "post-traumatic stress disorder."[20] The availability of an official diagnosis has been useful in bringing the Veterans Administration and Congress to acknowledge that the war remains a painfully unresolved experience for many. The official attention can be valuable, but calling the problem "delayed stress" is imprecise and misleading. It's not that the stress is delayed but that the signs of strain don't necessarily appear until months or years after the events that seem, in retrospect, to be the source of pain.

This time lag has prompted the popular image of veterans as "time bombs," their fuses set in the war, with the explosion to go off at some point in the future. This image is also unfortunate, for it implies that human memory is an instrument like a tape recorder or camera. In fact, memory is creative, not mechanical. In retelling the past, we cannot help selecting, arranging, and coloring what took place in the light of what has happened since. The past, as we relive it, is therefore as much a commentary on what and how we are now as on what took place some time ago. Ultimately, the cure has to address the person we now take ourselves to be, not just some thing or disorder rooted in a distant time.

The question for healing is how best to think about the role of the past in these "delayed" responses. In the face of extreme danger, people act and channel inner reactions in an instant, without deliberate thought. By censoring any response that threatened concentration on survival, most veterans pledged, in effect, to live up to an idea of themselves as tough and unbreakable. Later experiences, often intimate ones with lovers, wives, and children, call for a responsiveness that the hardened soldier decided long ago would make him too vulnerable. It is in these situations that the self-styled toughness is revealed as a cover, to hide what one fears is an underlying weakness.

At such times, vets may decide to let go, to allow a sensitivity that was formerly taboo. What happens for some, however, is that they then fall prey to a long-held belief that once they let themselves respond emotionally, the flood of feeling will be too much for them to handle. Believing that if they really open up they'd be overwhelmed, men worry all the more over emotional outbursts and haunting memories. The various correlates of this distress, from troubled sleep to loss of interest in life to guilt and other complaints, are now lumped together and called "stress disorder." What the diagnosis doesn't say is that if you're convinced that extremely strong feelings are a sign that you're sick or weak, then the only options you've got are to make yourself numb or let it all out and think of yourself as crazy.

Phrases such as "delayed stress" and other psychiatric jargon obscure the dual nature of postwar responses as both curse *and* opportunity. The rarely spoken fact is that however painful they are, these reactions also may serve as the occasion for men to evolve and update their ways of responding to life.

This duality is quite familiar to therapists who treat the everyday variety of human suffering. Consider the way Carl Jung put this point: "A neurosis is by no means merely a negative thing, it is also something positive . . . [for] it contains the patient's psyche, or at least an essential part of it. . . . His illness is not a gratuitous and therefore meaningless burden; it is *his own self*, the 'other' whom, from childish laziness or fear, or for some other reason, he was always seeking to exclude from his life."[21]

The tendency among many veterans and the public is to respond to talk of "stress disorder" with the seemingly logical but mistaken idea that what veterans need is to reduce their level of stress. This idea has the unfortunate effect of encouraging veterans and well-meaning supporters to think that men in pain should shrink from life. Or one might think that veterans need to change or reprogram their responses, when in fact their horror, rage, guilt, and desperation may be quite genuine, the signs of a reemerging sensitivity. Taking the direction implied by Jung and others, we can simply invite troubled veterans to revise their notions of what kinds of responses are admissible. For once a man grants himself the freedom to be appropriately upset by what he has seen and done, his reactions subside quite naturally, and he experiences himself as "more himself."

Retelling one's story is an ancient cure. It allows people to take a more livable stance toward what they've experienced, one that may not have been possible at the time the events originally took place. Retelling is likely to allow us to feel "more human" afterward, for recapturing the past in a sensitive way, often through the process of mourning, enables us to set aside our fearful self-protectiveness. In this way we overcome the greatest burden we carry away from shocking experiences: the limits we've placed on our capacity to care.

Fearful self-protectiveness is still very evident among the majority of Vietnam veterans. Most of the men my colleagues and I interviewed in our national study speak easily enough about the past. But they tell their "war stories" as self-congratulatory accounts, ways to keep people at a distance or to make themselves "look good." Among this reticent majority are a few who admit that they deliberately avoid or exclude a whole set of reactions. Take, for example, the ex-infantryman who recalled: "I got kind of sick the first time I

seen a VC cut in two. And then somebody says, ah, you get used to
it. I got so sick that one of the sergeants grabbed me by the collar
and pushed my face right into it. After a while I would do it, I would
push their faces into it, especially if they really broke down and
started crying. A lot of dudes would look at it and they'd panic.
They'd try to run away, and when they start doing that they're no
good to you because they're going to make mistakes. So when I
caught a new dude, and he says 'I'm not going to do that!' two or
three of us would grab him and say, 'Oh yes you are!' and initiate
him right then and there."

Earlier in the interview he had summed up his view of what happened to him over there. "I guess it's called adjusting. You know,
there's no sense in breaking down," he explained, and then recited
one of the most common keys to survival, "so you don't get too
close to people." Over and over vets will claim that they had to
restrict their capacity to care. Recalling the Vietnamese he saw killed,
a former officer said, "I felt sorrow but I didn't really have true empathy for them. I felt that it was kind of — those are the breaks."

The tendency to close down inwardly is particularly marked among
a small minority who recount, in an entirely detached way, gory
details of combat that would make most people cringe. They may
number no more than 5 to 10 percent of the men who served in
Vietnam, but given that 4 million men spent time in the combat
zone, this amounts to anywhere from 200,000 to 400,000. These are
the men who took part in massive killing, but talk as if nothing much
took place. "I don't let nothing get to me," is a common boast, as if
their lack of feeling is a great achievement. They don't seem aware
of the option of cultivating a more flexible strength — of having responses without being swamped by them. It's like the two ways not
to drown in water: You can refuse to go in, or you can learn how to
swim. Those who seem proud not to feel are like people who don't
go in the water and brag about staying dry.

We interviewed a former sniper who said, "I could give you a
running count of the Vietnamese I killed. My reaction was literally
pleasurable because I thought they were such crude little bastards."
Another vet who did similar work recalled, "Killing a gook was really
nothing at all. It didn't bother me at all. I could have butchered them
like nothing, really. I really had no feelings." Another veteran re-

membered that he "was very pleased when they fell, and if they still moved I pumped in a couple more rounds. I had no respect, no regard. . . . I was brought up to have respect for life but over in Vietnam I had no respect for life."

The first ex-sniper still thinks of his job in Vietnam as "the biggest challenge of my life. You felt a great sense of accomplishment when you succeeded." He described assassinating a high-ranking general: "That made my day. It was so precise, so critical that the human-life-taking aspect never entered my mind. I've learned to function under phenomenal levels of stress, almost made me immune to all sorts of dangers in life." The blockage of any sense of vulnerability is shared by other men. One said, "I knew I wouldn't be killed. It never fazed me."

Generally, men in this state say the war had no effect on them, and when asked whether they've experienced any symptoms of emotional stress, they say no. But given a chance to speak more freely about themselves, some will recall "a lot of drinking, dope smoking, wild times" when they came back. Others will claim that they are "well adjusted, no hang-ups, very content, the same old happy bum" in a tone that is hollow and eerie.

A large minority of veterans struggle to avoid thinking about the war, but are clearly aware of their inner conflict. They may say outright that they're trying to block out memories, questions, and feelings related to that time. Some say that "there's something going on," as if they were hexed by a curse. A former demolitions expert told us, "To this day I have no sad emotions. I don't worry about anything and it's bad. It's like half of me is gone someplace. I really don't know where it went." Since coming home he has been arrested three times, convicted twice, for assault, and invokes the popular stereotype, calling himself a "walking bomb."

Some veterans are reflective enough to acknowledge that they have troubling thoughts and questions they try to keep out of mind. A former Navy seaman said, "Dying frightened me. It was constantly on my mind. I saw a lot of dead guys because my job was to take them off the helicopters on stretchers. Like one time I saw a young Marine captain with both legs blown off and he lived and it just stayed with me." But when probed further about his reaction, this man claimed, "I didn't have any reaction, it just made you want to

go home sooner. I was at ah . . . well, things were moving so fast
that I . . . nothing stayed with me. I didn't talk about them, forget
about them, never thought about it 'til I came home and it was in
the past." Then, asked to say how the war affected his life overall,
he said in a detached way, "Mildly. It was an experience."

*I talked about my year in Saigon many times before I heard myself say
what was so upsetting about that night on the roof. It was easy enough
for me to know I was pissed at Robertson. Afterward I purposely avoided
him, not wanting him to have the satisfaction that he had gotten to
me. A few weeks later he was transferred out of the unit because of his
"attitude." I felt vindicated; he didn't know when to stop, not with me
or with anyone else. But I also felt sorry for him. He was a hothead,
and I knew he cared, though not in any way that showed or affected
others. He just looked around and called a spade a spade. The official
U.S. justifications for our being in Vietnam were lies, he said. We weren't
helping the Vietnamese; most of the soldiers and American civilians in
Vietnam wanted only to "get their ticket punched" — get paid, laid,
and come out with credit for wherever they were going next.*

*Most of all, it was the question he fired at me that stuck: "What do
you care?" At first I'd say to myself that I was there to fulfill my share
of the responsibility. Then the truth teller in me would let loose, and
"Bullshit!" would go the voice in my head. "You don't have anything
else to do with your life right now, and you're looking to cover your
ass just like anybody else. You wanted to get yourself to Vietnam so
that it would look as if you were doing the real thing, and then you
pull every move you know to get a job you thought would be safe. You
want it to look as if you've got guts, but you're as chickenshit as anybody."*

*"But I do care," I insisted to myself. "Look at how much more re-
spectful I am to the women and the Vietnamese than lots of the guys
around here." Then the voice would answer, "Don't give me that crap!
You're as much a bastard at heart as all the rest. You cringe when the
GIs walk down the street saying, 'Hey mama, want some fuckie-fuckie?'
because you know you're made out of the same stuff they are. You just
put a prettier face on it."*

*"But at least I'm not over here killing," was my one consolation.
"Yeah?" the voice would rip into me. "Are you so sure? You told peo-*

*ple before you came here that this is as much your war as anyone else's.
Are you taking that back now? What are you washing your hands of?
Remember McDuck?''*

*McDuck was the name we gave to one of the guys in our unit who
walked with a strange waddle and thought like Robertson. One day he
came up to me when I was about to send one of my spies into Cambodia and asked, "Did it ever dawn on you that Jean-Louis could get
killed doing what you're sending him off to?" I had mumbled something like "Sure. So what?" and walked away. But his question had
stuck, like Robertson's.*

*Months after I left Vietnam and was stationed in Washington, I read
an article in* Time *magazine about a French journalist who was lost and
probably killed in Cambodia. He had been my agent. Reading the article, I remembered McDuck and realized that I could continue to think
of myself as innocent only if I ignored what I had seen and done. If I
wanted the freedom that came with being truthful, I'd have to acknowledge that the war wasn't fought by some distant "them." I had
had a hand in it.*

People are forever telling stories. The question here is what, if anything, does this going back over the steps we've taken have to do
with healing? In asking myself this question, I've realized that it's
not just the past but time itself that is involved in healing, but not
in the way we assume when we invoke the cliché, "Time heals all
wounds." Time doesn't do that at all. Nobody ever saw time do
healing. When people say time heals, they usually mean the passage of time, the rush of many things that happen. If enough new
events crowd into our lives and capture our attention, we have no
time to think of old pains, which thereby subside into a background
gnawing. This is how we use time to dull pain, but it's not the same
as healing.

Healing occurs as we express ourselves genuinely, by saying in
some way what the past has been. In expressing how it was and is,
we make ourselves the witness — one who sees rather than one
who has merely been tossed about by passing events. In reaching
out to grasp a troublesome past, we cease to be at its mercy, and the
more we reach to make ourselves a witness to the past, the less we
are its victim.

Healing unfolds in steps, a series of which invariably takes time, leading people to say, in shorthand fashion, that time heals. But if you observe closely, you will notice that the healing doesn't occur by virtue of anything that time does to us, but rather through a shift we initiate in our relationship with time. With each bit of fresh telling we recapture the past, rather than merely lose ourselves in it through obsessions, daydreams, or absentmindedness. As the teller, we create a more expansive present, one that reaches to include the past. And the more we express ourselves in this way, the more time shifts from being a relentless master who dictates the pace and conditions of life to being the servant who offers us the time of our lives to live and relive as we see fit.

It may take many, many tellings of our lives and many, many moments of reflection to create a more ample sense of time. Each bit of retracing steps contributes by widening our grasp on what we've experienced, transforming memory from an intrusion to a reminder that the present is elastic and can expand to hold the time of our lives as a whole. In this way old pain is healed, but not because we forget. The more amply we reach out to grasp our past, the more we can look on old pain gratefully, recognizing it as the instigator that provoked us into growing to encompass it.

☆ 3 ☆

GETTING INVOLVED

War does different things to different men. It disables one, un-
balances the mind of a second, pauperizes a third, and makes
a fourth write great literature to ease his tortured soul.

WILLARD WALLER[1]

AFTER THEIR WAR some veterans are aimless and lost, some have physical and mental wounds that need attention, and many are seemingly unscathed. Almost all, however, have the urge to get on with life.

For most the goals are clear enough: They want a job, maybe more schooling, someone to love, and eventually a family. As for the war, most come home thinking of it as something to leave behind, and maybe, eventually, an experience they'll value — a time when they saw some of the world, proved a few things to themselves, got some craziness out of their system, and sorted things out so they could dig into life back home in a way they never could before they left.

Thoughtful veterans need something more than these concrete achievements to feel whole or "in one piece." For them life hangs together or has integrity only when they find a larger purpose, something that gives meaning to the past as well as the future. It is in approaching life this way that ex-soldiers confront the question of how to make sense of the killing and dying they witnessed or took part in.

Over and over commentators say that making sense of the war in Vietnam is difficult and painful, because we lost and because we didn't agree on what we were fighting for. Yet the same problem surfaced after an uncontroversial war and victory. During the "good war" of 1941–1945, historian Dixon Wecter knew that making sense of things would be the core challenge for that generation of veterans: "Whatever the cost to him personally of this war, in time and happiness and wholeness of body and mind, he [the veteran] wants to know that it has all been to some purpose. This war in the long view has got to make sense."[2]

One of the veterans of that war, J. Glenn Gray, served with Army intelligence in Europe. He was present at the liberation of several Nazi concentration camps and vowed that he would someday write about his experiences, particularly about the suffering he had seen. A decade later, while on his way to becoming a world-renowned philosopher, Gray wrote of his struggles to make sense of what he had lived through.

> The deepest fear of my war years, one still with me, is that these happenings had no real purpose. . . . How often I wrote in my war journals that unless that day had some positive significance for my future life, it could not possibly be worth the pain it cost. . . . I strive to see at least my own life as a whole and to discover some purpose and direction in at least the major parts. Yet the effort to assimilate those intense war memories to the rest of my experience is difficult and even frightening.[3]

Most veterans will put it more simply: They don't want to think that their buddies died in vain. Traditionally, a large segment of each generation of veterans has determined to *do* something — get involved or act in some way that matters — to help give the past a purpose. They join a veterans' post or march in Memorial Day and Veterans Day parades. Some take soda or food to the nearest VA hospital on Sundays. Most just pay a little more attention to the world than they did before, by reading the paper and following the news. A few reach the point of burning intensity to do something that counts, and turn their lives inside out in hopes that it will make a difference.

On May 10, 1970, my last year in the Army ended, and I left Washington and returned to my parents' apartment in Philadelphia. Waiting for me there was a letter from the student activists' committee of Eliot House, the section of Harvard College where I had lived during the early 1960s. The letter implored all alumni to write their congressmen and senators to protest the recent invasion of Cambodia. Fury at the operation in Cambodia had been seething in me for weeks, but I had held it in check. Like most of my buddies in our unit in Washington, I was disgusted by the idea of further military action, but unwilling to do anything that would get me in serious trouble. Now that I was discharged, I was free to speak out as much as I wanted. And the letter from people at my old school roused me as nothing had before.

For three years I had thought that once I got out of the Army I'd go back to Europe to study international economics. During the months I was stationed in Washington, I sometimes questioned that idea. So much was happening here. The war was front page news, and so were the demonstrations to end it. And there was Liza, my girlfriend in New York. She agreed to join me if I went to Europe, but she wasn't excited about the idea. I said we could get married over there. But the proposal didn't settle things. She told me what her friends were saying, that "he sounds like he doesn't really know what he wants." I didn't like hearing that. Other people's suspicions made me wonder about myself. What would I do over there? How would I pay for food and rent? How could I live like a wandering student and be a married man?

I read the letter from the students at Eliot House a second time. Suddenly the questions about what to do with my life fell away and a new plan came to me. I wouldn't leave the country. I'd stay and take part in the revolution that surely had to come. I'd work to end the war and to take care of the damage that had been done. I wanted to be part of building something valuable, not someday in the future, but now.

I called the VA hospital in Philadelphia. "I want to get involved, I want to do something, work with vets, help out, now!" One, two, three people listened and passed me on to somebody else. Dazed responses came at me from the other end of the phone. No one knew what to tell me, and they certainly didn't grasp the urgency I felt. So I concluded that Philadelphia, the place where I grew up, wasn't the place to be. I packed my bags and my typewriter and had my parents drive me to the train station. My father was concerned that I was throwing away my career as an economist. My mother said, "Whatever you want to do, dear," in a tone that meant, "You won't listen to me anyway, so what does it matter what I think?" I took a train to New York City.

Two blocks from Penn Station I found a YMCA. I checked into one of the cubbyhole rooms and went down to their counseling offices. There I met a gentle bearded man who listened intently. I told him that I was just out of the Army and had blood on my hands, but could be trusted to take good care of people. I wanted to dig in and do the hard, dirty work of tending to other people's pain. He introduced me to his boss, who asked about my background. I told him about Harvard, study in Europe, and the work I did in Vietnam and Washington. "Can you prove any of this?" he asked. I showed him my transcripts from school, my discharge, several letters of recommendation I had obtained from

old professors and from my commanding officers in Saigon and Wash-
ington. He looked through them and offered me a job in his counsel-
ing office.

The YMCA on Thirty-fourth Street in Manhattan is a transient hotel
for students, immigrants, and expense-conscious tourists, as well as a
way station for drug addicts, mental patients, and other wards of the
state. My job was to talk with people who came to the counseling of-
fice looking for advice about getting around the city or through their
lives. I met prostitutes of both sexes, pimps, addicts who taught me
words like skin popping and mainlining and spoons and Methadone
and copping heroin. I met bag ladies, battered teenagers, husbands on
the run, wives on the run, engineers from India looking to make their
fortune, students from the Midwest aglow with wonder at being at New
York. It was just what I wanted, a job that required compassion and
some wits and that made me confront every day an unresolvable heap
of human distress.

The second half of Homer's epic begins with the hero's first approach to his native Ithaka. On arriving, Odysseus hears a warning
from the goddess Athena, patron of the warrior, wise man, and spy.
She tells him that for the past three years "brazen upstarts" have
taken over his house and have been drinking his wine, eating his
cattle, wooing his wife Penelope, and plotting the murder of his son
Telemakhos. Athena tells him that his loyal bride has been using
various ruses to keep these suitors under control, leading them to
expect her to make a choice among them while secretly longing for
her husband's return.

"Patience, iron patience, you must show," the goddess counsels
Odysseus, "So give it out to neither man nor woman that you are
back from wandering."[4] Athena then transforms the mighty warrior
into an old beggar. In this disguise, he meets his son Telemakhos,
who has been waiting for his father's return for most of his life. At
Athena's command, the hero reveals himself to his son, and after a
tearful reunion, lays out his plan for retaking his home.

Odysseus goes among the suitors dressed in rags. They mock and
insult him while he appraises their strength. Late at night, when the
suitors have gone, Odysseus has Telemakhos hide all the weapons
that are usually on display in his house. He manages even to speak

with Penelope without letting on who he really is, telling her he has heard that Odysseus will soon return.

The next day, when the suitors return, Penelope calls for a contest among them. Whoever can string Odysseus' stout bow and shoot an arrow through a maze of twelve ax heads will win her hand. Each tries and fails, but now the man dressed in a beggar's rags has one of his servants bring him the bow. He strings it easily, shoots an arrow to its mark, and then fells one suitor after the other with the arrows he has left. Guided by Athena and aided by Telemakhos and two loyal servants, Odysseus slays the rest with spears and swords.

This fierce scene is an exciting climax to the saga. But what significance will a contemporary reader find in a tale of such primitive retribution? A psychotherapist, for example, might read the poem much as he or she would interpret a dream, in which all the characters appear as aspects of ourselves. Each of us has many facets, including metaphorical equivalents of the virtuous wife, the horde of social parasites, the cunning adventurer, and the voice that speaks with divine clarity. Seen in this light, *The Odyssey* tells the story of the inner revolution that follows our coming back or waking up to ourselves. This is a struggle that rages whether or not one has been to war. The challenge of healing is to overcome what is parasitic in ourselves, and to bring about an inner reunion, like the rejoining of the hero's family.

Healing involves more than contemplation. It advances through action taken to set things right, deeds that follow the guidance of what we call conscience. No matter how daring the moves we make, and how much we draw on wit and guile to cover our preparations, what reestablishes wholeness are the actions that spring from the voices within that the ancients called their gods.

People who had recently transplanted themselves from some faraway place were a common sight in the YMCA counseling office. As I talked with them, I'd often think of Monsieur Mui, the Vietnamese gentleman I spoke with almost every day during my year in Saigon.

Monsieur Mui was unusually kind. He would continually pray for peace, but he also had strong prejudices. Whenever we spoke he'd mention how erratic, superstitious, and untrustworthy the peasants were. He was an absentee landlord, an object of the peasants' resentment,

*and a potential target of any communist indictment of "enemies of the
people." I knew that if the communists ever took Saigon, Monsieur
Mui would be among those sent to work camps or a worse fate. When
I began thinking the insurgents had the nobler cause, I felt torn, as if I
were wishing bad times on a friend.*

*From observing Mui's plight, I drew the conclusion that things go
sour when the well born lose touch with their own people. I came
home suspecting that this lesson applied to me and others I knew,
those who were educated to hold a privileged position in society, but
only by being isolated from the trials and sufferings of ordinary people.
I viewed the counseling office as my finishing school, a place where I
hoped to undo years of social estrangement.*

*While I was there, the lesson was driven home through my meetings
with Guillermo, a Cuban who came from a wealthy family that had left
Havana when Castro rose to power. "My mother won't let us mention
Castro's name," he told me once. "But all of us know that things weren't
right before the revolution. We'd throw out more leftover food each
day than many, many poor families would eat in a week. We'd gamble
away enough money in one evening to buy food and clothes for a
dozen hungry kids for a year. But it was unfashionable to care about
such things. If you were rich, you had it coming. Nothing else mattered. It took one of our own kind like Castro, the son of a rich man,
to know things had to be straightened out between us and the people."*

*While I worked at the Y, Guillermo came to see me several days a
week to talk, to ask my opinion on his latest thoughts, to be his port
in a storm. His family had to leave everything behind in Havana, and
now he was supporting himself as a security guard. As a boy, he had
experimented with drugs and homosexuality, and his parents responded by sending him away to American mental hospitals, to Harvard summer school, to vacations in Europe. When the family arrived
in the United States in the early 1960s, Guillermo found work in an
advertising agency. He held a succession of ad agency jobs until he
was laid off in 1969. When the Y cut back on counseling staff, and the
last hired (me) was the first fired, I continued to see Guillermo once a
week at my place. He didn't pay me; we had an understanding between us. He had been in psychoanalysis in various countries since his
late teens, for more than twenty years. He would break me in, be my*

first long-term patient, and I would make myself available for the experience.

Months later, I moved out of the small room I had been living in to join some friends uptown. I sublet the room to Guillermo. He was pleased to be in my place, and I was glad to be able to do something concrete for him.

One day he didn't come to see me as we had agreed. That night I got a phone call from a neighbor in the old building to come quickly. I arrived to find two policemen at the door of my old room. "This is pretty gruesome but we need you to identify the body," they said. I went inside and saw what a corpse is like after it has been decomposing for a week in a hot room. Guillermo's remains, bloated to twice the normal size, had become a gray balloon, with even his ears filled up like bubbles. The place stank so badly I couldn't bear to breathe. He was lying in my bed, with reddish ooze coming out of his nose and mouth.

The next day I went back, after the morgue had come for his body. The mattress was still covered with gobs of stinking yellow pus. The living arrangement with my friends was coming to an end and I would to have to move back to that room soon. How, I wondered, would I ever be able to sleep in that bed again? The time came, however, when I had to. At first I cursed Guillermo for dying there, from what I suspected was an overdose of alcohol and drugs. Later I recalled the promise he had repeatedly made to me: "I'm going to initiate you," which is exactly what he did.

I was sad and tearful for days. Even worse, because it was hard to admit, my pride was hurt: He was my patient and I had failed to save him. I turned to my old boss at the counseling office for advice. He had been a Catholic priest who left the church in protest over being forbidden to marry the woman he loved. A kindly, wise man, he said to me, "Whatever you might think should have happened, Guillermo's destiny is clear now. You gave him what he seems to have wanted — enough comfort so that he could die."

Until then I had equated success in healing and in life with survival. What I learned from my experience with Guillermo is that death, like life, has its own logic, and that dying comes on its terms, not on mine. While mourning Guillermo I realized I was also mourning my former way of life, which I had abandoned after the war. Like him, I had grown *up thinking that I would be insulated from the suffering of the world. And like him, I found out that no privilege, no shrewdness, could provide certain escape from frailty, least of all from the greatest frailty, mortality. Guillermo had helped me see that I might as well make pain and death my friends, since I would certainly lose if I kept trying to banish them as enemies.*

Several years later, when I was a psychology intern in a hospital, I spent several months counseling patients in a cancer ward and made weekly visits to the room where medical students dissected cadavers. When nobody was there I'd go in and walk around the tables where the gray lumps were arranged, here a leg detached, there a belly cut open to reveal the brown gobs inside. It was as if I were waiting for a sign — that I had seen enough, that my dues were paid, that I was humbled enough, that I knew death firsthand and no longer had to search for what I had missed in Vietnam.

Eventually I realized that I'd never be cool about death and never be immune to grief. In fact, I never found anything to atone for, nothing to get over, for nothing would make my mortality and vulnerability go away.

I had left the Army in May. During the summer that followed I was often upset. News from Vietnam could drive me to distraction. One Saturday I turned on the radio and heard that the bombing had resumed over the North. I was supposed to go to work, but called and said I couldn't come. I put on my fatigues and combat boots, called Dial a Demonstration to find out where the protests were being held that day, and ran at full clip the thirty blocks from my apartment to the staging area in Columbus Circle.

It was several hours before other people came, sauntering along and smoking dope. I couldn't grasp their lack of passion. Bombs! I thought. We're dropping bombs on them again! Don't these people here get it? Can't anyone feel it? Do you know what B-52 attacks feel like even when you're thirty miles away? Do you know your feet feel unsteady as the ground shakes, your guts rumble, and if you have any imagination, you see bodies blown into the air and heaped in bomb craters like bloody trash? What is this, a picnic? Some revolution. I don't remember feeling especially out of place as the only person dressed in government issue combat clothing. I was already a complete misfit.

The following fall I audited psychology courses, studied on my own, and applied for graduate school in clinical psychology. I'd talk with fellow students over coffee. Not long after we met, I'd tell them what was on my mind. The war, psychological processes, and then more about the war and what it meant for American society. "You're really obsessed with that stuff, aren't you?" is what many people said to me during my first year out of the Army. On the upper West Side of Manhattan, everybody had been in protest marches, including taxi drivers and street kids. Demonstrations had been good places to cop dope and "off the pigs," but times had changed. The draft had ended. Things were getting quiet now, and people were into food coops, graduate school, and paying the rent. In this setting, preoccupation with Vietnam was out of fashion. I was weird.

I made a promise to myself. When my entrance exams to grad school were over, I'd find that group I had read about, Vietnam Veterans Against the War, the one place I thought I would fit in.

Over the past half century, several of the major developments in depth psychology, the various offshoots of psychoanalysis, came about as careful observers responded to the wars of their time. Freud's work was the first to register such a change. Departing sharply from his earlier focus on sex, Freud proposed in his later work that human existence develops through the interplay between two fundamental impulses: A life force moves us toward enhanced vitality, and a death force draws us toward quiescence. During this later period Freud also shifted his attention from childhood experience and family life to group behavior, religion, and the future of civilization.[5]

As with any such change, it was a complex development, traceable to the evolution in his clinical, theoretical, and personal concerns. However, one experience stands out more than any other in marking the divide: World War I.

The war was difficult for Freud, who was fifty-eight when it began. He had two sons at the front, and after some initial pacifist abhorrence at the very thought of war, Freud wrote and spoke to friends of his renewed patriotic feelings, and of his hopes that his native Austria and its "big brother" Germany would prevail. But he also had an enduring love for England, now the enemy, and his high ethical standards were affronted by the horrors inflicted by both sides. As the war dragged on, life in Vienna became difficult, as money, provisions, and good spirits dwindled. As many people he knew became weary and despondent, Freud's own views changed again. It was no longer pacifism or patriotism but a deep despair that came over him, countered by a realistic appraisal of how little chance there was of realizing utopian ideals in an imperfect world.[6]

In an essay written in 1915, Freud traced the wartime "melancholy" he observed in himself and others around him to the profound disillusionment among ethical people when confronted by their government's misdeeds:

> The individual in any given nation has in this war a terrible opportunity to convince himself of what would occasionally strike him in peace-time — that the state has forbidden to the individual the practice of wrong-doing, not because it desired to abolish it, but because it desires to monopolize it. . . . The warring state permits itself every such misdeed, every such act of violence, as would disgrace the individual man. It practises not only the accepted stratagems, but also deliberate lying and deception against the enemy; and this, too, in a measure which appears to surpass the usage of former wars. The state exacts the utmost degree of obedience and sacrifice from its citizens, but at the same time treats them as children. . . . It absolves itself from the guarantees and contracts it had formed with other states, and makes unabashed confession of its rapacity and lust for power, which the private individual is then called upon to sanction in the name of patriotism. . . . Well may that civilized cosmopolitan, therefore, of whom I spoke, stand helpless in a world grown strange to him — his all-embracing patrimony disintegrated, the common estates in it laid waste, the fellow-citizens embroiled and debased.[7]

At the time Freud wrote this passage, it was unusual to assert a relationship between psychological states on the one hand and ethical and historical concerns on the other. Most psychiatrists who worked with troubled veterans of World War I explained what was then called shell shock as the reaction of men with weak nervous systems to the overstimulation of loud noises and fierce explosions. Even when a group of Freud's followers proposed a radical change in this view, stating that the burdens were more psychological than physiological and stemmed from a conflict between a "war ego" and a "peace ego," their explanations assumed that the problems were ethically neutral and rooted solely in each man's personal sphere.[8]

Most psychotherapists did not view their patients as beings whose ethical and historical sense of things needed to be taken into account. Freud's essay, which is often dismissed as "unscientific" by contemporary Freudians, took the bold step of viewing people's inner turmoil in the light of their concerns about the larger world.

A generation later it was precisely this wider context that Erik Erikson insisted was crucial for understanding the veterans of World War II. Erikson had been trained in Vienna under the guidance of Freud's daughter Anna. His own life was deeply affected by the Nazi rise to power, which led him to emigrate to America. From personal experience, and from his exposure to the historical consciousness among Eruopean thinkers, Erikson proclaimed the importance of the cultural and historical context for understanding individual turmoil. He warned his fellow mental health professionals against directing their patients only toward handling their individual problems, since this narrowness would dilute the energy needed for the pressing collective tasks of postwar life.

Beyond the general point, that the historical context is crucial for individual lives, Erikson wanted to clarify the broad challenge that was facing Americans at the end of World War II, a challenge that we today have yet to face squarely. He wrote that Americans could no longer assume their accustomed role of being comfortably aloof from the world because, as he observed among World War II veterans,

> historical change has [now] reached a coercive universality and a global acceleration which is experienced [by these veterans] as a threat to [their] traditional American identity. It seems to devaluate the vigorous conviction that this nation can afford mistakes; that this nation, by definition, is always so far ahead of the rest of the world in inexhaustible reserves, in vision of planning, in freedom of action, and in tempo of progress that there is unlimited space and endless time in which to develop, test, and complete her social experiments. The difficulties met in the attempt to integrate this old image of insulated spaciousness with the new image of explosive global closeness are deeply disquieting.[9]

Erikson introduced into psychology a notion that has since become commonplace: People develop a consistent approach to life, an identity, by shaping their personal histories in light of the ideological and cultural currents of their time. What it means to be an American, for example, depends not only on our individual personalities and social structures but on historic changes and the way we as individuals come to terms with them.

One of the most prominent scholar-practitioners influenced by Erikson was Robert Jay Lifton, who served as a psychiatrist with the American military in Korea, and later studied Japanese men and women who survived the atom bombing of Hiroshima. He found that these people lived through personal upheavals of the sort that Erikson described as identity crises. Lifton also found that the historic and ideological challenge faced by Japanese people generally at the end of World War II was compounded for the Hiroshima survivors by a rupture of another order. They had seen family and friends incinerated, and had witnessed the obliteration of their entire city. For them it was the end of the world, and their sense of themselves was pervaded by this confrontation with massive death. They bore the distinguishing mark, the identity, of the few who survived. And through them, Lifton learned of the coherent themes that color the experience of those whom he called survivors.[10]

Lifton drew parallels between his observations of survivors of Hiroshima and reports from Germany and Israel on the survivors of Nazi concentration camps. These people all bore an inner stamp of death, in mood or preoccupation, and often asked themselves guiltily, "Why me? Why was I spared?" They became emotionally withdrawn, as if calluses had formed around their suffering, a state that Lifton named "psychic numbing." Some were unusually suspicious and prone to mistrust offers of assistance, seeing them as not genuine, because no comfort could be enough to relieve what they had lived through. And all were faced with the difficult lifelong task of making sense of an experience that defied explanation or justification.

The central task of healing for these survivors, Lifton concluded, is to give meaning to an experience that annihilated life's coherence. This is not simply an inward or psychological process; the shattering was not just of their sense of themselves but of their outer world and their connection with it. For them, involvement in the world took on special significance as a way to reconnect. To this end, many of the Hiroshima survivors became activists, campaigning not only for medical and economic benefits, but for peace and for worldwide nuclear disarmament.

By 1970 Lifton was recognized as a national expert on human responses to extreme situations. Testifying on "the Vietnam veteran" before a Senate Subcommittee on Veterans' Affairs, he stated that the difficult transition from the circumstance of war to civilian life was familiar after the two world wars and Korea. But there was undoubtedly another dimension to the problem, an aspect that was becoming known as the psychology of the survivor. Speaking about the returning Vietnam veteran, Lifton said: "His overall psychological task is that of finding meaning and justification in having survived, and in having fought and killed. That is, as a survivor he must, consciously or unconsciously, give some form to the extreme experience of war, in order to be able to find meaning in all else he does afterward in civilian life."[11]

Following this testimony, Lifton was invited to take part in the Vietnam veteran rap groups that began meeting in New York City in late 1970. Initially the groups were held in the offices of Vietnam Veterans Against the War. But within two years, the ideological commitments of the dwindling organization hardened, and it no longer provided a hospitable setting for the groups, which emphasized self-scrutiny and openness to all views. But even after the groups began meeting in space donated by an Episcopal seminary, many of the members remained active in protests against the war, and in various efforts to improve the life of their communities.

Three years after he first attended the rap groups, Lifton published a book based largely on that experience. A prominent theme of the book is the way personal healing from a moral and historic catastrophe brought veterans to an activist's commitment to constructive change in the world:

> For a number of [these veterans], and at varying intervals, political activities become inseparable from psychological need. Telling their story to American society has been both a political act and a means of psychologically confronting an inauthentic experience and moving beyond it toward authenticity. For such people not only is protest necessary to psychological help — it *is* [Lifton's italics] psychological help.[12]

It was a Saturday afternoon in December 1970 when I first made my way to the aging office building where Vietnam Veterans Against the War had its offices in three cramped rooms on an upper floor. The rap group was having its second meeting. About twelve guys were there, most of them in fatigue shirts, with beards, unkempt hair, and heavy looks. A few shrinks were in the room, antiwar types who had volunteered to sit in. A vet named Schmoo, who spoke with a strong Brooklyn accent, said, "We should get Sam to open up. Sam's planning a new demo, but I don't know. Something's funny in his head about this, and we ought to hear from him."

Everybody turned to the corner, where Sam was sitting on an orange crate. "Body language" wasn't a popular term yet, but I had done enough counseling to read the signs. Sam was the type who would stand out by trying to look inconspicuous — with his thick glasses, smoking a cigarette with yellowed fingers, blackheads on his nose, and gritty fatigues that looked stiff from dried sweat. "Sam, tell 'em what your plan is. Tell 'em what you told me," Schmoo said.

"Nothing really. Just leafletting the recruiting station. That's it."

"That's not what you told me, Sam. You said you were going to throw your body through the plate glass window if they tried to stop you. C'mon, Sam. Tell 'em."

"Nothing. That's it."

Nobody could get Sam to talk, but others readily spoke for him. "Suicide mission, it sounds like. He's not sure if he wants to stop the war or end his life," one guy said. Then another popped up, "Reminds me of my buddy in 'Nam. Weeks in Con Tien, mortars coming in every night. Eat and sleep in dirt, and every day a guy here and there gets picked off. After a point, he couldn't take it anymore. Put his M-16 to his chin and blew his brains out."

"I've thought about it many times," said a third. "But I figured if I was going to die in Vietnam, I'd want it to be meaningful. Not just kill myself for nothing."

Sam came to life at that point. "The only way death in Vietnam could be meaningful is if you're martyred, like if one of those helicopters that pick up shit houses and move 'em around got hit, and the shit house drops on your head."

Biting black humor was Sam's hallmark. Virtually the only time he said anything was to make a joke, at the expense of the government, the war, the military, or somebody in the group he didn't like. "By the time I spent a year over there I was saying 'Know why we have to stop communism? 'Cause that's what we've got in the Army and you can see how bad it works there.'"

The rap groups became known as the place where you could tell your story, even the most horrible parts, and other people would listen. One vet told about air strikes called in on his own unit by mistake. Friends died from so-called friendly fire. Another vet spoke about patrols that went into North Vietnam. "We were doing all kinds of shit that people back here covered up." Several guys echoed that concern. To die over there and have nobody back here know the truth about how it happened seemed worse than the dying itself. Almost in unison several guys talked about mutilating corpses — guys who collected VC ears.

Sam didn't open up in the group. But one afternoon he and I went for a pizza together and he told me about his nights on guard duty in a base camp, located a hundred yards from a Vietnamese village. "That's where I learned about gooks. Vietnamese weren't people. Didn't matter which side they were on. Slopes, dinks, gooks, it was all the same. You heard about patrols coming back with this many body count or that many body count. You knew they were counting pigs and anything else they could kill. The idea caught on. We'd go up on guard duty with that attitude — Vietnamese were no good, subhuman. The more you can kill the better.

"One night we're all smoking dope," Sam continued. "The moon is out and if you're stoned enough, a palm tree waving in the breeze with moonlight on it starts to look like something else. Like 'if the mother fucker moves his arm again I'm going to blow the shit out of him.' Then somebody says the antipersonnel radar, a useless machine, just picked up five VC in a rice paddy out to our left. Nobody checks to see whether it was anybody from our neighboring village. Everybody cocks their weapon. One guy fires a carbine, which makes a sound like an AK-47 [the Russian rifle used by the Vietcong], and that's all we needed. Everyone starts to fire into the brush. The sergeant comes running drunk out of the beer club and starts lobbing grenades into the Vietnamese village. We hear a lot of Vietnamese voices all of a sudden. The sergeant pops in another grenade. Then the voices stop.

"Nobody asks what happened. Nobody says out loud that maybe all we did was wipe out a bunch of our neighbors that night. Nobody goes to check it out the next day. And just to show you where I was at, I thought it was humorous more than anything else."

I was drawn to Sam. Everybody in the group wanted the war to end and was hurting in some way. But Sam was unusual in having an origi-

nal and articulate view. He'd carry leftist underground newspapers along with the National Review, *a conservative magazine, in the pocket of his fatigue pants. Bitterly opposed to continuing a war he saw as a total waste, he was just as bitter about radical rhetoric. "Knee-jerk patriotism and revolutionary fervor are the asshole religions of the twentieth century," he'd say. He wanted to know what both sides were saying, "so I could demolish either one in a debate."*

He was also unusual for having volunteered for Vietnam mostly for ideological reasons. President of the Young Conservative Club at a local college, he had thought of the war as a crusade. "Got to the point where it was bullshit to talk about it and not do something. So I went to stop the commies over there before we had to fight 'em in California." He enlisted to support artillery units in the technical branch that supplied wind and weather information to assist gunners. "I said I'd risk my life for my country, not commit suicide in the infantry."

Even outside the group, he never volunteered personal information. When I got to know him better, he told me why. He was suspicious of psychology, because "conservatives don't trust shrinks." But he knew he had something to get off his chest. It took weeks of meetings before he told it the first time. "Most of the Vietnamese you come across where I was wanted your money. Whores, shopkeepers, you get used to it." For that reason he was particularly touched by one teenage girl who used to polish boots for guys in his unit. All she wanted was to do her job well enough for the guys to be pleased and smile at her. She didn't know much English, but Sam grew fond of her through the sign language greetings they gave each other.

She rode from her village to the base and back each night in an open truck. Lots of stories about those trucks went around his unit. The mess sergeant used them to take food from the kitchen and transport it to the local black market. Another sergeant, the one in charge of the beer club, kept requisitioning lumber for the club and selling that down the road. A third sergeant, a confirmed alcoholic, had been assigned to driving the truck that brought the regular food shipments on base. But he had had so many accidents from drinking that they took him off that detail. Instead, he was given the job of driving the Vietnamese workers between their village and the base camp.

"One morning I was down at the beer club and the first sergeant comes in, grabs a medic, and tells me to come with him in a jeep to ride shotgun. I pick up my rifle and drive out there with him," Sam

recalled. *"Half a mile or so later we see the truck that the alcoholic sergeant was driving turned over in the road. The Vietnamese workers were sprawled all over. A bloody fucking mess. Right in the middle of it I see somebody's brains lying out there in the dust. It was the young house-girl, lying there with her head split open. I got sick and puked."*

He had already been protesting the mounting stupidity he saw around him. Not long before that morning, a new commanding officer had been assigned to his unit. During a mortar attack, he had ordered Sam to fill a hydrogen balloon for a weather reading. Sam had refused the order and later *"got busted, but not because of disobeying the order. The officer judging the case agreed it was a stupid order; the guy who finally went out to fill the balloon got hit. They busted me for attitude, for saying what a joke the whole thing was."*

He came to see the military machine as corrupt and incapable of doing much more than perpetuating itself. The Vietnamese people weren't being won over; there was no sustained victory over the opposing forces; inexperienced officers would be assigned to his unit for a few months, then reassigned and replaced by another set of inexperienced leaders. No cohesion. No spirit. And then the *"accident"* happened and Sam could no longer pretend he didn't care; he couldn't just go along with what was happening. It was horrible, awful, but also wrong. That's when his attitude became rebellious. That's also when he began to drink heavily, to keep himself numb.

Several days after he came home from Vietnam, Sam went to take pictures of an antiwar demonstration — *"just for laughs, you know, get a close look at these freak hippies."* His conservative friends had asked him to speak at a prowar rally, and he thought he'd gather some material about the *"flakos"* who were raising such a fuss. *"And then,"* Sam recalled, *"before I knew why or how, I was marching with them, shouting 'Out now!' I didn't see for a long time how it all fit together, how my arguments for the war were undermined by what I saw over there. All I knew was that the people were right who were calling it evil. It was the same thing that was happening back here, the students killed at Kent State, cops beating on demonstrators. It had to stop, and I was going to help."*

Veteran activism has a long history. Willard Waller, a historian of the veteran experience, wrote in 1944: "Many millions of veterans have come home to confront those who have betrayed them in matters great and small. Veterans have written many a bloody page of history, and those pages have stood forever as a record of their days of anger. Many times has their blind, understandable fury changed the course of history."[13] The Romans, with their knack for effective government, had a policy of settling former soldiers in the outlying regions of the empire. It was their way not only to protect against invaders, but also to keep those who were prone to political and military troublemaking as far away from the capital as possible.

The first American "veteran problem" began soon after the Revolution. Daniel Shays, an ex-captain in the Revolutionary militia, led a rebellion in Massachusetts among poor farmers and veterans who had received promissory notes but no payment for their services in the war. After the Civil War, veterans of the Confederate Army formed the Ku Klux Klan, which helped block racial integration in the South for a hundred years. Northern veterans had their greatest impact as a group by forming the Grand Army of the Republic, the first veterans' organization to secure pensions for ex-soldiers in return for political support of the party in power. A decade and a half after World War I, another generation of veterans caused a furor when twenty thousand of them, the famous Bonus Expeditionary Force, marched on Washington to protest unfulfilled promises of pensions. They weren't dispersed until General Douglas MacArthur was ordered to bring out regular troops, tanks, and tear gas.[14]

Earlier in this century, embittered German veterans of World War I formed volunteer units called the Free Corps Movement. First they fought against communists in the name of the Weimar Republic. Later they supported Hitler and were called by Hermann Göring "the first soldiers of the Third Reich." In Russia, roving bands of World War I veterans and deserters began as early as 1915 to fuel the social upheaval that became the revolution two years later. Since then, the Soviet Union has set an example for the rest of the world by taking scrupulously good care of its war veterans. During World War II, veterans of the defeated French army swelled the ranks of the anti-Nazi underground Resistance, and deserters from the Italian army lent their energy to the uprising that brought about the fall of Mussolini's fascist government in 1943.

In France during the early 1960s, veterans of the Algerian War fought in a bitter and occasionally bloody civil conflict. In 1961 President Charles de Gaulle called an end to the unsuccessful war against the Algeria National Liberation Front. Some of the elite paratrooper units bolted, under the leadership of right-wing officers who were determined to maintain Algeria as a French colony. The uprising was short-lived, but months after its end, procolonial paratroopers, joined by veterans of the earlier French defeat in Indochina, formed the Secret Army Organization (OAS). Over the next few years, the OAS was organized into small clandestine cells, in the fashion of a guerrilla underground, and terrorized Algeria and parts of France by assassinating leftist and Algerian leaders and bombing political targets.[15]

When activist Vietnam veterans came to national attention in the spring of 1971, they didn't conform to any of the then popular images of war veterans. They were closest in spirit to a relatively small and unknown group that was formed after World War II, the American Veterans Committee. The AVC began as a liberal organization dedicated to the founding of the United Nations and to creating a world without war. VVAW became the second generation of organized antiwar veterans.

VVAW was created in 1967 by six recently returned veterans who marched in an antiwar demonstration. Three years later a dozen or so chapters had formed across the country. The organization grew in a spurt during late 1970, after *Playboy* donated the space for a full-page ad soliciting new members and contributions. Then, in February 1971, one hundred and fifty former soldiers went to the Howard Johnson's Motor Lodge in Detroit to testify to the acts of brutality and unwarranted violence they had witnessed or participated in during their service in Vietnam. It was the first of dozens of such public testimonials held around the country in the following years. These events were called "Winter Soldier Investigations," a name taken from a bitter prediction by Thomas Paine, who wrote in 1776, "The summer soldier and the sunshine patriot will, in this crisis, shrink from the service of his country." VVAW members saw themselves as Winter Soldiers who would carry on during a bleak season, long after their official duty was done.[16]

It was in late April of 1971 that VVAW came to national attention. About two thousand VVAW supporters marched on the Captiol, flung their medals away in protest, and lobbied congressional lead-

ers for the week that preceded the May Day protests of 1971. At that
time the average VVAW activist was a college student with a working class background whose views had moved from moderately conservative before enlisting to strongly radical after serving in Vietnam.[17] Within a few years, most of these men had "moved on" to
concentrate on their personal lives, families, and careers.

Activist veterans, with views and agendas that span the political
spectrum, have continued to affect national life. According to the
1980 Harris poll, veterans tend, on the average, to be more involved
in political and community affairs than other men their age.[18] The
most conspicuous sign of the potency of their energy is the Vietnam
Veterans Memorial in Washington — the idea, fund raising, and ex-
ecution of which were provided largely by Vietnam veterans. It is
now the third most visited site in our capital.

After years of reluctance, Vietnam veterans have also been joining
in larger numbers the organizations devoted to veterans' interests:
750,000 now belong to the 2.7-million-member American Legion, and
500,000 to the 1.9-million-member Veterans of Foreign Wars.[19] The
Vietnam Veterans of America, with 20,000 members, is the first new
veterans' organization to be recognized by the Veterans Administration in a generation.[20]

The most active of all are a minority of veterans who take part
regularly in the political process — voting in local as well as in national elections, contributing to campaigns, attending rallies and
demonstrations, or working for candidates. These are also the ones
who join religious, professional, athletic, community, or fraternal
groups. The activists are more likely to have entered military service
by enlisting, to have served as officers, or to have begun their military careers before the war. And they are more likely to have finished college.[21] Their distinguishing personal quality is that they're
determined to "be involved."

The overwhelming majority of veterans do not fit this activist profile. The average ex–enlisted man is most likely to seem turned off.
He doesn't join groups, and if you ask why, he'll say it won't do
any good. He thinks we should've stayed out of the fighting in Vietnam, and that the war had a disastrous effect on the country by
undermining trust at home and reducing U.S. prestige abroad. He
is likely to agree with such attitudes as, "The people running the

country don't really care what happens to you," or "The rich get richer and the poor get poorer," or "People like me don't have any say about what the government does."[22]

These men are usually called alienated. Observers rarely appreciate, however, that veterans who express bitter feelings about the war and their government show a greater degree of emotional involvement with and concern for the world around them than their "cooler" and more blasé peers who've led more sheltered lives. Among people who believe that their thoughts and feelings don't matter to others, it is a form of activism to form and express strong convictions, even if they're negative ones.

The rap groups provided a private place where vets could talk of and listen to horrors they couldn't speak about elsewhere, except at the Winter Soldier Investigations held by VVAW chapters during 1971 and 1972. Former Marines might talk about boot camp, and how they were trained to "go for broke." "Your last day in the States you have a little lesson, and it's called the rabbit lesson. The sergeant comes out and he has a rabbit and he's talking to you about escape and evasion and survival in the jungle. . . . A couple of seconds after just about everyone falls in love with the rabbit the sergeant cracks it at the neck, skins it, disembowels it. He does this to the rabbit, and then they throw the guts out into the audience. You can get anything out of that you want, but that's your last lesson you catch in the United States before you leave for Vietnam."[23]

Some recalled moments of utter disgust. In one of the stories, a former Marine told of coming across a clump in the grass near a village that his unit had just attacked. "There was a tiny little form, a child, lying out in the field with straw over its face. It had been clubbed to death. Later we found out: the Marine that clubbed the child to death didn't really want to look at the child's face so he put straw over it before he clubbed it."[24]

Frequently we would hear about interrogations of prisoners aboard helicopters. "There were eight prisoners brought onto each helicopter . . . and an equal number of South Vietnamese [ARVN — Army of the Republic of Vietnam] troops as guards . . . five helicopters altogether, and I flew in the first one, the lead helicopter. We were to fly support for this mission to bring these prisoners to Saigon . . .

for their six-month rehabilitation program. We had radio contact with
headquarters in Saigon, and they said they'd have a greeting party
for us at Tan Son Nhut Airport. We all flew together in one nonstop
flight. When we got off the helicopter, there were exactly three prisoners left on one helicopter, and one prisoner left on the other. I
instantly realized what had happened and couldn't believe it. I went
over to the American door gunner of one of the transport ships and
I asked him what the hell happened, and he told me that they had
pushed them out over the Mekong Delta. . . . I said I couldn't believe it, and he said to go and look at the open doorways on the
ships. So I did. But after getting about five feet away I didn't want
to go any closer. There was flesh from the hands of the prisoners
when they were pushed out on the door jambs and on the door
frames. And there was blood on the floor where they had been
beaten."[25]

Most gruesome of all were the stories of torture and the hideous
mutilations of women. "There was this operation called Meade River.
Korean Marines, ARVNs, U.S. Marines and U.S. Army were involved. On part of the operation we had just gotten through making
heavy contact and we went through a bunker system. We found
hospitals and came across four NVA [North Vietnamese Army]
nurses. The Korean Marines asked us if they could have the nurses.
They would take care of them because we were sweeping through
the area, and we couldn't take care of any prisoners. While we were
still there the Koreans started tying them down to the ground. They
tied their hands to the ground, they spreadeagled them, they raped
all four. There was like maybe ten or twenty Korean Marines involved. They tortured them, they sliced off their breasts, they used
machetes and cut off parts of their fingers and things like this. When
that was over, they took pop-up flares (which are aluminum canis-
ters you hit with your hand; it'll shoot maybe 100–200 feet into the
air — they stuck them up their vaginas — all four of them — and
they blew the top of their heads off."[26]

Veterans who joined Vietnam Veterans Against the War weren't the
only ones to take action publicly by questioning U.S. policies in Indochina. Some of the most telling and implicative critiques have come
from people who served as officials in the State and Defense departments.

Former State Department official Richard Barnet traced the failure of American policy makers to notice and correct their own errors to the managerial ethos on our side that systematically excluded empathy and plain speaking. It was a style reinforced from the top by a small group of men who, from the beginning of World War II to the middle of the Vietnam years, were the managers of U.S. national security institutions. "Between 1940 and 1967, when I stopped counting," wrote Barnet, "all the first- and second-level posts in a huge national security bureaucracy were held by fewer than four hundred individuals who rotate through a variety of key posts. . . . Most of their biographies in *Who's Who* read like minor variations on a single theme — wealthy parents, Ivy League education, leading law firm or bank (or entrepreneur in a war industry), introduction to government in World War II."[27]

Antiwar critics called these men immoral for their responsibility for Vietnam. But Barnet was quick to point out that the charge was unfounded. Men like Dean Acheson, John Foster Dulles, William and McGeorge Bundy, Eugene and Walt Rostow, Robert McNamara, and Dean Rusk acted with firm convictions. Barnet argued that the post–World War II generation of national security managers were principled men. "Neither critics who insist upon discovering venal motives for murderous policies nor the participants' often honest defense that their motives were 'pure' are much help." It was simply that according to their morality, they were the elect, the ones who should command, and actions that appeared expedient to them were the ones to take.

Although these managers were widely traveled high achievers, their contacts were almost exclusively a narrow circle of foreign elites. Barnet saw this as a pervasive, institutional blindness. "As a class, [they] have not had the training or incentive to develop understanding, compassion, or empathy for people in different circumstances from their own. . . . This insulation from the real world, as well as their special brand of Calvinism . . . go far to explain the giant misunderstanding of the past generation: the nature and dynamics of revolution."[28]

Dedicated to managing, controlling and maintaining stability, these men were incapable of grasping the revolutionary aspirations of peoples throughout the Third World. "As a group, the national security managers have been so removed emotionally from the human desperation that afflicts a majority of the world that they cannot understand why people will join a revolution. Revolutionaries must be agents, dupes, or romantics. . . . Revolution, by definition, threatens stability and introduces uncertainty. It is therefore a threat that must be suppressed. It is this lack of understanding or feeling and the accompanying fear of the unknown which feeds the power fantasies of the managers and helps them to rationalize the use of terror, starvation, and intrigue to bring societies threatened by revolution back to 'normal.' "[29]

The managerial commitments of the nation's policy makers determined the strategies of the war and shaped the tactics used as well. Most military leaders followed their civilian managers' example. But some of the most dedicated career officers in the U.S. Army judged that their superiors betrayed the honor of the military tradition to buy bureaucratic respectability. In their memoirs, some of these dissenters have written bitterly about the lack of empathy among our military leaders for the people we were supposedly trying to help.

One of the few career officers to resign in protest over our war policies was William Corson, a former lieutenant colonel who supervised the Marines' operations in I Corps during his tour of duty. He wrote about the impact of U.S. policies on the local Vietnamese near his command: "We [Americans] had conspired with the government of South Vietnam to literally destroy the hopes, aspirations and emotional stability of thirteen thousand human beings. . . . This was not and is not war, it is genocide."[30]

In *Self-Destruction*, an anonymous Army officer, writing under the name Cincinnatus, indicted the Army's leadership for having conducted a war in ignorance of both its friends and foes. "Almost no one knew the first thing about the Vietnamese language, the country's nationalism or its politics, its culture, or the special problems existing there as a result of guerrilla activity. . . . Ignorant of the nature and culture of our enemy, oblivious to the realities of revolutionary warfare, unable to talk with South Vietnamese friend or North Vietnamese and Viet Cong foe, the United States Army forged ahead, certain that it knew the best way to secure a quick resolution of the military situation in Vietnam. The result was a debacle of its own making."[31]

The epitome of managerial rationality was the focus on tangible measures of success, untempered by an appreciation of the impact that these criteria had in shaping the war's strategy. The supreme indicator of progress was the body count; not the ground we gained or the readiness of the Vietnamese people to support the government we were there to aid, but how much killing we did. Sensitive observers at home were horrified. But what was unique about this war was that responsible military officers were horrified as well, though few of us knew about it until years later.

In 1977 Lieutenant General DeWitt C. Smith, commandant of the Army War College, was quoted as saying, "We study . . . the body count a measure of 'success.' . . . How did we ever come to use such an odious phrase? How did it come to be that some people allegedly changed statistics so they looked advantageous?"[32] Smith is known for having instituted courses on ethics soon after he took command of the college.

In a military history text now used at West Point, Lieutenant Colonel Dave Richard Palmer faults the Army's leadership, and particularly General William Westmoreland, for viewing the situation in Vietnam as allowing only one of two alternatives: annihilation or attrition. Claiming that it was the more feasible of the two, Westmoreland pursued his strategy of attrition, to wear down the enemy through "search and destroy" missions. Of this Palmer wrote:

> Attrition is not a strategy. It is irrefutable proof of the absence of any strategy. A commander who resorts to attrition admits his failure to conceive of an alternative. He turns from warfare as an art and accepts it on the most nonprofessional terms imaginable. He uses blood instead of brains. Saying that political considerations forced the employment of attrition [in Vietnam] does not alter the hard truth that the United States [Army] was strategically bankrupt in Vietnam.[33]

Cincinnatus drove home the point that the body count policy was not even good management. He notes that in wars throughout history,

> It was not always the side that lost the most men that suffered defeat. If such had been the case, the Union would have lost the Civil War. The Allies would have lost World War I and World War II. . . . But body counts were not only meaningless; they were also counterproductive. . . . Honorable officers were placed in situations where they had to com-

promise their word, their honor, and their oaths of office in order to satisfy their superiors. . . . The army's official position was [therefore] based
on lies, and no institution that builds on that kind of sand can long endure in a free society.[34]

Lieutenant Colonel Anthony Herbert, another military officer who
resigned in protest over this and other practices in Vietnam, wrote
of his horror over the body count policy. "Regardless of what a person might have been before he was killed, afterwards he was a dink.
Very damned few people ever reported killing a civilian, regardless
of how unavoidable the death might have been, and very damned
few dead civilians failed to be included in the body counts."[35] In the
battalion he commanded, Herbert rescinded the long-standing policy of giving extra leave to men with verified "kills." Instead, he
gave extra time off for live, captured prisoners. Unfortunately, his
example wasn't followed by others, let alone by those who commanded the war effort in Vietnam.

Corson, Herbert, and Cincinnatus were by no means alone. Many
of the Army's leaders during the war years came to see themselves
as having been corrupted by a "to get along, go along" frame of
mind. In 1974 Douglas Kinnard surveyed the generals who served
in Vietnam and found that "Almost 70 percent of the army generals
who led the war in Vietnam were uncertain what the objectives of
that combat were. Over 50 percent of those generals believed the
United States Army should not have participated in the Vietnam
war. An even 61 percent [say that they] were aware at the time that
'indicators of progress' such as body counts, kill ratios, weapons
captured, and so forth, were inflated and invalid."[36]

Cincinnatus asks: "Where were their voices when they were
needed? Kinnard suggests that they kept quiet because 'their careers
were at stake and they could not afford to make waves.' If generals
could not do so in order to call attention to problems needing re-
dress, how could anyone of lower rank be expected to step forth?
What sort of training and selection system allowed such men to rise
to the top echelon?"[37]

One of the most thoughtful Vietnam veterans I've met is retired Army
Colonel Reuben Nathan. During the 1930s he fought with the anti-

Hitler underground in his native Germany, and then, after fleeing, joined the U.S. Army, in which he served as an expert in psychological warfare in World War II, Korea, and Vietnam. Asked in an interview for this book why a man schooled in the classics, who has adhered all his life to progressive political and social ideas, would make a career in the Army, he said: "The Army is the most forward-looking national institution in the United States — the first to desegregate, the first to adopt liberal health and medical benefits, the first to insist on lifelong learning, and the first to institute effective ways to see that merit is near the top of the list for selecting people who are going to lead."

What went wrong in Vietnam? Colonel Nathan summed up a three-hour conversation about the war this way: "We failed because we forgot what the battle is all about. The only way this country, given what we stand for, can ever win in the struggle against totalitarianism is to *live* our principles. If we compromise principle to gain certain advantages we've lost right from the beginning." Later he added, "I'm only repeating the most ancient wisdom on effective strategy. Read Sun Tzu," he suggested.

Sun Tzu, a Chinese sage who lived about twenty-five hundred years ago, wrote *The Art of War*, a classic work on military strategy. Several years before the U.S. build-up in Vietnam, Sun Tzu's treatise was newly translated with a foreword by B. H. Liddell Hart, one of Britain's foremost military strategists.[38] "Civilization might have been spared much of the damage suffered in the World Wars of this century," Liddell Hart wrote, "if European military thought in the era preceding the First World War had been blended with and balanced by a knowledge of Sun Tzu's exposition. Sun Tzu's realism and moderation form a contrast to [the Western] tendency to emphasize the logical and 'the absolute' [as in] the dictum: 'To introduce into the philosophy of war a principle of moderation would be an absurdity — war is an act of violence pushed to its utmost bounds.' "[39]

For most of this century, Sun Tzu's work has been known among the more scholarly and thoughtful Western strategists. But official doctrine has followed the more rationalistic principles that Western military and political leaders have held as common sense. During the Vietnam War, American policy was dominated by computer-based logic systems and modern systems-management approaches to "inflicting casualties" and "neutralizing targets." Nobody heard or heeded the Chinese sage and his ancient warning: "There has never been a protracted war from which a country has benefitted."[40]

As one modern commentator has written, "Sun Tzu believed that the skillful strategist should be able to subdue the enemy's army without engaging it, to take his cities without laying siege to them, and to overthrow his State without bloodying swords." In short, "the supreme art of war is to subdue the enemy without fighting."[41] Such achievements are possible, however, only when the principles of war are carefully studied and practiced. For Sun Tzu the first principle is "moral influence . . . which causes the people to be in harmony with their leaders, so that they will accompany them in life and unto death without fear of mortal peril."[42]

What does this mean? A Chinese scholar explained it this way: "When one treats people with benevolence, justice and righteousness, and reposes confidence in them, the army will be united in mind and all will be happy to serve their leaders. The Book of Changes [the *I Ching*] says: 'In happiness at overcoming difficulties, people forget the danger of death.' "[43]

"Moral influence" is the clumsy English translation of *tao*, the Chinese word for "the way of the universe." According to the ancient teaching, success through effortless action arises by being in tune with this natural course; lack of harmony brings struggle and ultimately failure. Most modern people have lost touch with such wisdom. But over and over in the stories of Vietnam veterans, men reveal their discovery of some crucial ingredient, hard to name, that was missing on our side in the war. And because it wasn't there, no amount of good intention, American spirit, and material and military support to the people of South Vietnam could keep us from doing evil, and ultimately defeating ourselves.

Not all veterans talk this way, of course. Some even deny the problem. And a few are so dedicated to lauding the bravery, raw courage, and honorable action they saw among outstanding individuals in Vietnam that the larger horror is completely invisible to them. But the vets who came to the early rap groups brought with them, as an overwhelming residue from the war, a deep demoralization and loss of trust in their leaders, in the cause, and in the person they

were before going in. Years before the humiliating retreat from Saigon in April 1975, before the revelations of moral corruption in the
1973 Watergate hearings, and before the full exposure of official deceit and confusion in the Pentagon Papers, released in 1971,[44] many
guys just knew.

We made a distinction in the rap groups that is crucial for healing:
the difference between blame and responsible criticism. Blame jus-
tifies your aloofness or sense of impotence; responsible criticism involves you in constructive change. Many vets came to the groups to
complain — about their lives, the government, the war, their wives,
their families, the VA, American society, and the state of most people's consciousness. Given the critical views of most of us in the
groups, it was easy to find something to agree with in almost any
negative judgment. But condemning the world doesn't heal; it's much
more useful to assert one's concern and willingness to address what
you think needs attention. And so we often would point it out to
each other when we were copping out, using the war or something
else as an excuse to feel either superior or sorry for ourselves.

In the late 1960s it had become fashionable to harp on our national
shortcomings. At that time, the distinction between blame and responsible criticism was rarely made. For many men who came of
age during that time, this tendency still prevails. In studying the
interviews we conducted with veterans in the late 1970s, I found
that most of them still resort to blame, as if it were a way to relieve
themselves. In a few cases, I noted that veterans may point the
finger but are aware of trying to put their problem on somebody
else. In a rare example of such insight, one combat vet who took
part in our study explained that as long as he sees the war as the
fault of a former President, anything he did there is okay. "I'm
not bugged out like some guys are behind the blood and killing,
because, you see, I blame it on Nixon. If God asks me in heaven
about me killing people, I'll tell him Nixon made me do it. Not the
devil, Nixon."

Although most veterans seem unaware of their habit of trying to
use anger and blame for relief, observers can easily recognize the
tendency. One veteran we interviewed began with a classic statement of feeling bad for buddies who died in vain. "When I got out

I felt very, very bad for all those guys killed for nothing. It was a waste of taxpayers' money, just some namby-pamby thing. I mean we could've wiped out the whole thing, right up to Hanoi, but didn't." In the next breath he said, "It was just some racket for big business." The solution is to name the villain.

Most veterans blame the government. An ex-Marine put it this way: "I've come away with complete mistrust of any type of leadership of government. It's just public relations and put a front up, and no consistency between how things are and how they're related to legislation." Some push the point further, knocking the American people for not giving us a proper homecoming. "I don't think the vets got an even break. We didn't have any jobs, and it's a struggle for all of us, our families, ourselves. We're not properly taken care of. . . . I think I deserve more for doing what I did, and I want more for other vets who have less than I do. . . . We're the only veterans that came back that didn't have a greeting from the American people and that disturbs me."

The pain of homecoming is a common complaint. Some vets attribute it to people who were indifferent to them. "I had an okay attitude when I came back. It's just that I had a hard time looking for a job. I met a lot of idiots. They didn't care if I fought for my country. Nobody acknowledges the fact. They just look at you as one of the suckers and don't want me to have pride."

A large minority single out those who protested the war as a special target for bitterness. "The thing that messed it all up was these people that never saw the war and protested. They didn't know what the hell they're talking about. Why run to school just to get out of it? Nobody knew the war would be illegal. I didn't even know it and I was there. But they used that excuse and they're getting forgiven. It's not right."

These sentiments are easy to understand. Anger seems normal, even healthy, under the circumstances, and far preferable to the dull, numbed, and passive state of veterans who feel nothing at all. But men who habitually blame their distress on the past, or on some social entity beyond their reach, condemn themselves to impotence. They may have the details straight; it was not us but our leaders who declared the war, drafted us to fight, mismanaged the effort, failed to welcome us graciously when we came home, and neither prepared the public for us nor offered adequate services to prepare us for civilian life. So now what do we do?

Blaming others only reinforces our status as victims. To reclaim the power to lead our own lives we would do well to draw a different conclusion from the facts. Nobody is going to do it for us, so we might as well get on with healing from the war on our own.

Activity is a venerable cure. If you're busy enough, you don't have time for random thoughts, which lead many veterans to stay active to keep from looking back. Some are understandably proud of how well it works for them. "I keep on the go and don't let things get to me," they might say. People who believe that their only other option is to fall apart make certain to keep themselves distracted. When their time isn't taken up with work, they do something else — watch TV, or do anything to stay entertained.

Sooner or later, many discover another option. Instead of struggling not to be concerned with matters that don't fit their current life, they expand their activities to include ways to express those concerns. Many who find themselves still thinking about the guys who died, or who ended up worse off than they, say to themselves, "I've got to do something!" They may contribute to a campaign to feed orphans in the war zone, or join a veterans' post and help out with a fund raiser for the old soldiers' home, or write the President when they don't think he's paying attention to the lessons from their war.

What makes for healing isn't how much you do; it's the dedication and care you bring to whatever activity you choose. The more caring you express, the more you experience healing. Getting involved is what many vets call "giving a shit" and "doing something that matters." Whether it is a small gesture or a grand project, the essence is always serving others and the truth as you see it.

How is it that getting involved advances healing? It is an important question, too rarely discussed. Virtually all of the people who become counselors and therapists have known their own pain and have sought to emerge from their suffering by dedicating themselves to care for others. Similarly, most of the recognized experts on "post-traumatic stress" are men who mastered their own distress through the effort to assist fellow vets. And yet few of us openly acknowledge that fact. We spin theories and offer prescriptions for the way fellow professionals should treat veteran clients, and fail to emphasize what worked so powerfully for us: the shift from being a recipient to a provider of care.

Giving ourselves to serve others is a fitting antidote to what most diminishes our humanity — the refusal to care. The horrors of war haunt us only to the extent that we turn away, by constricting or numbing ourselves in hopes of limiting the pain. When my colleagues and I speak about overcoming this numbness or getting veterans to open up, we may sometimes mislead people into thinking that merely ventilating emotion will make them whole. In fact, however, the cure for a life diminished by the fearful refusal to care is to call courageously on that capacity and to express caring in ways that make it real. Only by getting involved in ways that are meaningful to us do we become the kind of people who warrant our own respect. And only then do we recapture the esteem that is the sense of being whole.

☆ 4 ☆

DIGGING INSIDE

A reflective soldier . . . experiences himself and his comrades as violators of the earth. The ruthlessness with which organized warriors deal with the order of nature in order to defend their miserable lives will appall him. . . . When his martial passions are kindled, this pygmy of creation is capable of defying the creative source of all life and flinging away all that he has formerly cherished. . . . Faced with this presumptuousness of the human creature, his closedness and dearth of love, the awakened soldier will be driven to say in his heart: "I, too, belong to this species. I am ashamed not only of my own deeds, not only of my nation's deeds, but of human deeds as well. I am ashamed to be a man."

J. GLENN GRAY[1]

Tiger got to hunt
Bird got to fly
Man got to sit and wonder "Why? Why? Why?"
Tiger got to sleep
Bird got to land
Man got to tell himself he understand

KURT VONNEGUT[2]

SOME VETERANS ACKNOWLEDGE their war service, talk about it readily, and even get involved in community life, yet still feel burdened by their experiences. Something still troubles them. These are usually the men who seek counseling, therapy, or spiritual advice. Often the first thing they say is, "It's time for me to get some answers."

Answers to what? If we interpret their statement as journalists would, we might think they want more facts. If we listen as propagandists or moralists, we might supply the arguments to help them decide whether they were right or wrong for what they did in the war. If we listen as scientists, perhaps we would give them an explanation for their pain. But if we listen in a healing way, we know they are ready for some new questions.

Usually the old question, the one that troubled survivors ask themselves over and over, is "Why?" It is a compelling question, for no sooner do you arrive at one answer, "It happened because of . . . ," than you begin to ask, "But why did *that* happen?" and so on, ad infinitum. The whole process leaves you no more satisfied than you were before it started. To makes matters worse, troubled people never ask "Why?" for merely abstract reasons. The question arises in a mood colored by the implicit conviction that the present and future are either refuted or unalterably ruined by what the sufferer now knows. Consider the following selection of the many possible variations:

Why did it happen? (The world's a hopeless mess.)
Why did I survive when others died? (I don't deserve to live.)

Why do human beings do such things? (People are disgusting.)

Why did I have to be involved in all that? (It must be punishment.)

Why did others get off so easy when I hurt so much? (Fuck them and fuck the world!)

What is the healing response to such pained self-questioning? Many responses are possible. Counselors and therapists, even those who espouse very different theories and techniques, generally respond similarly in one crucial respect. Essentially, they do not take the self-questioning as anything to be answered, and instead ask other questions or give instructions that shift attention elsewhere. The idea isn't to distract troubled people away from their pain. It is more like offering them a way to expand their repertoire. Instead of addressing questions that turn people more narrowly and frustratingly inward, therapists invite a dialogue by asking questions that convey a mood of enhanced possibilities, as in these common opening queries:

What happened? (Someone is interested.)

What hurt the most? (Pain can be shared.)

What's hardest to say? (Someone trusts that you can find the words.)

What do you want now? (Life goes on, and you are able to deal with it.)

The poet E. E. Cummings, a World War I veteran, wrote this line about poetry: "Always the beautiful answer who asks a more beautiful question."[3] As anyone who has experienced the power of therapy or counseling knows, his comment applies to healing as well.

In the rap groups, we accomplished this conversion to more "beautiful" or self-dignifying and life-enhancing questions more or less instinctively, without having any particular theory or set of rules to guide us. Men would come to a session preoccupied, asking "Why?" or "What did that war do to me?" If they came back regularly, sooner or later they would speak as if they had begun asking themselves different questions.

What did I bring to the experience to color it the way it is for me?

What is there to learn about myself from having lived through it?

What am I going to do now with this experience?
What about it am I going to carry with me for the rest of my life?

Sometimes the therapist isn't the one who asks the new question. He or she might simply respond in a way that prompts us to ask new questions for ourselves, opening possibilities for our lives that hadn't dawned on us before. And sometimes the most potent way to provoke such questions is through confrontation.

I never liked groups, and generally stayed away from fraternities, clubs, community organizations, and all the rest. In college I was curious about the experimental courses that were like encounter sessions, yet made a point of never taking any. After the Army it was different. I was drawn to the rap groups out of a craving for openness. Ironically, my appetite for it had grown from observing my undercover agents in Vietnam. They needed me because I was the one who hired, trained, paid, and supervised them. They also needed me to help them keep their sanity. I was the only person who knew who they really were. Having to "live their cover story" with everyone else they met, they had to be straight with me just to keep their minds clear. They taught me better than any psychology text that people who live behind a mask become prisoners of their own lies.

I went to the groups wanting to be truthful about myself. But it wasn't easy. It was embarrassing to tell strangers that for several weeks before I left the Army, I would be out for my morning jog, feeling so confused about where I had been and where I would go next that I'd cry out, often for my mother. It was also hard to talk about my feelings toward others in the groups. Few of them were college graduates; I was the only one who'd gone to an Ivy League school. I was reluctant to talk about it openly, feeling that the difference shouldn't have mattered so much to me. I was even more uncomfortable having to admit that however much I wanted my background to count for something, my hopes, fears, and pains were basically the same as everyone else's.

Most difficult of all was our being together. Sometimes it just felt too close. And none of us ever managed to acknowledge during the four years we met how much we craved this closeness, despite the discomfort. At times I was wildly excited that vets were together and I was part of it. Vets helping vets, creating a new way of healing ourselves. I would pronounce it almost as a battle cry. "We'll have rap groups coast to coast!" I prophesied one day. "We're inventing a new form of therapy! This country will never be the same in the way it deals with war!" I was on my soapbox, and having to listen to me bothered one of the therapists who had volunteered to sit in with us.

"You know, you're full of shit!" he said.

That stung. At first I couldn't imagine why he said it. He was there to help, not hurt. Who the hell did he think he was? And yet somehow I was grateful for his poking at me in a way I couldn't understand right away, let alone account for. He never came back, so I couldn't pursue the issue with him. But in a later session, one of the other vets I had often tried to help said, "You've gotten me to open up, how about us helping you now?" I backed off, saying I didn't need any help right then, but through these proddings I was seeing something about myself that I had ignored for a long time: It was much easier for me to offer help to the other guys than to let them help me. In a similar vein, as much as I helped and expressed my enthusiasm for the idea of rap groups in the abstract, the people I was with sensed that I was keeping myself removed.

The new question dawning for me was, "What is it to be real?" I knew it would take more than just telling the accurate story of my life. I also knew it called for something other than just spilling my guts. Without being able to say clearly what was involved, I sensed that the heart of it had to do with being genuinely open and available to other people.

"You're full of shit!" stayed with me. The words brought me to acknowledge what I hadn't considered before then — that I had developed the tendency to try to control situations by never letting anyone get too close. People had dropped hints: "You're not easy to get to know" or "Are you always on stage?" But only then, months after I had left the Army, did I begin to see it myself — the emotional barriers I had erected out of fear, and my ways of pretending to be real in hopes that people wouldn't notice I was putting on an act. I realized that the Army didn't have to train me for espionage; I was already an advanced practitioner of putting up fronts before I went in.

Once created, the rap groups were more than a place to meet for several years. They existed as an idea, an enduring possibility. When

Congress funded Operation Outreach for the Veterans Administration in 1979, the new program adopted rap groups as a major component. A nationwide program initiated by the Disabled American Veterans had done the same.

What happened in these groups? We talked, argued, made up, hugged, got confused, told stories, asked for advice, gave advice, complained, cried, and occasionally laughed. We followed no special formula and no set procedure. The one truth about the groups that we failed to appreciate then and never acknowledged when others asked "How do you run a rap group?" is that we improvised as we went along. The mix of ingredients included a measure of psychotherapy brought by the volunteer therapists, a dose of what we thought encounter groups and consciousness-raising groups should be, some political education, and lots of caring.

One vet would usually begin the conversation by talking about a problem he was having. Before long, another guy would respond, then a few more would take turns, almost like a jam session. There was nothing you were supposed to say, except that everybody shared a few common ideas: The war was a horror, and it's good to talk it out, but also to keep in mind the difference between real talk and bullshit. Nobody had to work hard to remember this distinction, though, because if you forgot, and lapsed into bragging, telling war stories, or just plain rambling, somebody else would point it out soon enough.

Most of us who took part in the early groups appreciated the value of psychotherapy as a response to our burdens. But for many veterans, the usefulness of therapy remains hard to grasp, partly because it is rarely made plain. In one of his later formulations, Freud wrote that the goal of treatment could be summed up in the phrase "Where id was ego shall be." Scholars disagree about what that means. It remains especially obscure for English readers, because this best known translation uses Latin words for Freud's German pronouns.

A freer translation, using the English *it* instead of the Latin *id* and *I* instead of the Latin *ego*, might read like this: "Whatever I have labeled as an *it* that impinges on me from beyond my control I will come to view as only having impact by virtue of the meaning *I* give to it."[4] Seen in this light, what troubles us about the war are the burdensome conclusions we've drawn from our experiences that govern our lives, usually from outside our awareness. The task of healing, then, is to reveal these conclusions to us, thus making it possible to revise them if we so choose.

This freer translation deliberately stresses the interpretive, rather than the scientific, claims to Freud's legacy. It is an emphasis that he encouraged quite explicitly toward the end of his life. In a 1934 interview he said: "Everybody thinks . . . that I stand by the scientific character of my work and that my principal scope lies in curing mental maladies. This is a terrible error that has prevailed for years and that I have been unable to set right. I am a scientist by necessity, and not by vocation. I am really by nature an artist."[5]

And what did he see as the goal of his art, in looking back almost forty years after his first psychological work? "To translate the inspirations offered by the currents of modern literature into scientific theories. In psychoanalysis you may find fused together though changed into scientific jargon, the . . . greatest literary schools of the nineteenth century . . . united in me under the patronage of my old master, Goethe."[6]

Repeatedly throughout his life Freud acknowledged the influence of Johann Wolfgang von Goethe. A century before Freud, Goethe achieved renown as a poet, statesman, friend of kings and great thinkers, and as a scientist in his own right. In his biological studies he advanced holistic views that foreshadowed by more than a century and a half some of the perspectives now emerging at the forefront of science.

Most of all Goethe is revered as a great spirit, a citizen of the world and champion of humanity. He saw his own vocation as serving life, and among his many maxims he wrote the following: "The most fruitful lesson is the conquest of one's own error. Whoever refuses to admit error may be a great scholar, but he is not a great learner. Whoever is ashamed of error will struggle against recognizing and admitting it, which means that he struggles against his greatest inward gain."[7]

These words suggest one facet of the age-old spiritual striving that spurs people on in psychotherapy: to learn the lessons that emerge from admitting formerly unacknowledged or only partially acknowledged wrongs. A kindred striving moved many of us in the rap groups. The idea was that those of us who fought in a lost and misguided war would have the most to gain inwardly by holding ourselves answerable for the wrongs we committed, witnessed, and acquiesced to.

You can't acknowledge the presence of something you habitually ignore. And so much of psychotherapy in particular and healing work in general brings us to attend to what we ordinarily don't notice. This is the "digging inside" or ferreting about in what psychotherapists call the unconscious, an unfortunate term that mistakenly suggests an actual place. What we find when we engage in such inquiry is not some fixed realm, but more and more reason to question whether any pat interpretation of the events of our lives is the whole story. Digging expresses the recognition that our personal myths, which we may have taken to be *the* truth, are in fact incomplete.

In the rap groups, the inquiry would frequently unfold as men recalled an event, then realized that although they were detached when it first happened, they were much closer to it looking back. Suddenly emotions would come, often pain, anger, or sorrow, as the men ceased feeling removed and let what happened touch them, as if reflecting on the moment at some later time allowed for a more intimate reinterpretation.

One evening we were joined by a veteran named Michael. He had heard about our group from a relative who read about us in a local newspaper. At the beginning he introduced himself as a former machine gunner, now an engineering student. Then he listened. Toward the end of that session he offered his observation about the way we spoke about ourselves: "You guys talk about feelings so much, feeling this, feeling that. I don't have feelings that way. I don't cry. I don't even laugh much anymore. But I laughed a lot in 'Nam. Like one time we were out on patrol and came across a village with lots of VC bunkers. The CO gave us orders to blow them up, so a bunch of us guys were walking along, tossing grenades into the bunkers. I was with a couple of buddies and tossed one in myself. All of a sudden this VC body goes flying in the air. The force of the explosion made his clothes come off at the same time. So we watched as his body went fly-

ing one way and his clothes the other and we laughed like hell."

A heavy silence followed. Then somebody asked, "How come you're not laughing now?"

"I don't know. It's the first time I thought about that incident in five years," Michael answered.

"Now that you've told us about it, y'got any feelings?" someone asked.

"Well, sort of. I don't feel good. I didn't think it was much of anything then, but it's real grisly thinking back on it now."

For many years, Michael would say the exchange that took place at that session was a turning point in his life. Up until then, he had a cool attitude about all that happened to him in the war. Afterward, he knew there was always much more about his experiences to explore.

When people would ask us what we did in these groups, one thing we said was "learn to feel." This is a shorthand way of saying that we would let ourselves recall experiences that we had glossed over in living through them, and then linger on them long enough so that whatever we were afraid to notice when they first occurred could register. The implicit question in all this was, "How would it be to feel what we used to think we couldn't bear?"

Saying that we were just "into feelings," however, is not accurate. We wanted to put things together in a new way, to see ourselves as answerable for what we did. Often that meant trying to grasp the part we played in the war within the larger context of our lives before and after. One of the unspoken questions that was never too far from our minds was, "How the hell did I get into that mess?" This question cut deep, and often led us from seemingly insignificant exchanges into deep personal probing.

After one of our sessions, Michael and I were riding in a car with a few of the others to a local radio station to be on a talk show about Vietnam veterans. We were "up," joking around, feeling good, even singing. At one point I broke into reciting lines from a German poem I had memorized during my stay in Germany before the war.

Bitingly serious, Michael broke the mood. "Cut out that German shit!"

I looked at him, amazed. "What's with you?"

"I don't like it."

"My grandmother doesn't either," I said, "but I figured that most of them were just like us, following orders, and didn't have real second thoughts, or not doing much about them until it was too late."

"I still don't like it."

"How come it gets to you so much?"

"My parents spent four years in a concentration camp."

"Holy shit! You've been coming to this group for months and you never told us that?"

That was the way Michael started piecing his own story together. Before then he could never figure out how a Jewish guy from Brooklyn could love an M-60 machine gun so much. After that night, he had a long series of dreams that mixed together the war, his parents, Germany, and life back in New York. One of his insights was that he grew up knowing his parents had a mysterious past, when all their relatives died. It was a dark, eerie part of life, horrible yet strangely inviting.

In probing himself Michael recognized in his childhood a longing he had never before discerned — to have a dark place of his own. Going to Vietnam was like an unacknowledged wish come true: Now he knew about horrors most people can't fathom. He also recalled that he had carried a chip on his shoulder as a boy, knowing that his parents' enormous suffering had never been avenged. After months in the rap group, and after learning to interpret his dreams, Michael looked back on the killing he did in the war as having had a personal meaning he hadn't seen before: It was his revenge.

"Know thyself" is an ancient prescription. Whether it's called confession or the pursuit of insight, reaching inward to reveal long-hidden truths has long been recognized as the way to inner liberation. One of the great healers of all time put it this way: "Ye shall know the truth, and the truth shall make you free."[8]

What is it about looking inward, or self-reflection, that has brought many schools of ancient and modern therapy to embrace it? How does digging inside bring about a cure? In the various approaches to therapy influenced by psychoanalysis, the search within is likened to an archeological dig, in which the seeker pokes beneath his or her own facade to locate psychological relics — old hurt and anger. This view assumes that what you're looking for comes ready made; hidden truths are thought to exist independent of your style, approach, and purpose in searching. But this isn't a very precise description. How could patients of Jungian therapists so consistently produce Jungian insights, and patients of Freudian therapists come up with Freudian ones if what we find through probing inwardly isn't conditioned by the way we search?

Healing reflection usually results in a more livable grasp of some troubling experience. What does this mean? We can't begin to answer until we ask what an experience is. Throughout the psychological literature, experience is commonly and unthinkingly lumped together with events or happenings of a particular time and place. But this is a mistake. Events are not experiences unless a human being is present, not just as another factor in the equation but as the essential requisite.

An experience is a human phenomenon with inexhaustible richness. We can peer into it and discover the role played by many different aspects of a given life. For example, we can reflect on an experience and find out how early childhood influences helped shape what took place. We can see impressions our parents left on us, the thoughts we were thinking at the moment of the experience, the expectations we had for the future, the people who touched us, the way we were influenced by our relations with others, the experiences that have happened since and have led to altered perspectives on the original experience. All in all, this is possible because an experience is a window on an entire life — including the situations, people, and structures that shape it — and on the human condition itself.

The new perspectives that result from healing reflection are, therefore, never just raw perceptions of reality. They are always interpretations. According to the view I'm suggesting, digging doesn't produce a grasp of what *really* happened. What we come up with through reflection are always new versions, new ways to shape and speak about what took place.[9] What rings true about a new version of this sort is not so much its close fit with some objectively given reality so much as its resonance with our present state, and with the commitments that have become second nature to us.

We can come up with many, many variations or interpretations of our lives, but only those that carry the conviction, "This is a view I will live by," mark junctures in our lives. The question is, then, what takes place at those moments when digging yields a major turning point? One answer is that we come up with much more than a new idea. It wouldn't be a turning point unless we accomplished something like a reordering of our entire lives, bringing about a more encompassing view of ourselves. Whether it is to acknowledge a wrong we committed, a long-overlooked personal shortcoming, a desire that has escaped our attention or seemed too loathsome to admit, with such insights we announce an expanded identity. In effect we say, "I now see myself as including what I used to leave out."

In listening to Michael a bell rang for me. Until then, I assumed about myself what some wisecracking sergeant said when I passed through basic training. "Headed for intelligence, eh? One of you rich boys, off to play it safe." If anybody asked me, "What's the real truth, why did you enlist?" I'd answer, "To keep from being in the infantry." Now another view was beginning to emerge for me, coaxed in part by one of my buddies in the rap group. After Michael spoke, Will, one of the original members of our group, said to me, "You had a Jewish thing going too. Why else did you bother to go to Germany before the war and then call youself Levy once you were in?"

His questions led me to review my past in a new light. I had spent the early 1950s growing up as a Jew in a Catholic neighborhood, where I learned about prejudice firsthand. But unlike Michael, I didn't rage at people so openly. My thing was to work harder to get them to like me. By the second grade I was already at it. A classmate told me what his parents said, that the reason people didn't like Jews was because they killed Christ. So I took a person-by-person poll of my second grade class to find out who thought the Jews killed Christ. By the time I finished college, I was concerned about different complaints against Jews: Jews are disloyal, or they're only loyal to Israel or the internationalist conspiracy or the Communist party. I wanted to make sure I didn't get tarred with that brush, and so I enlisted, thinking I was making the honorable choice — to make myself useful where a Jew like me belonged, in intelligence.

This was a new interpretation of what happened. But it was as consistent with the facts as any other, and had the virtue of emphasizing a certain striving in me that I no longer wanted to ignore.

Others in the group also began to see their lives from new perspectives. Most of the regulars in our group, those who came back week after week, had enlisted. Before coming to the group most would say that they went in because it was the thing to do, or because they would've been drafted anyway, or because it was a way to exercise some choice over what was happening. Nothing we said or did in the groups contradicted that understanding. It's just that one by one we discovered that our personal connection with the war could be understood in other ways as well, ways we hadn't appreciated before.

Sam, the quiet conservative, eventually told a story that gave some background on his prewar conversion to patriotism. He began by explaining that he had had a speech impediment as a little kid. At first he didn't know he had a funny way of talking. Nobody in his family told him about it. But when he went to the first grade, the kids started laughing at him. When he found out why, he was furious at his parents for not preparing him for it or correcting his speech.

In recent years he hadn't thought about his childhood, at least not until he got into the group. Listening to the rest of us, he came to see himself as a kid who resented being laughed at, and who became determined to turn the tables. He sketched out an underlying logic to the way he had developed the personal attitude of continually bucking the tide. In college, the kid with the speech problem became a first rate public debater. And because he never liked to go with the crowd, he joined the conservative club at his liberal college, just to be able to tweak the noses of the majority of professors and students, who walked around assuming that their progressive views were the one sure way.

Midway into his junior year, Sam felt various pressures building. The war was hotter than ever, but fewer people were enlisting. His girlfriend wanted to get married but he didn't. And his political friends wanted him to run for office, but he didn't want that either. His solution was to buck the tide again, this time to be the only one of his conservative friends to say, "I don't want to talk patriotism. I'm going to do something about it!" That's when he enlisted.

Of all the members of our group, I was closest to Will. He had come to the earliest meetings, and kept coming back from time to time over the four years we stayed together. But there were long periods when we didn't see him, so the fact that he never told us what the wrinkle was for him seemed understandable. He hadn't had a chance yet.

One night Will was there when a new guy came, a gentle man named Sal, who had served with the Army in the States. Sal said he felt uneasy being with guys who'd been to 'Nam. He said he envied us, but was also glad he didn't go. "I would've been too scared. And nothing could've made me shoot another human being."

Sal had always wanted to be a doctor, to take care of people rather than hurt them. "I never had any problem admitting being afraid," he explained, "because I was afraid a lot as a kid." Physical fears weren't so hard to own up to, he said, because he lived for years with something that was far worse: "I'm gay. But for a long time I lied about it or denied it. But not anymore. I've told my parents. I tell strangers. And I'm telling you because I hope you guys will be my friends."

One by one we reassured Sal that he could be himself in our group, and one or two of us thanked him for being up front. Will didn't say anything though, which was unusual. Usually he was the one who made large gestures, a natural master of ceremonies who'd be the first to welcome someone new. Instead, he was holding his head in his hands. When Sal was finished, somebody noticed Will and asked, "What's going on with you?"

We all looked. Will didn't say anything. We waited. He started to sob, then moved his lips, and the words came out. "Me too." Sal was sitting next to him. Will and Sal looked at each other. Then Will cried openly.

Later he told us that though his parents were poor, he went to a military school by winning a scholarship. He had no difficulty with the work, but had another kind of problem. His junior year he got very tight with one of his classmates. They did everything together — run, wrestle, play on the football team, listen to records, and talk about their lives. They were constant companions. By midyear their friendship had become more intimate. They would touch each other's bodies, and began to sneak to each other's rooms at night. One night the sergeant at arms caught them in bed together. The school expelled them both in disgrace. Will had never told anyone, even hid the details from his parents. He had made sure not to tell anyone that he could love another man in that way.

After the expulsion, he went to work doing men's work — construction, mostly heavy labor. Then he figured the one way to get it out of his system, to prove himself a man, would be to enlist in the Special Forces.

What he said next spoke for all of us. "It's what I thought I had to do back then." Reviewing our role in the war within the context of our lives brought us to a new appreciation of the choices we had made. As we came to take a wider view of ourselves, we realized that we had been blaming ourselves for what we now saw as the natural outgrowth

of our earlier lives. At the same time, a new basis for profound remorse
came to light. As Will put it, "It sometimes looks like Vietnamese peo-
ple had to die so I could work out my shit."

When mental health professionals speak as scientists, trying to explain the anguish among a minority of veterans, they refer to various symptoms. These are commonly said to be the later effects of
earlier causes in the individual's past — in the war, in prewar personality defects, and in further strains of the postwar environment.
From a healing perspective, however, symptoms among ex-soldiers
are the surface forms of the suffering imposed by an at least partially
awakened conscience. Only by carrying judgments about ourselves
into the present do we pain ourselves over the past.

People commonly call this distress guilt and talk about the effects
of guilt, as if the pain were caused by some objective force or feeling
that operates independent of the inner postures, commitments, and
views we hold about ourselves. From a healing perspective, guilt is
a catch-all term for the feeling that emerges from our belief that by
virtue of something we've seen, done, or lent support to, we are
unworthy or unclean.

With Sam, for example, it was his support for the war that he later
judged to be indefensible. From that revised perspective, the death
of the young Vietnamese girl through the recklessness of her American driver was especially painful. It stood, in his view, for his own
collusion and acquiescence to uncaring and unthinking acts. He never
spoke about the still more primitive aspects of that incident, but
many other veterans have done so. Many men who witness the death
or mutilation of women and young girls have later admitted that
they had been condemning themselves most of all for the flash of
erotic stimulation they had experienced as witnesses or participants.
It is as if they had said to themselves, "Anybody who gets off on
such bestiality is less than human and deserves to be eternally pun-
ished."

In my own case, the pain I carried away from the night on the roof
of our Saigon headquarters was a similar mix of self-condemnatory
judgments. I charged myself with getting off easy, for using deceit
and guile to land a job far away from the bleeding and dying, and
for being too cowardly to acknowledge how afraid I was. While Rob-

ertson spoke out and risked reassignment, I knuckled under to play safe. That I had criticized the crassness of grimy soldiers who walked the Saigon streets bothered me as well, for in doing so I denied that I had the same impulses, except that a privileged background provided me the luxury of holding myself as morally superior. As for more primitive urges, I too never divulged them in the rap group. But later I recognized that, like the sergeants who watched the gunships, I was fascinated and aroused by the power of raining fiery death from the sky. Helicopter gunships provided the ultimate supermacho fantasy — of gunners and pilots who squirted their death-dealing come on targets below.

For the purposes of healing, the surfacing of such judgments is as much cause for rejoicing as for compassion; it implies that, to one degree or another, the one who suffers under them has determined to hold himself answerable for wrongs he either committed, witnessed, or acquiesced to. This doesn't mean that people who do healing work want anyone to continue suffering. Rather, the pain is simply something to work with, a sign that a person has begun to wake up.

The man who suffers from his own condemnation is not necessarily aware of the source of his distress, nor do those around him necessarily see the moral striving implicit in his pain. Some veterans may even be so committed to punishing themselves that their lives are in danger, while people around them look on helplessly. Only a small percentage of the several million men who actually served in Vietnam are severely afflicted in this way, but their absolute number ranges in the tens of thousands. The wife of one of them wrote me this letter.

Dear sir:

Please can you help me? I'm sorry to bother you but it's really terrible, because my husband won't do anything I suggest. His headaches get so bad he actually bangs his head against a brick wall, and says that his depression and his nightmares *should* keep going. He says they're just punishment for the things he had to do over there. I know you can't help someone who refuses to make the first step. But now I'm getting crazy too. It keeps getting worse. Last night he came home so luded out [stoned on Quaaludes] he's lucky he didn't kill himself driving. He says that ludes are the only thing that make the pain go away. He's trying to get a gun permit now. I'm afraid that all he'll do is put a bullet through his head, and may kill me first. I don't know what to do. I'm afraid to nag him. But I want the pain to go away, and the drugs and booze to stop going in him, and I want us to have a normal life. It's all so hopeless though. So here I sit pouring my heart out to you, not knowing what to do. Thanks for being there. It helps to know there's someone out there who understands.

Most veterans have not reached that point. But it is not because they have questioned the war and themselves to the extent that they open-mindedly accept the past and their role in it. The conclusion my colleagues and I drew from our interviews with random samples of veterans from across the country is that most do not openly engage in such self-questioning. Ask vets at random about guilt and most will look at you and laugh. "It was a job to do" or "I feel proud of everything I did there" or "It was them or me" or "Guilt? I thought we should've kicked ass all the way to Hanoi!" Even among those who are clearly burdened, almost nobody says, "I judge myself harshly for what I saw or did in Vietnam."

For a sizable minority, the self-questioning has clearly begun, but the judgments remain implicit rather than clearly stated, so it often takes a trained observer to notice what's going on. In our national study, I found that about 20 percent of the veterans we interviewed would be termed "well adjusted" by most people because they have jobs, families, and stay out of trouble. Nonetheless, the lives of this group of men show signs of having a dull edge. For many of them, the problem seems vague — a loss of energy in the years since they've been back from the war. They seem turned off inside, usually without being aware of it, as if resigned to putting up with their discomfort. It's nothing they say outright as much as a background attitude of "I just can't help it" or "There's nothing anyone can do about it, so why even think about it?"

These veterans seem to feel that they deserve to suffer for their role in the horror. A few will say it directly, like the man who told his interviewer, "I wish I hadn't killed all those people. I found with all my strength and conviction I couldn't say 'Fuck you!' to the people who told me to shoot." The now legendary "survivor guilt," or feeling bad for living on after a buddy died, is also fairly common. Another man said, "I couldn't get over it. He got hit when they blew the bunker because that's where I told him to go. It's like I got him killed. I felt so terrible about it that when I got back I went to live with his parents for a while, trying to make the guilt go away."

The vets who talk this way usually mention other complaints, like nervous conditions, nightmares, drinking problems, and disillusionment. Often they talk about having changed since coming back. "I'm a lot more careful now. I was wild as a kid, but I'd never think of having a motorcycle now" or "I've become more nervous . . . anxious, you know, angry." Some seem to know about the changes only from what others have told them. "My mother says I'm not the same son she had before I went to Vietnam."

For each veteran who openly acknowledges that he has assumed a measure of personal responsibility for his role in the war, there are at least two others whose words betray their discomfort but who do not admit it directly. One man, for example, said early in his interview, "I never gave any thought to whether or not I killed anybody. I'd rather not know," only to say later that "I tried to figure it out afterwards, feeling bad maybe, but it was something that had to be done." He concluded by saying he's now trying to forget "the whole thing." Another veteran, who said he had nightmares after his friend got killed while "walking point" for him, said a few moments later that the deaths in Vietnam didn't bother him. "I took it. I'm strong. It fucks me up temporarily, thank God though it wasn't me." Later on in the interview, when we asked him about possible physical complaints, he revealed that he is still bothered by nervousness, quick temper, and the feeling that life doesn't mean anything.

One night an ex-grunt from Brooklyn named Bobby came to the rap group and told us his problem. He was living with one woman, having an affair with another, and told them both what he was doing. "They want me to choose between them, but I don't want to. I can't. I can't be with just one woman."

After the first few months, most of what we talked about in the rap groups wasn't the war but life in the present. And more often than not, the issue had to do with relationships, particularly with women. Problems with love and commitment were a continual theme. All of the regulars had some kind of difficulty in this area. Will was going through a series of troubled relationships, Michael was having weekly conflicts with his wife, and Sam and his wife were blowing up at each other almost every day. As group coordinator, I liked to think that I was above most of this trouble, but the truth was that I was having lots of it myself. I didn't blame my problems on the war; men and women all over the country were having hassles. And yet, something about the war was always there in the background.

What happened in the war wasn't all negative; the love and closeness I developed with Liza a few months after coming back from Saigon were more intense than any I had ever experienced. But I was open only to a point. After I came to New York and started trying to work out a life with her things went sour fast. She would want to be together. I would want to study. She was disappointed over the gift I gave her for her birthday. I was confused by her liberated woman talk one day, and by insinuations that her man wasn't taking good enough care of her the next. Soon all I wanted was to be alone. One day I met her for lunch and said, "It's over. We can't go on like this."

That was before the rap groups first met. Since then I had lived with another woman for a year or so and, after breaking up and dating for a while, had moved in with another. Two years later we got married, but that didn't settle things. Always, for me, it was the same issue. My dream was to be with one woman, but I couldn't be trusted, not by the woman and not by myself. As much as I tried, desire for others obsessed me. I had told Liza, "I can't stay with you; my head will turn," meaning that I couldn't promise not to go after other women. In my next two relationships my fears were confirmed. When I wasn't having an affair with someone else I was thinking about it.

I was always carrying on in secret, as if I couldn't keep myself from doing something underhanded behind somebody's back. From time to time the lying would become unbearable and I would tell all, and the result would be a crazy scene. I'd apologize, and later, when forgiveness didn't come, I'd defend my right to feel what I felt. Finally, when the frustration mounted, I'd find another woman on the side to fulfill the urges I couldn't satisfy at home, starting the cycle all over again.

Men who screw around are fairly common, and in psychology courses I got to read what therapists wrote about them. Alfred Adler, an earlier student of Freud's who later went his own way, wrote about the power struggles implicit in such behavior. He observed that one of his male patients had apparently patterned his life around trying to beat his mother for her having beaten him in the nursery.[10] I wondered if that applied to me. Having struggled for years to gain independence from my mother and sister, now I was no sooner getting involved with one woman than I was struggling not to let her have exclusive claim on me. But the Adlerian theory didn't account for my obsession with secrecy and being found out.

I had seen a similar pattern over and over in talking with men I had known in the Army. They seemed to be afraid of being found out by their wives. Their personal code was: what they didn't reveal nobody should ask them about — which I saw as an excuse to keep them from having to be answerable for what they did. Almost all of them slept around and kept it from their wives. It wasn't just the guys in intelligence work. Wherever I looked the idea seemed to be: To stay married you have to be a good spy.

The night Bobby came to the group I talked about these experiences. I said I hoped that one day I would be able to be faithful and trustworthy, but so far I wasn't doing so well. My buddy Will, who was often on to me more quickly than anyone then said, "So that's what it is for you. All of us get stuck on blaming ourselves for what we did in the war. You're no different. You were a spook, a sneak. No wonder you can't see yourself as trustworthy!"

Before that evening I hadn't noticed that the three years I had spent honing the skills of being covert, double dealing, and underhanded had left their mark. Will had touched a nerve. I wanted desperately to be honest, and even went so far as to talk about intelligence work publicly. But before hearing Will's observations I hadn't realized that I never told anyone how good I had been at espionage. It was as if I was afraid that if people ever found out how good a spy I had been they would never trust me. In fact, from the way I was still lying, cheating, and hiding in my relationship with my wife, I didn't think I could help myself, and didn't really deserve anyone's trust.

Most of the others had similar fears, particularly the guys who had been in combat. They didn't believe anyone could love a man who had killed as easily as they had. Moreover, they weren't certain that men like themselves deserved to be loved.

We knew it wasn't just us; many men and women were going through painful times. Being a veteran simply gave the distress a particular flavor. We had come home weary, wanting to be taken care of, and women were no longer waiting as they had before. Many of the women we met — on campuses, in demonstrations, and through friends — were locked in battles of their own, campaigning for new rights, against exclusively male prerogatives. They wanted equal privileges at work, at home, and in bed. And on that basis alone, intimacy suffered, since these women frequently went to their men not to give so much as to exact reparations for the indignities of a lifetime, for the entire history of female oppression by patriarchal societies. Often it felt as if we had to atone not only for the war in Vietnam but for the wrongs done by the males of all time in the battle of the sexes.

Although we needed women more than ever, and feared them more as well, we looked to them for leadership in a way that would have been unthinkable a short time before. We had the women's movement as a constant example, with their use of consciousness-raising groups as a major organizing tool. In the way we described them, the veteran rap groups were clearly inspired by women's groups: Not only were they a place to heal those who attended, but also a forum for getting the word out.

Psychotherapists often work with the residue of trauma by considering even such complaints as a troubled conscience as part of a person's unacknowledged strategy for living. The idea is that in any such approach there is always something gained and something lost, although the painful price of such strategies is usually more apparent than the benefit derived. The point of digging is to reinterpret the pain so as to uncover the bargain that the pained individual has struck with himself. Usually it goes something like this. Out of fear of further hurt, which might come from being vulnerable to others and to life, the sufferer has decided to keep himself barricaded like a guilty prisoner. The price is reduced connection with others and withdrawal from life; the gain is a sense of reduced risk.

During the four years we spent together in the rap groups, none of us rode this insight all the way home. We were still too committed to the polemical purpose of uncovering the role of war experiences in our lives to devote ourselves fully to overcoming our suffering. With regard to our troubled relationships with spouses and lovers, for example, none of us ever considered fully that we helped per-

petuate the difficulty as part of an elaborate, although unacknowledged, strategy for hedging our bets. Each of us had doubts that
we could ever be loved. And we relentlessly acted in ways that in-
sured we would never find out for certain, since we wrecked our
own chances before things ever got too far along.

People have good reasons for developing and adhering to such
life strategies. Invariably, the approach that minimizes risk by inflicting pain is based on a conviction that one is neither able nor
worthy of proceeding otherwise. Take the vets I knew well in the
rap groups; we didn't just *guess* that we might be unlovable. We had
good evidence from the past that we were capable of actions that
any civilized person would find horrid. But it wasn't just what we
did in Vietnam. Each of us went to the war already profoundly questioning our own worth: Sam the ex-stutterer bucking the tide, Will
trying to prove his manhood, Michael taking revenge on Nazis, and
me, the sneak, trying to prove I was not a disloyal Jew. Each in our
own way had come to view our participation, collusion, and acquiescence to the war as confirmation of our flawed nature.

I am proposing here a reformulation of the often-cited difficulties
many former soldiers have with love. The core of the problem is
never merely a matter of what one did, witnessed, or failed to do
during some traumatic incident. The reaction to such wartime experiences arises when one who judges himself harshly concludes
that his role in condemnable deeds serves as further reason to question his own worthiness to give and receive life's greatest gifts.

Such self-doubt has been endemic among many who've survived
a war, not just because lives were at stake there and because many
of us who were subjected to those extreme circumstances failed to
live up to our highest expectations for ourselves. The self-punishment ultimately rests on the case we made against ourselves from
the start and maintained all the way through. Many of us were willing to go off to fight in the first place only because we had not yet
"found ourselves." That is, the very reason we were willing to go to
such extremes is that we had been convinced that we were not yet
adequate for life. There was something we had yet to find out, to
do, to accomplish, to prove, before we could just live.

And so many who survive do not simply blame themselves for
living when others died. It is not even that we blame ourselves for

the initial sense of relief that came with being spared. Rather, it is that we had no way to justify how one whom we did not value highly, ourself, was granted the gift of further life. It is this gift, and the challenge to live as one who has been given it, that many survivors reject. People who believe themselves unworthy have no other consistent choice than to refuse to accept life graciously.

Digging inside ultimately heals by challenging our hold on this belief that we are undeserving of life and love. Searching inwardly for the source of our suffering may bring us eventually to notice that no single belief, no one way to characterize ourselves, ever provides more than a partial view. Successive realizations will supersede earlier ones, reminding us that the truth of whatever we think and feel about ourselves is only temporary. "The war did it" may be followed by the recognition, "I was already set up to be vulnerable before I went," followed by "I set myself up for it by the way I tried to play the game of life," followed by "Everybody I knew responded to things that way and I was just going along with a pervasive cultural trend," and so on.

What renders us whole is not any of these views. The cure lies in the looking itself — living out the commitment to the possibility that the truth is greater than what we presently think and say. Challenging ourselves this way serves as an antidote to narrowness, dogmatism, and identities that make us inaccessible to others. Eventually we dissolve even the belief that we are unworthy. We thereby shift from identifying with a particular view to seeing ourselves as being nourished by continually opening up to revisions in what we consider ourselves to be. For humans, being whole means acknowledging, thankfully, that we are still unfinished, on the way.

It is an ancient view that killing soils the killer, and even the warrior who kills for his king and with the blessings of his gods must purify himself. When Odysseus and his son take revenge against the suitors, the hero's home is soiled with the blood of the dead. To cleanse his hall of the taint, Odysseus orders fire and brimstone brought to where the slaughter occurred. Only after the bloody work and mopping up is done does he send word to his wife Penelope that he's home, and joins her in a loving reunion.

Since Homer's time, two major revolutions of the spirit have taken place. The first was the conversion to monotheism throughout the West. After this shift, divine power was no longer thought to take the form of godlike spirits who walk the earth as men and women, but to be an omnipresent ethereal essence. Murder was still a crime, and killing in war would have to be atoned, but the cleansing could no longer be a mere washing away of blood. It had to absolve the soul.

During the Middle Ages, in the time of the Crusades, wars were blessed by priests and popes. But soldiers who survived were nonetheless required to purge the defilement of war. To people who saw the entire world as God's kingdom, no war, no matter how sanctified, could erase the crime of murder. So after the battle was done, before a veteran could rejoin the fold of decent men, he had to confess and repent.

Historical records of that time include 'penitentiaries,'' or holy requirements imposed on all soldiers who had killed in war. One such list was issued in the year 1070 by a bishop for Norman soldiers who fought in the battles to conquer England. It shows that even after a "good" war, one blessed by the Norman church, penance was nonetheless required according to each man's sins:

> Anyone who knows that he killed a man in the great battle must do penance for one year for each man that he killed.
>
> Anyone who wounded a man, and does not know whether he killed him or not, must do penance for forty days for each man he thus struck.
>
> Anyone who does not know the number of those he wounded or killed must, at the discretion of his bishop, do penance for one day in each week for the remainder of his life; or, if he can, let him redeem his sin by a perpetual alms, either by building or by endowing a church.[11]

Most modern readers would find this list strange, the relic of an outmoded sensibility. This attitude testifies to the second great revolution since Homer's time. Whether we attribute the change to the triumph of science, or to the Reformation and the successful challenge to priestly authority, today only the minority of very devout citizens look to any ministerial class as competent to absolve them from the taint of war. Modern communities no longer provide ritual cleansing for their surviving warriors. The task of absolution has become a thoroughly personal matter, and what has emerged with the increased burden is both the widespread pain of postwar trauma and the individualized cure, which brings some ex-soldiers to the radical step of renouncing the cult of war.

The healing we sought in the rap groups, although new in form, was not original in spirit. Forsaking violence is the cure proposed by modern as well as ancient prophets. Even before a generation of disillusioned soldiers turned pacifist after World War I, one of the great authors of the nineteenth century paved the way for the warrior's self-absolution by renouncing war.

Less than two decades after writing *War and Peace*, a celebration of the vast drama of the Napoleonic wars, Leo Tolstoy wrote of a personal conversion after realizing that the true intent of Jesus' injunction, "Resist not evil," was as a thorough critique of the cult of war. "I was taught to judge and punish," he wrote in 1884. "Then I was taught to make war, that is, to resist evil men with murder, and the military caste, of which I was a member, was called the Christ-loving military, and their activity was sanctified by a Christian blessing."[12] In a pamphlet entitled *Church and State* he wrote that "Christian state" is a ridiculous term, for it either refers to no state at all or to one whose Christianity is a sham. For him the Christian teaching is hostile to governments, and those who profess the Christian way ought to renounce, nonviolently, the evil requirements imposed by states.[13]

While few of the famous writers who emerged from World War I reported conversions like Tolstoy's, many of their bitterly antiwar statements carried his message. Ernest Hemingway wrote, "Never think that war no matter how necessary nor how justified is not a crime. Ask the infantry and ask the dead."[14] What is the crime? The answer is implied in the title of his book *For Whom the Bell Tolls*. It is taken from "Meditation XVII" of John Donne, the seventeenth-century poet whose way of serving the divine at the dawn of the scientific age was to enunciate the invisible connection that links all of humanity. In writing about the funeral bell that announces the death of an unknown neighbor, Donne warned:

> All mankind is of one author and is one volume. . . . No man is an island, entire of itself; every man is a piece of the continent, a part of the main; . . . Any man's death diminishes me, because I am involved in mankind; and therefore never send to know for whom the bell tolls; it tolls for thee.[15]

All killing, no matter how thoroughly sanctioned by ideology, priestly authorities, or the state, is a violation of the unseen relations that bind all to all. This violation, and the readiness to hold oneself answerable for it, surface in every successful rap group I have ever attended or read or heard about. We saw no suitors to vanquish; we trusted no priestly class to dictate our penance. But we felt defiled by acts that were only possible for men with hardened hearts. Our way of cleansing ourselves had much of the flavor of modern, psychologically informed self-scrutiny. But our digging into ourselves and into each other had a timeless purpose. It was to open our hearts to love.

REACHING BOTTOM

It is not society that is to guide and save the creative hero, but precisely the reverse. And so every one of us shares the supreme ordeal . . . not in the bright moments of his tribe's great victories but in the silences of his personal despair.

JOSEPH CAMPBELL[1]

Thus play I in one person many people,
And none contented . . . but whate'er I be,
Nor I nor any man that but man is
With nothing shall be pleased, till he be eased
With being nothing.

SHAKESPEARE[2]

SOME VETERANS SAY that nothing makes the horror go away. They've tried everything they know — talking about it, getting involved, probing themselves — but the trauma is still with them. To hear them tell it, they'll never be the same.

For men like these, the pain is more than a personal matter. Insight into their wrongs, real and imagined, will never entirely deliver them of their suffering. Freud's idea, which still pervades the literature on trauma, is that distressed people keep going back to troubling experiences in hopes of mastering them. In countless recollections, while both awake and asleep, a constructive energy keeps battling a destructive energy and continually loses. Battling over what? What is the horror at the core of traumatic experiences? What, at bottom, is trauma? And what is there to master in these experiences? In the end, we say, people have to grab hold of themselves. But what is it about ourselves that must be grasped in confronting such experiences?

Most people who are engaged in healing work don't ask such questions explicitly. Instead they draw on the intuitions they've developed from living through their own traumas and coming out on top. To make healing more widely available, however, and to reach out more effectively to those still in pain, we should ask what it is that competent peer counselors and therapists have learned for themselves.

Many veteran counselors say, "I know because I've been there." In part they mean, "The guys can't put me on; I can tell the real from the fake." But they also imply that they know how to be genuinely compassionate, even when it means being unusually direct and tough, rather than feeling sorry or indulging a troubled person's self-pity, which never helps. What is this knowledge based on? How does one come by it?

Saying "I've been there" suggests that it's the shared war experience that confers the special connection with fellow vets. But if asked, the most experienced counselors and therapists would admit that people who weren't in the war can be effective too. The special connection has less to do with being there physically than with having suffered and learned. Where is it, then, that they have been? Some will say, "in a bad place" or "in the pits." In the phrase made famous by Alcoholics Anonymous, they've "hit bottom" and come up. But what is the bottom? What happens there?

After four years, almost two hundred vets had come to the rap groups at one point or another. Several score had come back often enough for us to notice that they were getting something out of it. We succeeded in several ways: Some of us made friendships that would last for life; the group had been a precious haven during painful years, helping us to begin understanding ourselves; a few would look back on it as the place that launched us on careers of serving others; and the therapists who volunteered touched many of us deeply — as mentors, friends, and colleagues. Most of all, we had established rap groups as a reality, a model that others could use.

We also failed in many respects: Only a tiny fraction of the vets in our area ever participated; while we met (from 1970 to 1974), no nationwide movement sprang up; and for all the probing, questioning, and endless dialogue, we never fully resolved what was so troubling about what we had gone through. In fact, most of us were still messing up our lives. My buddy Will had recently tried to kill himself. Sam and his wife had just had their first kid and were separated and fighting more wildly than ever. Michael was still having nightmares and threatening to leave his wife. And I was fighting with my wife even more than before. For all of us, life at home and at work was still a constant battle. Nobody said that Vietnam was doing it to us. But the evidence was clear: We were still at war, at least within ourselves.

Yet I knew something was changing for me. It is one thing to talk and think about the devastation over and over when it might help stop a bad war. But I could no longer find a purpose for living in pain, and

my obsessions began to seem hollow. I couldn't just stop them, though.
For one thing, I wasn't sure what I'd be if I gave up the one thing I had
going for me. I was afraid that if I stopped being a troubled vet I'd be
nothing at all.

The most pervasive problem among veterans is not any clear set of
symptoms. Rather, it's the feeling that life is a downer, the personal
version of the black hole. Individual descriptions vary in degree and
emphasis. But in general, it's the feeling that life is hopeless. Life
seems meaningless and empty, or at least *your* life seems to have no
purpose.

One way into the hole is to punish yourself long and hard enough.
Many travel a different path, approaching despair by repeatedly
thinking that their life is pointless, like the war that killed their buddies and drained their pride. A large minority of veterans, men who
disagree bitterly over whether we should've fought all the way to
Hanoi or stayed out of the war altogether, would shout in unison
that the way the war ended was "royally fucked." They'd add that
what they've got to show for their sacrifices and pain is nothing.

People in this state think everything is a mess. Nothing is worth
anything. For many, it's not something they can tell their buddies.
If they're going to think about it at all, they go off to do it by themselves. Since nothing matters, it's senseless even to talk about it. It's
as if saying anything would dilute it, turning it into lies or half truths
that other people could easily dismiss.

A sense of meaninglessness is nothing new in human experience,
and it's especially common among young adults, people in their teens
and twenties who haven't yet settled down and established their
direction in life. But it's even more common among veterans and
other survivors of mass horror than among people who've never
been wrenched from the preoccupations of their immediate sur-
roundings. For the survivor lives in the midst of an appalling void.

A century ago, Nietzsche wrote that it is not suffering, but meaningless suffering, that exacts the greatest toll.[3] And after World War
II, Viktor Frankl, a psychiatrist who survived a Nazi concentration
camp, developed his own approach to psychotherapy based on this
idea.[4] But the lesson still needs to be learned. Since Vietnam, neither
the American public nor the mental health community has yet rec-

ognized that the primary psychological burden among veterans is a profound emptiness.

A national Harris poll documented the widespread failure to recognize the problem clearly.[5] Veterans, in fact, are as unaware of it as others who were interviewed. When asked to speculate about Vietnam veterans as a group, the vets were similar to the general public in saying that the greatest psychological burden was "emotional and mental difficulties" usually associated with psychiatric disorder. But when Harris asked the same men to talk personally and focus on what they knew for certain about themselves, he found that the veterans' most common psychological complaint was "not knowing what you want out of life."

This was a phrase coined by Louis Harris and Associates. Psychotherapists of different schools will debate how to explain and understand it best, but on its face the problem is clear enough. It's not seeing any sense, direction, significance, or purpose to life. It's the polite thing to say when life lacks coherence. Saying "yes" to a stranger on the phone who asks, "Have you ever had the problem of not knowing what you want out of life?" is easier than saying, "Look, you want to know my problem? I'll tell you. Life sucks. After what I've been through I don't see any point to the whole damn mess!"

In studying the interviews my colleagues and I conducted with veterans across the country, I found that most who spoke of meaninglessness trace it to profoundly troubling experiences. Some pinpointed the trauma quite distinctly. "I still picture the expression on his face when he got shot, just seeing the three bullet holes over and over in my mind." Most, however, talked about the original trauma as having spanned a period of time that included recurring events. "It was the fear of just being there, being killed or whatever, the thought of losing an arm or leg," or "The experience of walking in the woods. It's nerve wracking. Somebody's out to get you at all times," or "Rockets, that got me, because you never know when they're coming."

Men who spoke of meaninglessness often mentioned the fear of death and injury. One vet explained it as "always feeling uneasy, because you never know when somebody, the next guy, is going to drop, or will it be you." Another said, "It's happening every day

. . . what makes you so special that it can't happen to you? So you got to feel strongly . . . a mental strain." All who referred to trauma were very aware of the dying. Some recalled intense reactions when they killed. "I damn near broke down and cried." Another put a common sentiment this way: "I guess nobody wants to kill or train to be killed, but sometimes it gets to the point of either you or me. Pray it's not me." Often the most terrifying thing was the possibility of being maimed. "I'd rather come back whole or not at all," said one man. Another put it as, "You get killed and it's over. But to see yourself with no arms or legs, that was the bad part."

Not all vets were aware of one original traumatic experience. Some conveyed a feeling of emptiness without registering any specific complaints or recalling any troubling memories. But after reviewing the course of their lives in a three-hour interview, most of those who spoke with a hollow tone came to recognize the change they had undergone as a result of the war. One man concluded, "I guess since Vietnam I'm more of a loner type. Just like to leave home, go sit in the park and watch the cars go by, relax, get carefree. Before I used to like a lot of company and running around. Not anymore." Another said, "Maybe sometimes I think about getting old, you know. Like left on my own, an old man in some tenement, just slip out without nobody even caring or knowing who you were."

Nowhere in my search through the vast professional literature did I find an answer to the question "What is trauma?" that satisfied me or enabled me to respond to others' pain the way I wanted to. I did find many intelligent explanations of the kind that read, "Men are traumatized by . . ." followed by a list of various events that people would agree are profoundly upsetting. But what is so traumatic about such events? I didn't want an explanation by someone detached from the experience. I wanted a way to go to the heart of it, a way that would make me a reliable guide for plunging the depths with others.

My quest became part of my doctoral research in psychology.[6] I began by studying what I believed to be one of the most encompassing theories of human motivation then available — a scheme developed by Professor Aaron Hershkowitz consisting of a matrix generated by three overlapping dimensions that allows for fifty-four interpretations of any human action.[7] I added two more dimensions, thereby expand-

ing the scheme to include 486 possible interpretations, which I used
to provide enough "slots" in which to place hundreds of observations
made in past decades about war trauma.

Once I began using this interpretive device, I discovered that some-
thing crucial was always left out. No matter how far I expanded it, the
system had no way to include what was most essential — that some-
thing about trauma doesn't fit into any scheme. An experience is trau-
matic when it bursts into your life and you can't make sense of it in
any comfortable way.

The literature on trauma has not yet confronted this dilemma. Most
observers are content to say, for example, that "death is traumatic," or
"massive death" is what makes so stark an imprint, without asking,
"Why death?" or "What is it about death?" It's not anyone's death that
is so troubling. It has to be someone who gets close to us in some way,
not necessarily physically close, but a death that somehow matters. It
has to be a death that comes across as refuting something fundamental
in us. What is that? What touches us? Loss? Okay, but what do we lose
exactly?

Traditionally, psychotherapists have left such questions to philoso-
phers, spiritual guides, and poets. And so I turned to these other sources
to point the way.

On his long return from Troy, Odysseus meets up with Circe, a
goddess who bewitches men and turns them into pigs. Aided by the
god Hermes, the warrior thwarts Circe's powers and becomes her
lover, staying with her to feast and drink for a whole year until he
and his men, grown fat and languid, long for home. Circe speeds
him on his way but warns, "Home you may not go unless you take
a strange way round and come to the cold homes of Death."

Odysseus' journey follows her prophecy, as he eventually passes
through Hades, the place where dead men's shadows dwell. There
he meets the ghost of Achilles, the greatest of Greek warriors who
fell at Troy. Odysseus praises the fallen hero and pays tribute to the
ideal of a glorious, honorable death, one that redeems the pain of
dying.

> Was there ever a man more blest by fortune
> than you, Achilles? Can there ever be?
> We ranked you with immortals in your lifetime,

and here your power is royal
among dead men's shades. Think, then, Achilles,
you need not be so pained by death.[8]

Achilles' ghost soberly chastises Odysseus for making ignorant statements about a state he hasn't yet reached, and tells him that the idea of a glorious end is a dismal fraud.

Let me hear no smooth talk
of death from you, Odysseus.
Better, I say, to break sod as a farm hand
for some poor country man, on iron rations,
than lord it over all the exhausted dead.[9]

The message from the dead is that hero worship offers only false hope. Many modern soldiers would say the same. Among American survivors of Vietnam, disillusionment runs high. The veterans who joined the rap groups spoke of the war itself as bitterly sobering; its brutal realities flew in the face of their old beliefs about American goodness and human decency. In the groups we sought to strip away more illusion by unmasking the blindness that led each of us to take part in what we later condemned. But where does this searching end?

People who examine life relentlessly eventually find that their questioning boomerangs. At some point the unanswered questions turn in on us, challenging the ground beneath our feet, leaving the possibility of having nothing to stand on.

In our time, poets have sung the praises of such groundlessness, this pervasive nothingness. Nikos Kazantzakis is best known in the English-speaking world for his novel *Zorba the Greek*. He is especially revered among Greeks for his epic poetic sequel to Homer's *The Odyssey*. In Kazantzakis's masterpiece,[10] the hero returns to Ithaka but doesn't stay long. He is still restless, hungry for some great quest, and sets out on a spiritual journey.

In the early 1920s, a decade and a half before he completed *The Odyssey: A Modern Sequel*, Kazantzakis traveled alone in postwar Europe. Struggling to give voice to a spiritual message that could inspire modern humanity, he wrote a short book called *The Saviors of God: Spiritual Exercises*, which became the philosophical foundation of his epic poem. In this confession, the poet tells of the journey through his own personal hell, where he confronts the nothingness he carries within.

> . . . "Dig!
> What do you see?"
> "Men and birds, water and stones."
> "Dig deeper! What do you see?"
> "Ideas and dreams, fantasies and light-
>   ning flashes!"
> "Dig deeper! What do you see?"
> "I see nothing! A mute Night, as thick as
>   death. It must be death."
> "Dig deeper!"
> "Ah! I cannot penetrate the dark parti-
> tion! I hear voices and weeping. I hear the flut-
> ter of wings on the other shore."
> "Don't weep! Don't weep! They are not
> on the other shore. The voices,
> the weeping, and
> the wings are your own heart."[11]

As he digs within, eventually confronting the obsessive urge to dig, the poet thinks at first that the darkness haunting him is death. Penetrating further, he sees the longings of his own heart and then the dark Invisible that is his heart's source. Here Kazantzakis joins contemporary thinkers and ancient sages in saying that we cannot define, set limits on, certain crucial matters such as the pervasive yet unnamable nothingness that pervades our being. Some writers call death our ultimate challenge, but the most thorough probing reveals death as only a pale metaphor. In living our lives we do not know the reality of death before the moment of dying. We know only mortality — what we take death to mean. In moments of penetrating insight we can peer into the ultimate, which is beyond all we think and beyond all we see, hear, taste, touch, and smell. There we find the awesome nothingness that Kazantzakis calls the dark Invisible.

During my last months in the rap groups I talked about my wife of those years. Initially I had thought getting married meant that I was cured. But as the months passed, things between us got worse instead of better. Nothing I was doing seemed to help, not even talking about the problem in my rap group.

She and I had met in one of our graduate school classes. Like me, she was studying to be a clinical psychologist. After the first few months of our marriage, the romance faded and our moods would conflict. We'd fight, then one of us would go off to our therapist, loosen up, and come back more accommodating. Then we'd make up and the cycle would begin again.

We loved each other. We were also fierce opponents, sometimes screaming and vicious, but mostly sullen. Friends asked me why I tolerated such a life. My study of psychology gave me a rationale: Psychoanalysis tells you that you can't relieve your pain by changing locale or partners. You confront the same inner torments, over and over, until you work them through. You either deal with problems as they confront you or they'll turn up again wherever you go next. That was the principle I thought I was applying.

One summer we went away for a few weeks. She wanted to be on the beach while I wanted to be with my books. She wanted to talk about money and I didn't. I wanted either to be left alone or for us to be together romantically, and she wanted us to take care of business. Neither one would do what the other wanted graciously, and frequently we'd fight.

One rainy afternoon as I was reading I heard her sob. She was sitting at the table where she usually set up her books and course notes, tears pouring out. We weren't fighting just then. I couldn't imagine what was bothering her now.

"What's the matter?" I asked. She didn't answer. But she didn't seem angry with me. I didn't think it was anything I did, so it felt safe to go to her.

"What is it?" I asked more tenderly.

"I was just thinking. Is this it? Is this all there is?"

In a few words she had said it all, the bitter truth. I wanted to feel compassion but it wasn't there, and I didn't try to force it. Instead I sneered inside. Finally, I thought, she's starting to see the big picture. She's finding out that there's no use waiting for the good fairy to make life sweet. It isn't sweet. It sucks. Too bad. Doesn't matter what you were hoping for. What you've got is what you're going to get.

That incident gnawed at me. I had drawn a disturbing implication

from what she said — that I wasn't enough for her, that she was dis-
appointed and felt stuck with me. It didn't matter that I often felt the
same way. I didn't care that I had a double standard — that she should
adore me no matter what I felt. I began thinking I would have to leave.

After that we fought even more. She would look at me and say,
"You've got daggers in your eyes." Uncannily sensitive, she could al-
ways read me right. During one of our worst flare-ups, when some-
thing she said ripped all the way through me, I kicked down a door
and shoved her halfway across our bedroom. Reaching for the most
foul below-the-belt insult, she shrieked, "You crazy veteran!" Not long
after that I told her what I'd been thinking for some time: We were
through.

In the first months after we separated, we'd occasionally talk on the
phone or meet for coffee. Once we even managed a passionate date,
almost a year after we split. Then we cooled and became distant ac-
quaintances, and again I started wondering if the war would ever be
over for me.

Vets with haunting memories aren't the only ones who feel diminished by the war. To judge from our research, many men who grew
up in the 1960s express their widely divergent attitudes about the
war with a heavy mood. The war seems to weigh on them from
some dark corner of their lives. Some see it as a personal problem,
something they have to atone for. But for most it is a kind of unfinished business that burdens them in an impersonal way, looming
out of the shared domain of relationships, institutions, and the larger
society.

Although many of the men who didn't go insist they were not
affected personally by the war, almost all make a point of identifying
the ill effects it would have had. "The war didn't affect me one way
or another, but if I had gone, it probably would've done something
to me. I probably would've come back a junkie, half crazy, and half
something else."

Many confess that they have tried not to think about it, hoping to
avoid the unpleasantness, with only partial success. "It didn't affect
me much at all, and the reason is I try to block it out of my mind. I
didn't want to get involved with the Vietnam War if I didn't have
to. But I couldn't help hearing things, making you feel opposed to
it, leaving me with a bad taste in my mouth about Vietnam."

This "bad taste" comes in various flavors. For some, it is the reluctant admission of error. "I hate to say it, but I really think the
whole thing was wrong. I didn't disapprove when we were there,
but I've changed after the communists just ran it over. If I had to do
it all over again I'd say screw it, what does anyone want to do that
for, what did all these guys get killed and wounded for? I hate to go
against the country, but I think everybody realizes we were wrong."

Many, a clear majority, say something that suggests what public
opinion polls from the mid-1960s to the early 1980s have documented with overwhelming consistency in the country at large: a
marked decline in respect for established institutions.[12] "I never really
thought about the war at first. I was pretty gung-ho, believed in
John Wayne, you know. But then things started changing, and my
views started bouncing back and forth, trying to understand the reasons why they got into it. I had to start challenging everybody, from
the President on down. Things get pretty shaky when you do that,
like who can you trust?"

Many men who didn't go express regrets. The tendency of the
less fortunate among them is to feel worse off for having missed the
training and advantages for later life that might have come had they
served. "Like everybody else, I felt they should've escalated faster
and gotten over with it. I didn't like the killing, but my brother and
my friends who went, nothing bad happened to them over there, so
I didn't look at it as the worst thing in life. I'm sure I would've been
better educated if I went into the service, probably ended up with a
better job."

The regret expressed by the more fortunate tends to be in the form
of nostalgia for the spirit, commitment, and high ideals common
during the war that have dissipated over the years since. "I'm per-
petually disgusted with how little of the things I once admired are
still in existence. It wasn't embarrassing to be idealistic in the 1960s
but it is now. I'm a bit of a romantic at heart, but there is no place
for it now."

A few of the men who didn't go portray themselves as personally
accountable for the war as a whole. "I didn't like the idea that the
government was doing something in my name and everybody else's
that I was dead against. I didn't like the feeling of responsibility for
that. But I couldn't wiggle out of it. It was sort of like the point we
kept making to the Nazis during the Nuremberg trials. What was

the difference between me and some German who didn't do as much as could've been done to stop it all?"

Many who stayed home mention the veterans. Men who took some deliberate action to avoid serving especially express regret for the suffering of those who went. "I feel real bad for the people who got killed. I was afraid to go, afraid I'd get killed. So I told them about my asthma. I really did have it when I was young. When they asked me when my last attack was, I lied and said last week. I got my doctor to write a letter. He didn't lie, he just said I *had* asthma, but that led them to think it was still a problem, so I got off."

Some feel pity for vets, believing that the men who served are now impaired. "The guys over there, they were doing something they had to do, you got to obey the laws no matter how much you disapprove. But I feel sorry for them, a lot of veterans I've met, it really affected them. They have a strange type of attitude about life, a lot different from mine. They're more callous, unsympathetic to different things."

Others feel sorry while disapproving of the war and condemning the most publicized atrocities. "I had concern for the guys who were junkies or who came back and suffered, and for the mistaken bombings. But how can you kill so many people by mistake? Take this guy Calley and My Lai. We were supposed to be supporting democracy, but we were doing the same dirty work as the other side. I would've gone if they called me, but not to Vietnam and not to die in vain. Only thing is, I feel bad about all the guys who had to go while I was at home enjoying the best of life."

A few recognize that some vets have matured through their experiences. "By me not going in I was able to get my life more together, have a chance to set my own pace. The people who went over there had their lives disrupted. But then again, some made out. They gained knowledge, some got a trade, so basically it depends on the person."

Most of these remarks convey a sense that the war is still a burdensome weight for the men of this generation. Some speak of personal regrets. But for many the burden is an unbreachable gap, separating those who went from those who stayed home, and those who favored the war from those who opposed it. Their implicit lament is the difficulty facing men whose experiences are so divergent. How can such people understand one another, let alone share values, goals, and responsibilities for the common good? It's as if the very basis for community has been undercut by a wound that extends more broadly than any psychological diagnosis can reach.

My own attitude toward the war protests went through several dramatic changes. I resented the demonstrators only during my first few months in the Army. Once in Vietnam, I thought they were doing important work. After coming back and joining in the protests myself, I thought I had found a home. But soon a new source of resentment began to creep in. I'd cringe when I heard people who had never been near the war say things like, "I don't feel any responsibility for what went on in Vietnam. I've been protesting since the beginning!" — as if being on the right side made their hands clean and put them above the rest of us. After the humbling changes I'd lived through, I couldn't accept that sense of rectitude, the cocksure attitude of "our side has the right answer, always has and always will."

I was still searching for a way to enhance my life. I wanted to succeed in my work, establish a relationship, raise a family, and have more say in things that mattered to me. But I knew then that working things out for myself would not be enough. I wanted a way to cure others of the war's curse. And even if I could personally affect only a tiny fraction of the people who needed help, I wanted to know that there was a way that would work for the others. Without that broader possibility, there would be no cure, just social and psychological Band-Aids. Unless the whole world could heal from war, we would never be able to get beyond the cycle of getting over the last one well enough to prepare for the next.

By the mid-1970s I knew that none of the causes I had championed for curing the world's ills would work. The traditional conservative belief I developed in college — that the world needed the protection of American power — disintegrated as I witnessed the abuses of that power in the war. Then the counterbelief, the liberal critique of American interventionism as inherently evil, began to seem terribly shortsighted as I tried to assimilate the news coming out of Indochina.

In April 1975 Vietcong and North Vietnamese forces took Saigon, renaming it Ho Chi Minh City. Weeks later, in neighboring Cambodia, the communist insurgents known as the Khmer Rouge marched into

the capital of Phnom Penh and overthrew the U.S. backed govern-
ment. For centuries, the Cambodians had been known as peace lov-
ing, warm, and hospitable. But the new communist government under
Pol Pot changed that. They began a campaign to drive millions of Cam-
bodians back to the land and to expunge all Western influences. What
followed was a slaughter that ranks with the most hideous brutality of
all time.

If you wore glasses you were killed. If you spoke a foreign language
you were killed. If you had a profession, such as law or medicine, you
were killed. If you were even related to an intellectual, or if you could
read and write, you could be killed. It is estimated that between one
and two million Cambodians were murdered or starved to death by
their own people.

I saw film footage of the cells where the prisoners were tortured, the
blood turned black on the cement floors and walls. Endless rows of
mug shots taken before the prisoners were slaughtered documented
the deliberate policy of eliminating "bad elements."

I didn't run out to join any protest about Cambodia. To my knowl-
edge there were none. I barely said anything about what I had learned,
because at first I was speechless. I had cheered for the people who
wanted to liberate Indochina, and now the liberators of Cambodia had
become far more murderous than the regime they ousted. I felt be-
trayed and ashamed. I had laughed at the conservatives who warned
of blood baths in Indochina if U.S. forces left, and I now had to admit
my naiveté in so blithely dismissing their concerns.

I refused to accept the leftist line of blaming the new horrors on U.S.
policies of half a decade before. Some of those policies certainly de-
served to be criticized; I still disapproved of our bombing of Cambodia
in the late 1960s and early 1970s. It was a face-saving gesture, an effort
to buy time for the retreat we were making in the guise of Vietnamiza-
tion. It was a cruel sham that cost human lives, an unstatesmanlike
effort by our leaders to prove they could be as ruthless as those they
opposed, and in the long run amounted to only an impotent gesture.
But bombs don't turn men into brutal murderers.

In arguments with friends from the antiwar days, I'd point out that
we bombed the Japanese and the Germans during World War II and
the North Vietnamese far more intensely than we did the Cambodians,
and nobody ever claimed that the slaughter inflicted by the Germans,

the Japanese, and the North Vietnamese was caused by our bombs. Some of my friends called me a turncoat. When I wouldn't mouth the old slogans on a TV show, and spoke instead about respecting service, one person even sent a scathing note calling me a "born again hawk."

That friend had jumped to the conclusion that I was pushing conservatism. But in fact I didn't think the right had any better answers than the left. Conservatives blame the horrors in Indochina and elsewhere on communism. After Cambodia, I too felt a need to consider the critique of totalitarianism more closely. But I never felt enlightened by the way this argument is usually made. Rightist dogma is no better than the leftist variety at grasping the origins of collective violence. Mass slaughter didn't begin with the followers of Karl Marx. Hitler wasn't a communist, nor was Napoleon. For many centuries, systematic murder was carried out by sworn Christians in Europe, in crusades against Moslem "infidels," then against "heretics," and later still against one another. The slaughter that followed Indian independence in 1947 was the work of Hindus and Moslems, and many of the murderously repressive regimes of recent decades — in Indonesia, Argentina, Uruguay, Chile, Haiti, South Korea, El Salvador, and Guatemala — have been run by staunch anticommunists.

As I grew dissatisfied with fashionable political doctrines, I came to believe that the origins of war and slaughter have a much deeper source than ideology. Some people see a biological program for human aggressiveness, supporting the view that war is innate. But the evidence doesn't support this view either. In 1973 Erich Fromm, in *The Anatomy of Human Destructiveness*, presented findings from physiological studies, psychological experiments, anthropological field research, and history to challenge this belief in biological determinism. According to Fromm, the traditional assumption — that human beings are innately equipped to act aggressively — is correct to a point. We do have the capacity to be aggressive, whether to defend ourselves from attack, protect our families, search for food, or pursue other goals of our choice. But the evidence is that organized and massive violence has developed through history, and it is no more innate than the preference for meat and potatoes or rice and beans.

In fact, anthropologists now say that wars as we know them only entered human experience about six thousand years ago, with the advent of centrally ruled, hierarchical communities. And although the common prejudice is that modern civilization is far more humane than its ancient precursors, the evidence indicates the contrary. The number of battles and people killed in warfare has risen steadily over recent centuries, not the reverse.

War must therefore be a cultural phenomenon, not an inherently biological or even psychological one.[13] The relevant question for healing is: What in our present culture predisposes us to war? In raising this question, I wasn't asking for a political scientist's inquiry into the causes of war, some explanatory list of diplomatic, political, economic, social, and ecological factors. I wanted to know what it is about our way of life — among we who end up fighting — that makes war possible to begin with.

Once this question became clear, I realized I could study the roots of war by looking in my own life, turning from cultural questions in the abstract to searching my own experience. Something crucial had horrified me in the midst of the war I had known. I suspected that what I was looking for would elude me until I got to the bottom of what it was that I couldn't bear that night on the roof in Saigon.

During my last year in graduate school I attended a lecture given to a psychology class by a professor who was a practicing Buddhist.[14] He said, "You psychologists try to deal with human conflict by changing people's behavior, thoughts, and feelings. But all your remedies fail because you ignore the fact that all our predicaments are rooted in the nature of mind."

One of the students then asked how we could fix the mind. The professor became very excited and walked up to the student, almost shouting: "You're asking about the mind as if it's a motor in somebody else's car, and we're a couple of grease monkeys trying to fix it. You're asleep! Don't you see? The question is coming out of a mind! Yours! You're stuck in the predicament you're asking me about. How do you expect to make any headway if you don't wake up to at least that much of it?"

Later he said there was an ancient way out of this dilemma. "You can't grasp what I'm saying like some new idea to understand. You have to begin your own course of study of the mind. And the only way to do that without fooling yourself is to watch your own. That's the point of meditation. Find a teacher who can give you instruction in watching your mind. Almost anything else we say is self-delusion."

I knew that the student who asked the question could just as well have been me, and if this professor was right, I was just as deluded as the next person. So I went up to him after the lecture and asked where I could get the kind of instruction he was referring to. He gave me the address of a meditation center run by the students of a Tibetan lama named Chogyam Trungpa.

Several years before, I had gone for instruction in transcendental meditation. The idea there was to say a Hindu word over and over for ten or fifteen minutes at a time. It was supposed to relax you. I did it for some months but didn't get much out of it. Buddhist meditation was supposed to have a point to make about the mind. That sounded more interesting.

I went to the meditation center expecting to find a bunch of freaked-out religious fanatics prancing around and chanting. Instead I met about a dozen intelligent middle-class people, most of them about my age or younger, drinking tea and waiting for the meditation to begin. One of the women took me aside and gave me the basic instruction. "Once we begin, sit on your cushion, and whatever comes to your mind, say 'thinking' to yourself and bring your attention back to your breathing. We finish when the gong rings."

For one hour we sat. Nobody said anything. The guy in the front of the room, who was sitting facing everybody else, scarcely moved the whole time. I couldn't believe it. How could he do it? Five minutes into the session my legs were killing me. I crossed them. A few minutes later I stretched them out. A few minutes after that I tried grasping my knees with my arms. And then I repeated the cycle again and again until the gong rang, none too soon. I didn't learn anything through all of it, except how uncomfortable it is to sit for an hour doing nothing. I told that to the woman who had given me the instructions. She said, "That's the point. You're doing fine."

For several years I read, attended lectures, and about an hour a day sat on a cushion "doing nothing." After some practice, I had no trouble observing my thoughts. Later I was able to observe my observing. Later still I would observe, observe myself observing, and notice that as I did a kind of roominess would be present. I'd feel relaxed all through my body, but that was a secondary result. More prominent than the body sensations was the expansiveness. Some people called it "space." In having more "space," I wasn't so easily unsettled by things. But somehow I had more control of "time," and ability to slow down the fastest action. I seemed able to notice fine textures and gradations of experience that had formerly eluded me. At times I saw the change as a new capacity to discriminate among my thoughts, like the fine agility it takes to catch an arrow in flight. What I was catching were the movements of my own thinking.

It is difficult to capture this expansiveness in words. It's a sense of reality opening up and widening, with everything becoming fluid and commingled. Meditating, sitting on a cushion, observing breathing, noticing sensations in my buttocks, stiff legs, dim candlelight, slight sound of breeze outside, all of it intimately interwoven, already together, needing no synthesizing or integration or thinking. All of it is, immediately, just there.

In just such a moment the time came back when I felt the piercing fire on that Saigon night. A resonance emerged between these two times, separated by half the distance around the globe, six years, and an uncannily wide shift in mood and circumstances. Yet as I sat there, I was in Saigon too, and it was a night in the war, all separations vanished, no "it" and no "me," just whores below and fiery death out there, lust and concern, all together and intimately connected, unavoidably here.

The original experience was an instantaneous flash. Now I could play it back, slowing it down and putting words to what initially came as a shattering silence.

"It's not close. It's on top of me. It's me, I'm it. No question of whether or not to be involved. It's already decided. What looks like it's out there touches here, all the way through."

A split second later questions come flooding in. "How could this be? How will I ever be safe again? What chance do I have if stuff like this keeps penetrating? No peace, no security, no room to maneuver. I'm pinned down, trapped, can't get out. I'm finished.

"And look at it! Fire, death, killing. People don't give a shit who burns and dies. They just keep doing it. We all look on. It's acceptable! We could just as well go to the whorehouse and fuck and forget. People incinerate people as if it doesn't matter. Somebody's trying to make a point, and the point is more important than human life.

"What's to preserve life? My life? Any life? Life can't go on like this. There has to be some guarantee, some catch, something, someone who'll keep things safe. But no! Nothing. There's nothing. It's real, this horror. And even worse, I can't get away from it. How will I ever get relief? I didn't ask to give a shit about this! I don't want to care. It hurts too much. It makes me uncool. I feel like a jerk!

"Nobody cares that I care. It doesn't do anything. 'Fly shit in the ocean.' So what? I'm puny, nothing. I don't matter, nothing matters. Shit like this, this horror justified by trumped up logic, keeps going on. And look: People just watch. It doesn't mean anything. Nothing means anything. Forget about hope!

"Nobody gets out of life alive. But now I know. Even life might not make it. The whole business is doomed. Fuck it!

"But how do I turn off the caring? I'm trapped, caring but able to do nothing. Living is torture, I can't bear it.

"Only one thing I can do is never forget. I'm never forgetting! Nobody can make me. That's it! I've got something now! Something to hold on to as mine. I've seen the bitter truth! Nobody can take that away from me!"

Sitting there recalling what had taken place, I realized that I never said the words, "From now on, I'll be a standard bearer for the bitter truth!" in Saigon or anywhere else. But I could see, looking back over the better part of a decade, that I acted as if that had been my vow. The stark reality that I confronted one night in the war challenged my most precious hope — that my life, and life in general, were taken care of. As a child and a young adult, I had always believed that I wouldn't have to worry about the basics; somebody else would do the hard part. In watching my countrymen carry out the sanctioned murder of defenseless villagers — going after Vietcong infiltrators hiding in the area — I saw clearly that nothing is guaranteed in this world, not my life or anybody else's, not even the sanctity of life itself. It's all expendable. No safety, no security. Not now, or ever.

Working my way back to recapture that moment didn't make anything secure. I just saw more distinctly than ever the posture I had assumed toward the insecurity, how I had accepted it only partially, under protest, and used my bitterness as the justification I hoped would give meaning to my life. I had finally unraveled the contortions I had gone through to contend with what I'd seen. It was as if I had declared:

"Look world, you're not going to make my reality meaningless, my

hopes for security worthless! Watch this trick! I'll take your damned insult to all I hold dear, and I'll use it to set myself up even higher, more exalted, less vulnerable, because now I'll be cloaked in good-ness! I'll trade on moral indignation, and righteous disgust with all your horrors! So what if I have to live a bitter life? That's better than a mean-ingless or insignificant one. At least now I'll have some way to justify my existence, as witness to the horrors of humankind."

Looking back, I could appreciate that I had responded as best I knew how. For years I had been struggling to find a justification for my life, a way to define myself and to have something to stand for. Only in looking back did I finally appreciate that this struggle had grown out of a search for a security that one key experience revealed as illusory. That night in Saigon I refused to admit what I saw, that the struggle I had made the center of my life was pointless and vain.

By peering into my own experience, I saw that trauma is something more profound than individual breakdown. To be sure, individuals are hurt, but in trauma the pain is more than personal; our culturally taught strategy for contending with life fails to work.[15]

In our culture, which now encompasses most of the world, we take ourselves to be this or that personality, identity, or self. We construct our identities narrowly enough so that none of us has to answer for the human condition, and so that each can entertain the hope that in claiming only some limited turf we'll be safe, right, and invulnerable to attack. Regardless of our official religion, we wor-ship privately the fortress self, latching on to whatever group affili-ations enable us to belong somewhere and to set ourselves apart, and we hope above, the mass of others.

This identity or self is our set of stratagems for trying to "make it." Everybody has a unique agenda, though we can recognize ten-dencies and similarities among those we group as common "types." Some people criticize themselves in order to keep others from at-tacking them. Some try to make it by being especially good and above reproach. Or they become avid critics of others and cloak them-selves in self-righteousness. Others concoct a strategy around the claim that they don't care what others think, and then, in hopes of convincing everyone, do things that are considered bad. Some peo-ple want to be ignored so nobody can ever make demands on them, causing them to portray themselves as failures. And a few, in a mixed display of defiance, foolishness, and courage, strive for prominence by deliberately taking positions that leave them open to other people's attacks and demands. We call these few our leaders.

Common to all strategies is our culturally prescribed assumption that to be worthy you've got to *be* somebody, which means *making something* of yourself. To be your own person, you have to be unique and have a personality all your own, even if it is a flawed one. The idea is to make some identifiable, objectively presentable face you can show the world. But for this whole operation to be successful, you have to "believe in yourself," that is, present the face as if it's really you. To convince others, you have to convince yourself that your persona — the concoction of stratagems, life stories, and lessons you've drawn from all that has happened — is the real thing. You must ignore the fact that you put it all together or else the conviction will drain away. So you play the act, forget who wrote the play, and then you can say, "I'm somebody."

Trauma takes place when an experience reveals the lie in this whole game. The pain comes with having to confront what we, in this culture, struggle to ignore: There is never any safety or security we can take for granted. When we observe very closely, we see only the interpretive schemes we've created for making sense of things, which we so often fool ourselves and others into taking for great truths.

The problem comes not when someone says, "You're full of shit!" We don't take such charges seriously unless we've already begun to question whether the face we present to the world is really us. The real trouble starts with any experience that fundamentally challenges not just our particular stratagems, but our underlying basis for creating a self. For example, great catastrophes show us that life proceeds with no rules at all, at least none of the kind we want to establish in order to feel secure. Suddenly we see there's no terrain, nothing to believe, nothing to know, nothing to profess that will make us inviolate.

What we call traumatic responses are the new strategies we concoct after being shocked into realizing that life doesn't play by our rules. When we can no longer pretend that life confirms our favored identity, we take on a negative version of our old self. We respond like children who visit a new neighborhood and, finding that the kids don't play by familiar rules, say, "If you're going to do that, I'm not playing." In trauma, however, it's not just the other kids but life itself that violates our rules. And traumatic responses are our way of looking on the horror and saying "I'm not playing" to life.

Ironically, "I'm not playing" is nonetheless a way to play. It is a life strategy not unlike the posture struck by people who play "hard to get." They make us struggle to get through to them, and if things between us and them don't work out, they are well prepared to walk away thinking "I knew it wouldn't work right from the start." In other words, "I'm not playing" is a way to hedge your bets; you don't risk disappointment if you always expect you'll be rejected in the end.

Troubled people never say, "I don't like the terms life offers, so I'm going to live only halfheartedly, under protest." Friends and relatives who want to help by trying to convince the survivor to get in gear will usually hear in response, "I can't." Pleading with a troubled person to live more fully doesn't have much impact, because such common sense advice attempts to get the sufferer to do precisely what he is committed not to do. He won't *say* he is committed to stay the way he is; rather, he'll insist he is incapable of doing otherwise, not because he wants to mislead, but because he genuinely believes that his traumatizing past has demonstrated his impotence for all time.

When we view traumatized people as the authors of their own dramas, we can choose either to blame them for their pain or to use this understanding to help us respond with the most thorough compassion, which means seeing that people have the power to reinterpret their lives. By being compassionate, we can recognize traumatic responses as attempts to deal with dreadful experiences in the most immediate way, by an inward protest or turning away. The alternative is healing. But to see this option clearly, it is useful first to ask: How is it that turning away comes so readily? And why is it that war and traumatic responses go hand in hand?

Never is trauma so prevalent as during war, and few people are ever as preoccupied with their war as those who remain traumatized afterward. For purposes of explanation we can say that war causes trauma, by one or another theorized mechanism. But for the purposes of healing we'd do well to probe further, into the possibility that war and trauma share a common source.

War is the ultimate expression of opposition. All willing participants of war agree that opposition to the enemy is more important than their individual lives. How is it that people who are so ready to kill one another manage to agree so completely on war's essentials? For all the differences among the world's peoples, humanity in this age shares a common underlying understanding. We all know the difference between friends and enemies. And we all know how to determine who our enemy is: anyone who stands for what we're dead set against. In this perspective, war ultimately rests on drawing lines, on setting up a life-and-death separation between what we are and what we're not.

And so, just as our strategy for making identities predisposes us to trauma, so does it orient us toward war. Dividing up the world into our turf and the rest is the precondition for battle. "I am this, not that" means we habitually define ourselves by, and stand out to the degree that we are opposed to, what *we* say we're not.

War breaks out when we place these identifying differences above life itself. To protect and raise ourselves higher, we put down murderously the people we oppose. This much is readily clear. Less obvious is the underlying reason why we are susceptible to threat in the first place.

The culprit again is our very strategy for defining an identity, the attempt to establish a separate self by cutting ourselves off from whatever we negate. This generates fear because it insists we are the opponent of what we consider alien. Our dependence on this strategy makes a threatened existence inevitable, because it forces us to depend on antagonism as the only way to know ourselves. We have to be something, this thing and not that thing, and certainly not nothing.

These clarifications are useful only for people who have employed this common strategy enough to perceive its limits. Others are so caught up in trying to be somebody, at almost any cost, that they don't see the source of their anguish. The pain is especially disquieting for veterans who resorted to and even relished brutality in the war and can't explain to themselves why. We are so used to thinking that vile deeds are committed only by terrible human beings that we fail to grasp how much evil is done by men who want desperately to feel worthwhile.

After I had published some writings on veteran trauma, I was called to examine a Vietnam veteran being tried for hideous crimes. One night ten years after coming home he went on a drunken rampage, stabbed his wife after he forcibly sodomized her and bit off her left nipple, and then killed his two children by plunging a knife into their hearts. Why? his lawyer asked me.

The vet was a seemingly calm man who had been written up in his local newspaper as a model "house-husband" only a year before. Women's lib had hit the working class in his small conservative town, and he'd stay home, clean the house, and take care of the kids while his wife worked. Nobody could figure how such a man could be so evil.

I spent a whole day talking with him in his jail cell. He told me what he had never told anyone. In Vietnam he had been sent on missions to "mop up" after raids through Vietnamese villages. The Vietcong were nearby, so his squad was told to kill survivors with knives rather than with noisy weapons. This man found a teenage girl lying wounded in her hooch. He raped her, then killed her by plunging his bayonet, grasped in his fist, into her heart. He recalled the blood squirting over his arm, its sweet smell. He killed several children the same way.

Two more times during his tour he was sent on similar missions, and he raped and murdered the same way. "It might sound awful to you," he told me. "But one time I saw a bunch of airborne troops doing something worse. They held a young girl and scalped her alive before raping her, all ten guys, while she was screaming and bleeding from the top of her head. Only when all ten were finished did they put her away."

For years this man had been having nightmares of his mother bursting in on him in a rage while he was forcing women to have sex. For a decade he had drunk steadily, managing most of the time not to think about what he had done. In his night of horror at home, he had, in effect, acted out the primitive justice of an unforgiving law. He communicated in deeds what he could not reveal any other way; that he should not be spared what he made others suffer. It was as if he carried out his own condemnation and punishment for what he did in Viet-

nam. He would not be survived by children because he had deprived others of that possibility. And he would perform, for all his family and neighbors to witness and contemplate, the same horrors he had tried to banish from memory through heavy use of alcohol.

Neither the extremes of the war nor this man's description of his early life were enough to account for what he did. He had gotten into trouble as a boy, but only for minor mischief. He had also played sexually, and sometimes even forcibly, with his younger sister. But this, too, was common in communities like his. He had driven himself with another obsession in a way that only came clear to me by reading between the lines of what he said.

He had a lifelong fear that he would amount to nothing. He saw himself as going nowhere, a zero who mattered to nobody. Most men who feel this way don't resort to violence, but express their bitterness in other ways. And except for three episodes in his thirty-five years, this man contented himself with the usual remedies: He'd keep himself distracted with boring routines, and then relieve himself at night by getting drunk. But always he was capable of going over the edge, of lashing out, violating others, especially women, those who got close enough to stir tenderness and make him feel need. He couldn't stand the intrusion. A nothing, a nobody who had so little going for him, had no room for anybody else to get near.

Now he has lots of help in keeping himself thoroughly walled in. A life in prison is only part of the sentence. As long as he is there he will be constantly threatened by fellow inmates, who loathe crimes like his. For now he needn't worry, for where he is, nobody and nothing will get too close.

We do not heal ourselves from war or trauma by treating symptoms, memories, bad feelings, or underlying fears, just as it doesn't work to turn away from them. Healing must involve an alternative principle, a fundamental stance that turns us toward and includes all that's there, a posture that allows us to be at home in the world, rather than being rigid, antagonistic, and threatened.

Meditation reveals the essential balm, the healing that takes us beyond inner and outer battles.[16] It is the practice of "turning toward" whatever is there, to observe rather than turn away by separating ourselves and categorizing things. What appears through meditation? Sounds, feelings, thoughts, body movements, and more noises, sensations, and things to think.

Questions arise too. Who am I? What is this "I"? Can "I" appear as other than an identity, not needing to be defined by what it is not?

Closed eyes make for easier observation. Try to observe the I in action. A noise comes from across the room. Who hears it? The I? How? How does the sound come from there to here? The answer isn't clear. Simply from sensing what's there, there's no way to rule out that the I went over there to pick up the noise and bring it back.

Then comes a thought about something. From where? Recollection says it came from a book. Who brought it here? Did the book put the thought in the I's head? Again no way to tell. It could just as well have happened the other way around: The I reached into the printed page, read the author's mind through his symbols, and took the author's thought into itself.

Elusive business, this I. Watch closely, sense very carefully what usually seems to be the outer edge of this I, the skin. With eyes closed the sensing is even more acute. Breathing is clear: Chest moves, belly does too. But skin? Can't tell. Neither skin nor outer edge is clear. Pressure from the seat on backside is clear; rumbles in belly are too. But outer edge is indistinct. No sharp separation between the I and everything else.

A new sound comes from the other end of the room, and quicker than a wink the noise and I are linked together in an instant of hearing-the-noise, with no way to tell which went to meet which. In fact, watching closely turns up no way to separate where this I reaches and where it doesn't. For as soon as anything is present as sound, or thought, or image, the I is already joined with it in hearing, thinking, or seeing. Whatever is there the I includes, for anything perceived must already be joined with the I who perceives it.

Meditation is healing, in that it provides a way for us to engage wholes, by opening a seamless perspective on all that's there. What's present is real and vivid, but not because I have defined anything by what it is not. Anything that appears stands on its own, without any need for me to draw lines. And as for myself in meditation, I too am unmarked by battle lines or separations, and emerge to myself as nothing more or less than the presence in which whatever appears comes to light.

Of all modern thinkers, Martin Heidegger pressed furthest the search for a new grounding for humanity in an age when we are threatening to destroy all of life.[17] Heidegger traced the logic of the atom bomb to the underpinnings of perception in our culture, the strategy of making something by splitting and dividing it from what it's not. He called for another, more meditative way of thinking. He did not want the experience engendered by meditation to be isolated from the mainstream of life, but rather incorporated into the specific ways we think and act in this culture. For Heidegger, meditative thinking is a way of engaging ourselves with "what at first sight does not go together at all."

What, at first sight, does not go together at all? Reality. All that is. In his life work, Heidegger's goal was to challenge the official Western view of reality of the past twenty-five hundred years. More probingly than any thinker since Aristotle, he asked, "What is being?" That is, given all the phenomena around us, what lies at the heart of their existence, or, as he often put it, what is the Being of beings? He insisted that only so probing a question could bring us to appreciate in a wholly fresh way what it is to be human.

For Heidegger the question, "What is being?" is more important than any answers that he or anyone else could provide. He suggested that the question serves to bring us into contact with all that is, with being itself. By its nature, the encompassing presence of all that is cannot be reduced to any interpretation, yet remains accessible to intuition.

To cultivate an intuition of being requires us to overcome a deep prejudice that comes down to us as self-evident truth. The traditional approach to the question of being is to ask about particular things, things that are well defined. Science, rationality, and common sense assume that we can speak meaningfully only about things that are first clarified as having identifiable features, that is, are defined and thus separated from what they are not. Heidegger insisted that we observe for ourselves the effects of this prejudice. As long as we attend only to things we've already defined, we never confront being itself. Being, in its most encompassing sense, is the possibility for phenomena to come into existence. We can apprehend this limitless possibility only by attuning ourselves to the indefinable, to what does not exist in any explicit way.

How? The indefinable does not announce itself like a familiar object. It first dawns on us, Heidegger wrote, as a pervasive sense of nothingness. This isn't some abstract notion like zero. To appreciate the nature of nothingness we must relax our impulse to turn away from it, for nothingness first comes upon us in the experience of dread. Dread is distinct from anxiety and worry, which are concerns about something specific. Dread does not have a particularized focus. It is the sense of everything falling apart, the ground slipping from under our feet, or the entire structure of our lives being whisked away. It's not that everything disappears. We don't just see a blank. Rather, in the slipping away everything remains, but in a way that leaves nothing for us to hold on to. That is what overwhelms us: the experience of being in the presence of nothingness itself.

Reflecting on this experience can provide another insight into the connection among war, horror, and trauma. War is a mass ritual to exorcise the nothingness, to defy the possibility of ever having to take a view of ourselves that is at once so humbling and so far reaching. In war we fight to defend our rigidly defined selves and battle our enemies firmly believing they alone threaten our security. What rips into people's self-assurance in moments of horror is the nothingness that wars and crusades try to conceal. And traumatic responses are the ways people constrict themselves so they don't have to confront the nothingness ever again.

Heidegger's question, "What is being?" points to healing. He meant to raise the possibility of engaging possibility itself. This engagement includes nothing as an essential facet of being. Rather than attempt to avoid all contact with the void, we can be open to the gaping presence of all that is. Extending ourselves willingly brings forth a reflection of our own receptivity. Nothingness then appears without any negative quality. What emerges is a welcoming presence.

In embracing openness as home ground, we free ourselves of any vestigial longing to find our worth, security, or protection in some thing, identity, structure, or otherworldly essence. In reaching the bottom of nothingness, we outgrow the need to imagine a source of security beyond ourselves, discovering the possibility of letting ourselves *be*.

Throughout the ages most people have lived as if life went on in the shallow end of a great pool, with firm ground under their feet. The great achievement of our time is that many people are recognizing what the sages have always known — that we are already in deep water, over our heads. Until we embrace this groundlessness as home, we won't face the only choice there is — to swim or surely sink.

People who see the choice clearly know that war — killing and facing death — is not the ultimate experience. The most indelible moment comes in facing nothingness, which leaves you thoroughly alone with yourself. At that moment you see that your life means nothing except what you make of it, and the only thing to ask is what you're going to do with what you've got.

For many months after the end I mourned the wreckage of my first marriage. During that time I dated a number of different women. One in particular affected me deeply. Her name was Sondra. We went out on weekends and cared enough about each other to suspect we might have a long future together. A serious commitment, however, was the last thing on my mind.

I was down a lot — ruminating about my broken marriage, trying to figure out what went wrong. I was also troubled about my career. Having finished graduate school, I now had to earn a living, and was feeling more at the bottom of the heap than ever. It was the late 1970s and jobs for psychologists were scarce, patients for beginning therapists even scarcer, and the research project I had initiated was so badly in need of funds that none of us who worked there could expect to earn a living from it. Much of what was going on in my life gave me reason to be depressed, and I never hesitated to tell Sondra how bad things really were.

She was usually patient with all of this. Then one day she asked me to meet her for a walk in a nearby park. "I want to be with you, but not if you're always going to be in mourning," she said. The words didn't come with the tone of an ultimatum, but the message was clear enough: Either I cut it out or she'd leave. I couldn't believe what I was hearing. How could anyone ask this of me? Who in their right mind would re-

quire someone to overrule their feelings? Did she want me to blot out my history, to ignore the war and all the traumas that had happened since?

I was on the verge of saying all this to her when I looked at her closely. She seemed firm but very open, and I caught a glimpse of my reflection in her eyes. This woman had no trouble finding men, I realized, and wouldn't settle for someone else's emotionally drained ex-husband. Then another thought came: Her words are an invitation. She means for me to be the one for her.

I lingered for another moment, and reality widened to include both of us, as if we were meditating together. Though the words had come from her mouth, I suddenly felt that it was our being together that had spoken, telling me it was time to stop mourning. What was now possible between us had as much to do with my being open to her as with her openness to me. The feeling there had endless reverberations, like the infinite reflections in two mirrors placed face to face. At that instant I was struck not by anything in particular so much as by our simply being together. The intimacy moved me, as if there was nothing else I'd ever want or hunger for.

Then, with an assurance that was new for me, I said, "I got the message." I didn't know how I'd do it, but I knew I would stop mourning. Being with her like that mattered more than anything else I could think of. And in choosing to be with her I saw a possibility that had never been so clear before: I could leave behind the "mourning veteran" and his preoccupation with the meaninglessness of things, all of which had kept me aloof. Instead I could be there, available for another human being.

In the following weeks and months I had many chances to show her that I did get the message. Something would remind me of my first wife, or of the great sadness I felt for the Vietnamese, the vets still in pain, or the hopelessness of ending bloodshed in the world, and I'd glance at Sondra and realize again that I had a choice. I could wear my concern like a suit of armor that imprisoned me and prevented us from being close, or I could say what was on my mind in a way that didn't demand that she show pity or feel my guilt. I began to see myself as a reformed "agony junkie," facing a choice similar to the one that alcoholics and heroin addicts know well: Either break the habit or lose someone you love.

Reaching bottom means living out the worst and also penetrating to the essence. Once we've hit bottom and begun the ascent, the experience of "the worst" appears in retrospect as having revealed an essential bottom line truth.

The bottom itself, the moment when the "negative trip" stops, is not a predetermined point. Nobody can say whether or when the bottom will come for someone "going down." It appears only when the person suffering says "Enough!" or "I'm not going on like this!" or "I'm going to handle things, now!" In this sense, reaching bottom and beginning the ascent occur in the same instant. The constant refrain on the way down, "Nobody cares about me, so why bother?" becomes "If I don't take care of things, they won't get taken care of!" or "It all rests on me." At the bottom, we see that we alone have the power to go on by taking care of whatever in our life needs attention.

Bottoming out, and beginning the ascent happen at the moment when people intervene in their own lives with fresh conviction. They may have heard and recited "I know it's up to me" over and over on the way down. But these are the words of a spectator, not of the author of the drama. The shift that ends a downward spiral occurs when someone who is going down stops merely observing his or her life and starts acting as the one who leads the action. At that point one not only knows but also lives the truth of "It's up to me; nobody and nothing will do it for me."

For people whose "downer" consists of an activity that they and others can readily observe — drinking, using drugs, whoring, and so on — what there is to stop is obvious. But in cases of primarily inward suffering, the basis of long-term, post-traumatic pain is the struggle to avoid the emptiness at the heart of the original trauma. The bottom comes when we stop running away.

Once we stop trying to flee the horror, we can look back on traumatic experience as having led to a life-enhancing revelation. At the moment we declare "Enough!" we transcend our own sense of affliction. We give voice to the power to re-create our lives. By opening ourselves and reaching toward it, even the inescapability of nothingness appears in a new light — as the spaciousness in which life unfolds, a fertile opening, empty in itself but the source of infinite richness and possibility.

TURNING
IT AROUND

Most great cultural traditions . . . far transcend in scope and content any one trait or theme or any one injunction to Man. Otherwise they could not do justice to all the richness of the human spirit, and the wonder of human life. But one theme, one injunction, one duty do we find in all — in Buddhism, in Hindu Scripture, in Ecclesiastes, in the Gospels. The vulgar English phrase is "come off it," do not assume such an air of superiority. For the Greeks it was . . . "Man, know thyself," and in . . . the Gospels it is, "He who would find his life must lose it."

ROBERT OPPENHEIMER[1]

Most impressive . . . for me [are] those astonishing moments of insight [that carry] the conviction that this entire unspeakable world is "right," so right that our normal anxieties become ludicrous, that if only men could see it they would go wild with joy.

ALAN WATTS[2]

FOR A SMALL BUT INCREASING number of veterans the trauma that was once present is now gone. These men have found a way to transform a terrible experience into one that now enriches their lives. Rather than being overwhelmed, oppressed, or diminished by the past, they seem in command of themselves. And rather than protest or demand something in return for what they've lived through, they're committed to finding value in what they did and experienced, regardless of their opinions about American policies.

How have they turned that experience around? What's the key to this transformation? Most people who ask these questions do so with an eye toward cataloguing the various factors, traits, beliefs, or circumstantial details that distinguish veterans who have made it from those who haven't. Although the answers explain the differences between the haves and the have nots, explanations don't heal. The task for healing is to bridge this difference — rather than account for it — by revealing its source in such a way that others can bring about the transformation for themselves.

I first came across veterans of this sort in my research. Among all the ex-soldiers I knew, they stood out as unique. I had met men who said, "Heal? Who needs to heal? I'm fine!" and who simply skirted all the tough questions. And I had dealt with many others who appeared troubled but refused to talk about it, or were caught up in blaming the world, and pitying and punishing themselves. The veterans I found most extraordinary were not resentful, resigned, or emotionally distant. Most striking was their attitude that no matter what they had gone through, they would put it to use in their lives.

Many in this group had been disillusioned by the war, which crashed in on them with devastating disruption. What makes these men different is that they do not or no longer invoke those unsettling changes as a reason to live less fully now. If they have reservations or second thoughts about the war or the way it was conducted, they include themselves among the responsible parties by talking of *our* war and what *we* did or might have done differently.

Those who speak of "our" war and of what "we" did in Vietnam generally do not espouse any of the stereotypical hawk or dove attitudes toward the war. These veterans seem to have thought the issues through for themselves, attempting to weld together what they see of value among competing points of view.

For example, one of the veterans interviewed in our study said, "We were there, we had something to do, but we should've been more aggressive. If people are going to die, we might as well fight to win" — a statement that sounds prowar. But when we asked this same man about people who protested against the war, he did not give any of the customary prowar responses. In an open-minded and generous tone he said, "I respect all those who stood up for what they believe. Every man is different and has to go the way he sees as right. I wouldn't've protested, but I can see why some people did."

In a similar vein, some of the veterans who object strenuously to the war nevertheless value the idea of service to their country. Among veterans who fault our policies in Indochina are many who favor compulsory military service, which they regard as a maturing experience, a necessity in today's world, and a responsibility of citizenship that shouldn't be left to volunteers who can't get decent civilian jobs. "Don't leave the dirty work to the poor and uneducated," is a common sentiment even among men who disapprove of the war and criticize the military.

One veteran provided a graphic example of how unpleasant duties can be turned into inspiration. "The living conditions in Vietnam had a big impact on me. I literally was put on shit details over there, you know, taking the shit out of the latrines, pouring gasoline over it and setting it on fire. Burning shit over there was the most disgusting thing I ever did in my life, and that, and being close to death, it made me appreciate my life and the lives of others more."

Even the most harrowing experiences are amenable to being transformed. Like many who eventually spoke out against the war, a former helicopter pilot described how his difficulties began with bitter disillusionment over U.S. policies. "As a chopper pilot I had a unique position for observing things over there. The Vietnamese, I could see, didn't want to fight. They wouldn't leave the choppers when we landed for a firefight. And I could see from the air the confusion in so many of the battles and how poor the tactics were and panicked the decisions often were. I saw the violence between officers, vendettas against one another over the loss of their friends. And I got to talk with Vietnamese officers who were frank with me about why their people didn't want us there."

For him, as with so many others, the constant threat of death became an overriding consideration. "After my first day, when we got caught in crossfire, I thought my chances of getting through were nil. So many pilots got killed, I felt it was only a matter of time before I would get zapped too." He became deeply opposed to what he was doing, but pushed on out of a sense of obligation and powerlessness to do otherwise. "They used to call me Lucky because I only got shot once. I'd go in under fire and do all kinds of crazy things with the chopper to avoid getting hit and I'd get medals for it. But it was only because I didn't care anymore. I'd fly anywhere, even though it was killing me, losing weight, nerves going, couldn't sleep and pouring out emotional strain and conflict all over the place. It was tearing me apart and I knew it."

After witnessing wanton killing, he became intensely critical of U.S. tactics and strategies and of the war as a whole. "After a number of situations where I saw people killed needlessly, I spoke out, got angry, and sometimes screamed and yelled. I became a dissident in my group, against almost everything."

As bitter as he was, he came to recognize that the way he is —not just the attitudes he forms but the basic stance he takes toward life — is up to him. When the interviewer asked him to sum up how the Vietnam War affected him, he gave an ironic answer. "Well, I'm succeeding at what I'm doing now. If it keeps up like this, then you might say Vietnam was good for me. If things fall apart, then you might say it hurt. But I know who it rides on."

Most of the men who talk like this have gone to college and come from middle-class families. In the statistical analyses my colleagues conducted, social and economic status is strongly associated with psychological well being. In fact, the differences in adjustment between whites and blacks and between people from disadvantaged and well-to-do families are much greater than the average differences between veterans who went to Vietnam and their peers who didn't.

But once again it is crucial to emphasize that statistical studies focus on a fictitious "average veteran." Averages are calculated by ignoring the vast qualitative differences among people and by attending only to certain things about them that can be measured in a common way. If averages are all we look at, we blind ourselves to the possibilities open to individuals. So in our work we studied veterans on a case-by-case basis, which reconfirmed a truth that is too often ignored: Economic and social advantages don't guarantee access to healing, and poverty and discrimination don't prevent determined veterans from pursuing it successfully.

One of the men we interviewed in a black ghetto area provides a revealing example. This former infantryman, who received four Article 15 punishments — for minor infractions of military law — during his year in combat, told his interviewer that he was "scared as shit" during his tour and that he "freaked out" when one of his high school buddies who went to Vietnam with him was killed in action. He came home too confused to have any plans for school or work. All he could think of was "joining the brothers in making a revolution right here" in America. Months later he was disillusioned all over again, this time at the lack of commitment among the "so-called radicals." After many months of kicking around, he enrolled in school and got a job in a city welfare agency.

He spoke about the horror of the war, but insisted that the experience was valuable for him. "I left the Army feeling a new competence. I had an experience behind me that helped me overcome a lot of the inner conflicts and allowed me to see myself as someone who could control my own destiny." Since leaving the Army he has practiced various disciplines, psychological and spiritual, that "teach you to develop your inner self." When asked what inspired him to try these things, he said, "I still take it right back to Vietnam. That's what pushed me into seeking. The war, well, it made me have a clearer view of myself."

This new strength wasn't based on blindness to the horror. "It made me see what atrocities man can commit." But he didn't stop there: "I also got a lot of things off my chest just talking to people over there. So it showed me too the incredible love in the soldiers themselves, not the shit love on TV or movies, real love. And just that experience alone gives me hope for a better world, helping each other with problems and things."

The possibility of transforming the most horrible of experiences is not new. It is one of the themes of J. Glenn Gray's *The Warriors*,[3] a book based on his observations during and after World War II. A decade after he came home from that "good war," he wrote:

> In moments of clarity nothing is more apparent than the fact that the best and worst of men are different in degree only, not in kind. The soldier who is moved by sentiments of friendship and preservative love can reject the soldier-killer, for example, but he cannot in justice deny common humanity with him. Nor should the soldier of conscience . . . fail to recognize the potentiality of similar awakening in the most reckless or ruthless of his comrades as well as in the enemy. There is too much evidence of such transformations for any of us to doubt.[4]

He explained the key to the transformation this way:

> Why men fight without anger and kill without compunction is understandable at all only to a certain point. A slight alteration in consciousness would be sufficient to put their deeds in a true light and turn them forever from destruction. It would require only a coming to themselves to transform killers into friends and lovers, for, paradoxical as it may seem, the impulses that make killers are not so different in kind from those that make lovers. I know no other explanation for the notorious linkage in war between the noblest and the basest deeds, the most execrable vices and the sublimest virtues.[5]

Gray gave a vivid illustration of the kind of transformation that is possible with an incident he recalled toward the end of his war. His unit had liberated a German concentration camp, and Gray, as an intelligence officer, was able to mingle with the former prisoners as they were released from boxcars and wandered through a nearby town to be fed and cared for. All of them gravitated to one man, whom they hailed as the leader who had kept up their spirits over a period of years. Talking with the numerous French prisoners who spoke this man's praises, Gray was surprised to find out that the leader was a German, a political prisoner of long standing. Gray made a point of interviewing him and wrote, "Deprivation had accomplished that rare thing, a cleansing of all hatred and revenge from his heart, leaving him almost uncannily sane and wise."[6]

Transformation in this sense is not merely a shift in thought or feeling; it is an inherently spiritual phenomenon, a point made repeatedly by Carl Jung.[7] Jung broke with Freud over this point, complaining that the founder of psychoanalysis tended to take his own psychological metaphors too literally, and didn't subject his thinking to rigorous philosophical questioning. Jung used this questioning to strip away any idea that profound human change could be interpreted in terms that ignored the spirit. In his work Jung explored the connections between his observations of patients and the transformations depicted symbolically in the world's religions, in dreams, in mythology, and in the visual arts.

Transformation is the goal of the hero's spiritual journey in *The Odyssey: A Modern Sequel*. In the prologue, Kazantzakis declares that this goal requires nothing in particular, for *everything* is grist for the spiritual mill:

> O Sun, my quick coquetting eye, my red-haired hound,
> sniff out all quarries that I love, give them swift chase,
> tell me all that you've seen on earth, all that you've heard,
> and I shall pass them through my entrails' secret forge
> till slowly, with profound caresses, play and laughter,
> stones, water, fire, and earth shall be transformed to spirit,
> and the mud-winged and heavy soul, freed of its flesh,
> shall like a flame serene ascend and fade in sun.[8]

The entire poem praises this search to distill spirit from the stuff of life. A dramatic climax comes after the great hero has led his comrades on a journey through the African jungle to the place where he will build his ideal city. He climbs a holy mountain to commune with his spirit guide. After several fitful days and nights haunted by phantoms, Odysseus awakens to recognize that he and all men are bridges between past and future. He comes to see the phantoms within him as spirits of the dead, the living, and the unborn. He realizes that his accustomed image of himself is a pale hint of his life's infinite possibilities, and that he must struggle to open up to his true nature.

Expanding in spirit as passionately as he once rushed into battle, the modern Odysseus reaches out to embrace his ancestors, then people of all races, and then the animals, birds, fishes, rocks, water, all of the earth, and ultimately the great cosmic void. At the end of this inner ascent, he sees that it is the divine spirit in himself that yearns to be set free. "Some call it Love, some call it God and Death, and some have called it Outcry that leaps from flesh to flesh and shouts: 'I stifle in all bodies . . .' "[9]

At this point the poet congratulates his hero on recognizing the cosmic essence within. For Kazantzakis, the spiritual journey is the singular calling of the mighty one who fights until death, whose struggle for freedom is not against some worldly opponent but from the fetters of his mind and the dullness of his flesh. He must overcome his reluctance to see the entire world as an extension of himself. His unceasing challenge is to break out of the chains of his own pettiness.

Kazantzakis took a cue from Nietzsche, who declared that "God is dead,"[10] meaning that our materialist culture had killed off any sense of holiness. Existentialists often took Nietzsche to mean that man must therefore save himself. Kazantzakis thought of self-saving as too low a calling. The great task facing us all is to save God, to create consciously what primitives and naive believers assume without question: a holy presence in the world.

The Odyssey: A Modern Sequel is a prayer for a new global commitment. It is a poignant cry from a world that yearns for the holiness of healing, a call that can be met only by those bold enough to take it on. Transforming the horror and meaninglessness of life is our ceaseless task, which asks of us continually to be open to our awestruck vulnerability, the source of spiritual fire.

Awakenings of this sort do not arise out of the circumstances of time and place but from a call from within. People can have an awakening anywhere, anytime. Some veterans used the war as their occasion; others have taken up martial arts training or some other spiritual discipline. But awakening does not require any particular props. Even the most unlikely situations can be opportunities for enlightenment. This was never so clear to me as when I took a two-weekend workshop called the est training.[11]

My training began when a woman walked to the front of our group of about two hundred and fifty people and called out, "There'll be no talking!" She was barking like a drill instructor in basic training. Some people sitting near me started whispering, and suddenly a man walked quickly down the aisle from the back of the room. "Don't you listen?" he shouted. "She's telling you the ground rules. Bathroom breaks every four hours, and one meal break late in the day. Leave your watches outside the room, and no talking while the training is going on."

I was stunned by so much regimentation, but amused as people asked questions like, "But what if I really have to go, I mean to the bathroom, before the break comes?" and the man, obviously the trainer, said wryly, "You people are like kindergartners. Notice? We've got to spend all this time reassuring you that in a few hours you won't starve, and won't pee in your pants, and that we won't keep you up past your bedtime. Children!"

A friend of mine, a managerial consultant, recommended the training. I had gone to him complaining about the burdens of success. I had received the grants that made my research project a national study, and I was also being hired by the Urban League to run a pilot project for four veterans' outreach programs across the country. I had to manage several teams of people and was suddenly in over my head, bickering with my colleagues and fearful that I couldn't do the job. My training as a therapist had only prepared me to work with people who think I'm saner than they are. I needed a way to resolve things when I was in the soup as much as everyone else. My friend said this training was the best crash course he knew.

I had heard lots of criticism of est. Many psychotherapists spoke of it as authoritarian or harmful. In the end I trusted my friend who had been there more than the opinions of people who criticized it from a distance. I wanted to see for myself.

Soon after our session began, an older woman raised her hand and the trainer called on her. She stood up and said, "You're crude, insulting, and demeaning. People shouldn't have to listen to your vile tone!"

"You're right. Nobody has to be here. You can leave right now."

"I just might do that. I would never talk to my patients the way you talk to people here," she said.

"You're a doctor?" he asked.

"I'm a psychologist."

"It can be pretty humbling to see that there are ways of doing things other than yours," he snapped back.

"If this is the way you're going to be, I don't want any part of it."

"Then leave," he said, at which point she left the room.

I felt bad for the woman, and felt the challenge to psychologists personally. I stood up without waiting to be called on. "I second that," I said loudly. "That's no way to talk to people."

"Take a microphone," he barked.

"Screw your microphone. I can talk as loud as you can!" I yelled.

He walked over to me. "You know, Arthur," he said, reading my name tag, "it doesn't take much to see you've got a little issue with authority."

"Yeah? It's called a year in Vietnam," I said with a sneer, expecting that my reference to the war would make him back off.

"Is that right?" he asked, with even more irony in his voice. "Would you be willing to discover you've put one over on yourself with that one?"

I gulped, as if caught with my hand in the cookie jar. Someone was challenging me in public on my "veteran trip" — me, an expert on healing trauma! I didn't know whether to be insulted or flabbergasted. I thought my problems with the war were over now that I had stopped mourning. Suddenly an old question came back: Had I been fooling myself again? Could there be something about healing I hadn't seen before? What was this trainer getting at?

"Yes, I'd be willing to consider that."

Sitting there afterward was uncomfortable. What were people thinking? That I let myself get pushed around? Or that I was flexible enough to consider a new viewpoint? After going back and forth a dozen times I realized it was a dead end. They'll think whatever they want — I can't stop them. Other, more useful questions then came to mind, like what was that confrontation about? What use could I make of it for my own healing? What was the lesson in it?

As I watched and listened to other people respond to the trainer, I noticed that each person was acting as though the trainer would meet certain of their expectations. But whatever they seemed to expect — for him to be understanding, tough, considerate, informative, entertaining, or whatever — he would refuse to be pigeonholed and would *throw their expectations back at them. I realized that I had expected him to be "nice," and when he wasn't I made him out to be a bad guy who'd back off when righteously challenged. But he didn't accept that role either. And when he pointed out that I had been interpreting his behavior according to assumptions that had nothing to do with him my next move was to invoke the war as a justification for my response.*

There it was, the war again, and here I was, dragging it along with me. Suddenly I saw an opportunity to unravel my postwar identity in a way I never had before, an identity that allowed me to meditate, philosophize, and even write about the most profound matters, but that in a crunch had me resorting to the same old strategies. One of them, I realized suddenly, was to try to distinguish myself from the baddies of the world by being nice, by being a goodie who'd resist the bad guys, as if doing that would make me worthy. If anyone around me was wronged, I had to protest to prove I was a good guy. Living out this identity didn't leave me any room to consider that there ever could be a more fitting or useful response.

Okay, I thought. So I had fallen into that trap and got caught. What's the big deal? I've had insights like these before. So what if I'm a jerk, playing world redeemer sometimes? Isn't everybody? What's this got to do with why I'm here? How does this help me manage things in my life?

As I asked myself these questions, I began to realize that I was really on to something. The truth was that I was still using the war to explain myself: The war had thrown reality in my face; the war had taught me about human cruelty and frailty; the war had shown me how to care; the war had forced my hand; the war had set me on my life course; and because of the war I had to help the other guys. Even if I kept myself from mourning about it, I was still using this web I had spun as my way of being something, being somebody. And as long as I kept it up, I wasn't free simply to be.

It began to dawn on me that this whole business was a myth I had created. I could see now that other people had similar myths, and that they and I had helped spread them, so that most of the country felt sorry for Vietnam vets. In my version, veteran experts like me were badly needed; this followed from the assumption that I and other vets were damaged by the war. And there it was! My self-importance was based on proving we were screwed up. If I gave up believing we were damaged by the war for all time, I'd lose the justification for my life that I had cooked up a decade before. No wonder my work was so hard. No wonder people thought of me as heavy. No wonder I was having trouble finding joy and sharing it. Curing veterans, having us heal completely, was a threat to my very identity!

Though I had suspected all this before, I never knew what to do about it and so never bothered to articulate it clearly. As I listened to the trainer speak about choice, I saw that I could choose to hold on to this myth or not. Or I could rework it, leave it behind altogether, even cook up a new one. Then I realized even that insight was not enough; no new insight would ever save me. What I'd probably do is cook up a new myth, then live it for a time and get trapped in that one too. Being alive meant risking losing my cool, getting tied up in another myth I'd spin for myself, and having it all thrown in my face when I'd least expect it. What if there's no place to get to? What if there's never any good reason to be joyful and fulfilled? What if this endless struggle is all there is?

This time the answer came with a giggle. Maybe I'd join the human race. I'd do my work and be with the people I was close to without having to make it all some great burden or weighty cause. And since there's never any reason to be joyful, there also isn't any reason not to be. This was a new possibility. Why not be ecstatic, for no reason at all? For the first time I got the joke that people appreciate in enlightenment experiences: We might as well smile as frown.

Enlightenment, cosmic consciousness, transformation — never before has so much been written and said about such matters. There are many different approaches to higher human development, but scholars have noted a core body of knowledge common to all great teaching traditions, which has been passed down for thousands of years. This knowledge is often referred to as the "perennial philosophy," a term Aldous Huxley used as the title of his book, published in 1945, containing lengthy annotations and quotations from the sacred writings of Buddhists, Hindus, Sufis, Taoists, and Christian mystics. Huxley took the title from Gottfried Wilhelm von Leibnitz, the great seventeenth-century German thinker, who noted the striking overlap among the mystical teachings known to the most advanced practitioners of the world's religions. These teachings point the way beyond suffering to an enlightenment that comes only by training ourselves to perceive the limitlessness of the realities we face.

A wave of interest in enlightenment disciplines began to swell on the West Coast of the United States during the late 1950s and early 1960s, partly because of the influence exerted by Huxley and a group of other Europeans, mostly Englishmen, who settled there during and after World War II — men like Christopher Isherwood, Gerald Heard, Alan Watts, Gregory Bateson, and Robert de Ropp.[12] Since then, Japanese Zen masters, Indian swamis, Tibetan lamas, and Sufi masters have arrived there and elsewhere, drawing on and further fueling this interest. Millions of new adherents in North America and in metropolitan centers throughout the world's industrial democracies have been inspired by these teachings. According to some reports, a similar awakening is stirring in the Soviet Union as well.[13]

Widely thought of as "Eastern religion," the perennial philosophy has ancient roots in the West, though they are still largely unrecognized. In his 1975 book, *The Transformative Vision*, José Arguelles traced the development of the European and American expression of cosmic consciousness in the arts. He noted that the "journey to the East" is a symbolic voyage. Going eastward became necessary for seekers in the West only as our culture became blinded to the wider reality of psyche and spirit. The East became an antidote to rampant industrialization and to the accepted reality of post-Renaissance materialism only when the West became narrowly preoccupied with technology and progress.

Arguelles echoed the challenge posed by Friedrich Nietzsche a century ago. Our materialist culture, which spread from Europe since the Renaissance, has affected the entire world and led inexorably to world wars and to the nuclear "balance of terror." The predicament did not begin in Europe, but in ancient times. Nietzsche traced the problem to the "slave revolt in morals," the debasement of Christ's original teachings, which occurred when Christianity became a doctrine to believe, rather than a call for spiritual growth. Arguelles leveled a similar charge, that our culture suffers from a slavish tendency to worship our greatest teachers rather than follow their example:

The failure of Christian civilization — or any other — has been its inability to live by the example of its teachers. This failure has plunged us into the nightmare of "His-story"; instead of living Christ's story ourselves, we have others live it for us. Thus civilization must have its special personalities — the saints, the geniuses, the madmen. Our reliance on them to seek ultimate reality is necessitated by our own abdication of vision, of the creative powers, of the spiritually regenerating forces by which the individual alone might become not merely an animal or a good citizen — but a fully conscious being.[14]

Yet history has another face, the mounting revolt, which erupted in the sixteenth century with the Reformation. At that point, the idea that had been declared heresy for a millennium surfaced with such force it could not be ignored: Individuals can achieve personal knowledge of the ultimate without mediation of priests or doctrines. In 1901 William James, the father of American psychology, surveyed the last few centuries of religious evolution in the West and concluded that this individually pursued enlightenment was becoming increasingly accessible without the trappings of formal religion, priestly control, or ritual.[15]

James described the key experience as a shift that brings "excitement and heat," so that a new "hot place in man's consciousness" forms. Notions of higher purpose replace the more limited concerns with personal gain, at least as a first priority. Enthusiasm, from the Greek word meaning "inspired by God," is a natural result. James used the term "self-surrender" to explain the release from narrow or selfish preoccupations that characterizes these experiences.

Another moment in the est *training marked a dramatic turn for me. A man in his forties, a bank clerk, stood up and spoke about how much his life was marred by his wife's infidelities. No training could help him, he said, because nobody could change what she had done. The trainer then said, "That's right. Nobody can change the past. But you can choose whether to keep suffering or to forgive her."*

As the man paused to think I was drawn into thoughts of my own. Forgive? How's that possible? Forgiveness didn't fit with any psychology I had ever studied. The concept was foreign to me except as a religious notion and certainly not something I made a point of practicing. I had always associated forgiveness with either weakness or saintliness, but now I was struck by the boldness of it. Could someone simply say, "I forgive you," and the most hideous wrongs cease to weigh on either party? As a rational thinker I objected. "How's that possible? What's to keep you from forgiving the wrong kinds of things? What if the person you forgive goes out and does something wrong all over again?" In pondering these questions, I was struck by the power of forgiveness: Whenever forgiveness is granted it overrules logic and flies in the face of the countless reasons against it.

None of the psychotherapists I knew raised the possibility of forgiveness with their patients. No wonder people's hurts have to be studied, analyzed, emoted about, desensitized, pored over, but are rarely cured. For in the end, there is no answer to profound hurt except, "Yes, that must have hurt a great deal. Now what?" What do we say to the "Now what"? Nothing in the repertoire of psychological techniques and philosophical arguments I knew came close to the power of forgiveness. Only "I forgive you" has the potency to put an end to the recriminations and self-recriminations once and for all. It was so simple, and I felt embarrassed to admit how long I had been oblivious to it.

But what in us has the right to forgive? What in us has the power to shift so profoundly our relationship with the facts of what we've lived through? I couldn't answer. The questions pointed to impossibility: Only a saint or a megalomaniac could forgive the kind of horrors I knew. Wouldn't anyone who dared to say, "I forgive the people who declared that war" be setting himself up as ridiculously grandiose? Wouldn't that give license to more of such horror? Aren't blame and recrimination among the few restraints on evil impulse that we have left?

My questioning went on until I noticed that I was begging for some code or rule to guide me to the "right" choice. "You want to reduce living to some correct formula, don't you?" I laughed at myself. Clearly, I'd have to learn the ways of forgiveness as I had virtually everything else, through trial and error.

What if I forgave my mother for not having understood me better as I was growing up? What if I no longer blamed her for not having known then how to deal with me? By just asking these questions I realized that the real absurdity was in not forgiving her. To blame her for not having known more than she knew was pure pettiness. Yes, I really did hurt from her not knowing me better. But why continue to blame her for that? For years I had understood that I was often a difficult son. Understanding had eased the tension between us, but it never relieved me altogether, and I finally saw why: I had never raised the possibility of forgiveness. Once I did, the way to go was obvious. I imagined a conversation with her in which I said, "I forgive you." She melted and held out her arms to me, and I began to cry and to embrace her in a way I hadn't done in twenty years. I knew then that it wouldn't be long before I'd actually say those words to her and ask her to forgive me for not saying them sooner.

More answers then came to me. Something happened in the moment of granting forgiveness that I had never known until I actually did it. A long time would pass before I found a way of putting that experience into words, but in that instant I already had a clear intuition. Who I am, the nature of what I'm being, is transformed in the moment of granting forgiveness. Since that first time, I've observed the transformation repeatedly. The very act of forgiving calls forth a new relationship with life, and with it, what I take myself to be expands to include possibilities of being with others that weren't there before.

The last two decades have been marked by an "American awakening" according to Walter Truett Anderson, whose recent book describes the impact of Esalen and the human potential movement on American culture.[16] Contemporary scholars who look back from within that cultural shift have begun to identify the undercurrents of enlightenment in the West that have been banished for several centuries from our cultural mainstream.

In a forthcoming book, James Moffett, a nationally known educator, traces the perennial philosophy through the mystic teachings of many of the sects persecuted for heresy during a thousand years of ecclesiastical domination by the Catholic church in Rome.[17] Moffett also describes the influence of the perennial philosophy on Shakespeare and other giants of the Western tradition, and calls for teaching American history with an appreciation of the spiritual background that gave rise to the founding of our republic.

The ideas in the Declaration of Independence originated in the spiritual Enlightenment that swept Europe and North America in the eighteenth century. After almost two hundred years of factional hatred and religious wars in Europe, gifted artists, thinkers, writers, and statesmen joined an international movement called Freemasonry, which was dedicated to the principles of universal brotherhood and freedom of the human spirit. Its membership in the late eighteenth century included Schiller, Mozart, Frederick the Great, the *philosophes* and revolutionaries of France, as well as Franklin, Jefferson, and Washington. Fifty-six of the fifty-eight signers of the Declaration of Independence were also members. All were steeped in the perennial philosophy.

Many of the artists, poets, and writers in our tradition are revered with little appreciation of the profound and ancient inspirations that stirred their work. The quest for enlightenment — the transformation that heals — appears as a theme in the works of William Blake and the Romantics, then in the writings of the first renowned American authors — Emerson, Thoreau, Melville, Hawthorne, and Whitman — up to the great English-language authors of the twentieth century — Yeats, Lawrence, Joyce, and Eliot.

Edgar Allan Poe provides one example of how little is known of what inspired these authors. Most people think of Poe as a writer of fantastic stories and eerie poems. Sixty years before Einstein published his theory of the unity of space and time, Poe wrote, "Space and duration are one." Poe envisioned the universe as a great pulsing unity, "Swelling into existence, and then subsiding into nothingness at every throb of the Heart Divine." As for the ultimate nature of this heart, he wrote, "It is our own."[18]

For Poe, as for all the sages before and since, history has only one great purpose: the fulfillment of the promise that all people will eventually embrace the consciousness that has, from the dawn of civilization, been available only to a few:

> The sense of individual identity will be gradually merged in the general consciousness — that Man, for example, ceasing imperceptibly to feel himself Man, will at length attain that awfully triumphant epoch when he shall recognize his existence as that of Jehovah. In the meantime bear in mind that all is Life — Life — Life Within Life — the less within the greater, and all within the Spirit Divine.[19]

It is not only the great artists who have been inspired by the mystic perception. Gifted scientists have also come to view the entire cosmos as the ground of each individual's existence, and each individual as capable of sensing the whole within his or her being. Ken Wilbur has recently republished mystical writings of some of the great scientists of our century, including Heisenberg, Schroedinger, de Broglie, Jeans, Planck, Pauli, and Eddington.[20] Albert Einstein put it this way:

> The most beautiful emotion we can experience is the mystical. It is the sower of all true art and science. He to whom this emotion is a stranger . . . is as good as dead. To know that what is impenetrable to us really exists, manifesting itself as the highest wisdom and the most radiant beauty, which our dull faculties can comprehend only in their most primitive forms — this knowledge, this feeling, is at the center of true religiousness. In this sense, and in this sense only I belong to the ranks of the devoutly religious men.[21]

And what is the goal of such enlightened perceptions? Einstein's answer:

> A human being is a part of the whole, called by us "Universe"; a part limited in time and space. He experiences himself, his thoughts and feelings as something separated from the rest — a kind of optical delusion of his consciousness. This delusion is a kind of prison for us, restricting us to our personal desires and to affection for a few persons nearest us. Our task must be to free ourselves from this prison.[22]

In our time, the way of openness and the tradition passed down from ancient sages is becoming the basis of a new psychology, one that draws on the perennial philosophy. The idea for it was announced by Abraham Maslow in 1968:

> [The] "higher" . . . psychology [is] transpersonal, transhuman, centered in the cosmos rather than in human needs and interest, going beyond humanness, identity, self-actualization and the like. [This] may very well offer a tangible, usable, effective satisfaction of the "frustrated idealism" of many quietly desperate people, especially young people. These psychologies give promise of developing into a life philosophy, the religion surrogate, the value system, the life-program that these people have been missing. Without the transcendent and the transpersonal, we get sick, violent, and nihilistic, or else hopeless and apathetic. We need something "bigger than we are" to be awed by and to commit ourselves to in a new, naturalistic, empirical, non-churchly sense, perhaps as Thoreau and Whitman, William James and John Dewey did.[23]

I was like a little kid with a new toy. I wanted to try out forgiveness, particularly on the greatest wrong I had ever suffered and helped perpetrate, the war. I began to consider who there was to forgive. I was long past the point of blaming one side or the other exclusively. For all our country's blunders and crimes, I didn't regard the "liberators" of Indochina as faultless. Yet the cruelties of the war remained, even if there was nobody in particular to single out, even if I had to admit that in the greater scheme of things, the war in Indochina was another instance of an ancient, bloody ritual played out in contemporary terms.

In taking inventory, I recalled that I had blamed not only all the parties to the war, myself included, but the culture that — in my more recent sophistication — I saw as making warfare possible. The very idea of granting forgiveness on such a scale, even if I never told anyone about it, made me blush. I felt like a child who thinks he might be President someday, or as I sometimes felt in synagogue as a little boy, when singing one of the ancient chants gave me goose bumps, that I had some personal role to play in advancing the cause of the most holy.

I sat there in a hotel ballroom, listening to an est trainer, contemplating a step that seemed more daring and more blessed than any I had ever taken. I would no longer hold myself, my former leaders, the world, life, history, the human race hostage for the pain I knew about, witnessed, and felt. I would forgive — not in response to a promise that it wouldn't happen again, but as a gift, as an ennobling act, the only gesture that had the power to be thoroughly healing for me.

I closed my eyes and saw myself in Saigon, standing on the roof next to that whorehouse on a summer night. I said "I forgive you" to everyone and everything that had conspired in that moment. I saw myself at Arlington Cemetery, where I had marched the next year with Vietnam Veterans Against the War, and pictured myself saying "I forgive you" to all those who had a hand in killing those men. And I pictured myself at my typewriter, composing the dozens of scathing letters to Presidents, congressional leaders, and military men, sending off a follow-up to each one that said "I forgive you."

When that was done another task became clear. The next one in line to be forgiven was the biggest fool in the drama I had lived. In an instant replay of decades I could see him hungering for some way to feel important. As a boy he had tried on the colorations of one group *of buddies he thought cool, then another, and another. Wanting to be on the right side of things, doing what he thought would help him make it, he went to war halfheartedly, hoping to hedge his bets. Then the hollowness in his pose backfired. In revulsion over his own moral failures, he took up the slogans of the great moralizers* who condemned his war and the people who failed to recant the way he had. A few years later, there he was again, embarrassed to admit that events had partially vindicated those who had favored the war after all. Stripped of any moral refuge, he stood before me naked, having to admit his uncertainty about what's right.*

It was not a pretty portrait I painted of myself. And I saw what made it so disfigured. I had withheld from myself for so long the very forgiveness I was now contemplating. To forgive myself, to call a halt to self-blame as a way of managing the vulnerability I couldn't stand about myself — the possibility was dizzying. Again I closed my eyes and began a conversation that was different from any I ever had with myself.

"For a long time you've been looking to call the shots right, haven't you?" I asked myself. "Well, you don't have to worry about that anymore. I'm no longer going to hold it against you whether you get it wrong or not. I know what you've really been up to all this time. You give a shit, don't you? Isn't that it? Isn't that what you've been afraid to admit outright? Isn't that what hurts the most? People, the world, all sorts of things can get to you, especially when you don't want them to, right? And you're the one who has to carry the pain, and it never looks cool. I forgive all the contortions you've put yourself and others through to try to make it look as if you've got it all together.

"Even more I know what you want, what you've been striving for — dignity, right? You want self-respect. You want some way to express your care, to feel as if it matters, as if you matter. And I know that whatever happens, you'll persist in that quest. I've never paid tribute to your persistence, and so, in addition to forgiving you for all your foolishness, I ask you to forgive me. I've never recognized and appreciated that it's not what you make of yourself but just you, what you can't help being, your humanity, that's of value to other people and to this life."

That freed me. I no longer felt I had to do anything with my life. From here on I could live playfully. Even death had lost its heaviness, for I seemed to have stumbled on my own personal version of the last rites. I was forgiven, and as I got the message I saw that I wasn't just speaking to myself. What came about was a new relationship with life, in which I no longer expected anything and had realized the possibility of appreciating everything, even the worst horrors. I had used horror as fuel for my searching. Horror had touched me as deeply as anything on earth and brought me to confront my own caring. I had no way to fit this realization into a moral code, but the truth of it was inescapable: I was appreciative even of horror — not that I wished it on anyone, but it had served me well.

At that moment my relationship with the war changed. It was no longer a great wrong I had to condemn or hold against anyone, nor was it a justification for my life. I no longer needed any justification. I could live or die or go on to do whatever I chose. The sense of obligation I had always felt had dissolved in forgiveness and acceptance. And what now emerged was an unprecedented possibility for me: to make life as challenging, as exciting, and as exalting as I was willing to have it. I could be whatever was closest to my heart, and have my life be the gift I'd give to acknowledge the appreciation that now filled me.

As soon as the possibility became clear, I saw immediately how I'd realize it. I wouldn't make myself into some new personality. I'd let myself be free so that I could live to fulfill a purpose that went beyond any particular role. From now on I'd stand for what I had lived at first hand — the possibility of healing from war. I'd find ways to communicate it, share it with other veterans, spread the message to others. I'd join with everyone who knows that mass bloodshed and state-sanctioned violence must soon be things of the past.

In making this promise to myself, I noticed transformation at work again. A seemingly impossible task, taken up in the spirit of no obligation, nothing to prove, suddenly appeared feasible. I knew I could fail, and fail miserably, and I wouldn't hold it against myself. To live as my purpose — the possibility of healing from war — would simply be a fitting way to give of myself in the decades I'd have left. At that moment my life took on a clearer direction than ever before, and I appreciated the irony that it came when I no longer felt any need for it.

Based on impressions from our research, a significant minority of Vietnam veterans have had moments of enlightenment, conversions, and other crucial points at which they turned traumatic experiences into sources of renewal. A review of veterans' writings yields a similar impression. Most memoirs and novels deal with the war experience or with unsettling, if not traumatic, homecomings. A few accounts, however, focus on the struggles of healing, demonstrating that some portion of the veteran population knows what it means to turn suffering to joy.

Rick Eilert, a former Marine rifleman, was hit at close range by a grenade and rifle shots in Vietnam. More than a decade later, he wrote a memoir of the thirty-nine operations and the painful periods of recuperation that it took to piece him together.[24] He was determined to get his girl to marry him and to walk again on his own. Almost every page of his story includes lines like, "I didn't think anyone could feel as bad as I did and still be alive." With shrapnel embedded in every area of his body, an arm and a leg severed, he had to learn to walk all over again, which was an excruciating trial.

Eilert recalled one day in his long years of rehabilitation. He was working out on parallel bars the day after a dental surgeon had cut shrapnel and bone fragments out of his gums.

> I tried to concentrate on moving down the bars, and fought my way along. . . . I began gasping for air. All the cotton in my mouth hampered my breathing. Shultz didn't care. He pressed me even harder to finish the exercise. I was near the breaking point, but not the quitting point. Shultz's smug expression made me more determined than ever to make it. I pulled and pumped my arms, dragging my heavy plastered legs, inch by agonizing inch, until I reached the chair.

> By now blood was trickling out of the corners of my mouth. More blood ran from my toes as the toenails continued to dig into the swollen flesh. And I was gasping for air.[25]

Eilert tells the willful side of healing. Determination carried him through, as time after time he turned pain, setbacks, disappointments, and more pain into opportunities to laugh or to show what it means to be courageous.

By itself, determination works up to a point. Beyond that, healing calls for letting go of willfulness or the urge to control. Max Cleland, another veteran who was seriously wounded by a grenade explosion in Vietnam, wrote a memoir that emphasizes the self-surrender that was crucial to his healing.[26] For Cleland, who had lost both legs and his right arm, the letting go was the culmination, which occurred only after he too had willfully pressed himself to live, to mend, to walk again, to drive a car, and to resume an active career in politics.

The turning point came when he acknowledged that his many accomplishments weren't enough. He had already been an aide in the U.S. Senate, and was on his way to becoming a Georgia legislator, the youngest man ever to head the Veterans Administration, and then Georgia's secretary of state. Past achievements and future promise hadn't kept him from feeling "restless and unhappy in my spirit." And he remained that way until he came back to his traditional religious education, which had new meaning this time. It was then that Cleland saw how his enormous pride and self-preoccupation had consistently kept him from acknowledging any source of inspiration beyond his own egocentric desire to control things. Suddenly he heard new significance in words he had read in a newspaper a short time before: "Let go . . . and let God." Cleland describes how his dissatisfaction turned to inner peace as he was driving his car on a rainy night:

I had never let go of anything I wanted in my whole life. Instead I wanted to be in control of everything. . . . How could one let go and let God — and still be successful? I realized though that maybe this was faith — not a clutching, but a letting go! . . .

My eyes began to fill, and emotion surged through me. The tears burned as I strained to see through the steady beat of the windshield wipers.

'God forgive me! God help me!'

The words came out suddenly, a deep inner cry of my soul bursting through the controlling nature of my will.

Tears streamed down my cheeks.

Then something happened inside me. My racing heart suddenly slowed. The knot of tension and frustration began to dissolve. I could feel changes taking place in my physical body as a feeling of peace spread through every tissue.

Nothing was changed on the highway outside . . . but the glow within me remained. And with it came a revelation. Though I had departed from God, He had never abandoned me. Though I had ignored Him, He continued to love me. And now when I reached out to Him, He came to me. . . . It was an opportunity for a new life.[27]

Cleland saw his transformation as a return to a traditional Christian community and form of worship. Others I know speak of similarly enlightening experiences in nonreligious terms. Sam, my buddy from the rap group days, took the *est* training soon after I did. He too describes a change in the way he feels, but he emphasizes the change as having to do with his perceptions of others. For the last ten years he has held various positions at a social service center in Harlem. After *est* he was promoted to supervisor, and now has the reputation of being the one who can handle the weirdest, most difficult people who come around complaining about their welfare checks.

"It's different now," he says. "I see the human being through all the garbage and I just respond to that. Everybody else still gets caught up in the act these people put on when they don't expect anyone will treat them decently."

When I began working on this book, I asked Sam how this turn affected the way he views his experiences in the war. He said:

"I got to appreciate something about Vietnam when I started asking myself what the truth is about life. You take the abstractions away and stick your nose in the crap. That's the way the war trained a lot of guys. After Vietnam you could act blasé, like I did at first. But deep down I knew I was being touched like I never had been before. It was a situation where you can't half-step your way through. Looking back, I think it was a privilege to be with guys you could trust your life to, people who'd carry you to bed when you were too drunk to walk, or who would listen when you were real down.

"The thing I loved about the *est* training is that people saw life stripped down to its core, the way we did in the war, without having to go to Vietnam or some other hell hole. The one worry I always have is that people will think that because they didn't go, they can't feel or know or understand.

"Of course there will always be something special for me about the war. But I couldn't see it for a long time. It looked so horrible I felt contaminated. I would try to make it less dirty to ease the pain. Then I saw that the killing, the whorehouses, cheating at poker, the awful drunkenness weren't all of it. The worst of it still couldn't keep me from remembering the good times, the things I'll never regret, like the way we dealt straight with each other over there.

Now it's to the point where I'm glad I went, for the way I opened up through that, and all I've learned about it since."

I asked him how he had turned his suffering around. "It happened when I stopped beating myself over the head. It began with saying that the war had bad parts, good parts, horrible parts, just like any other big experience. But in the end, whether it drags on me or not is my choice. When I saw that, I turned.

"So I say that the process of going through Vietnam and dealing with it I use now. It works for the rest of my life — not anything in particular that happened over there, but what I learned from grappling with the experience afterward. Everybody's got to face death, love, ambition, frustration. Every day people get married, break up, have kids. You can only take what comes along. What came my way was Vietnam, is the way I see it. That's what I had to face. In the end, though, it's no more special than anything else. I keep hearing vets say what we used to, but now it sounds stupid. 'You can only relate to another vet, somebody who was there.' Sure we got a special connection with each other. But it's not some exclusive thing. If you know how to look, there's magic no matter where you turn, and people to share it with."

In the years after U.S. forces withdrew from Indochina, the possibility of putting a wrenching national experience to good use dawned on some of the Army's more insightful officers. One of them, Colonel Harry Summers, wrote a review of the war from a new perspective.[28] His book has been used in courses at the war college, and has been read by many U.S. military leaders. Though it is not an official Army publication, the book nevertheless conveys a point of view that has broad appeal.

Summers reappraised U.S. strategies enacted during the war. Although he did not say so, the presentation itself can be read as a strategy — to transcend the domestic divisiveness and to bring about a breakthough in the way the war is remembered. To appreciate this strategy, it is worth noting what Summers did not do in his book.

First, he did not make the argument that we lost the war because the politicians wouldn't let the Army win. He didn't rest his case on evidence that President Johnson refused General Westmoreland's request for reinforcements, that details of bombing missions had to

be cleared with Washington, that the White House was overly involved in military affairs from the beginning of the war.

Second, Summers did not contend that the Army, the war, and
the nation's institutions were sold out by traitors from within. He
did not blame the war's critics for helping the enemy by pointing
out the moral failure on the U.S. side. He did not argue that war
reporting was biased by liberals in the American media. And he did
not base his case on blaming guilt-ridden students who, in their
draft-exempt status, tried to ease their conscience by protesting the
war in which others died in their place.

Essentially he wrote that our great failure in Vietnam was poor
strategy, and that the people who are ultimately responsible for it
were the military leaders who advised the President and directed
military operations. As for the domestic factions that fought bitterly
at home, Summers dealt with them in turn and, in effect, made a
case that each group was correct to some degree.

Some kind of intervention in Vietnam would have been justified,
Summers said, as long as national policy was "containing communism," because events ultimately bore out the initial assessment that
we were dealing all along with an expansionist communist power in
North Vietnam. He argued that American reporters essentially did
their jobs, reporting the facts in spite of the chaos and horror around
them. The response at home was not due to distortion of slanted
news coverage. Where others had seen evidence for a conspiracy,
Summers saw only that a civilized nation that was not whipped into
war fever greeted the facts of slaughter for what they were — signs
that Americans were killing in cold blood.

Summers did fault the Army's way of fighting the war and the
failure of military professionals to advise the President of the consequences of his choices. He claimed that our military experts not
only should have known better, but did, in fact, know better than
to try to do the job that properly belonged to the South Vietnamese — that of forcefully policing their own people. He then proposed an alternative war strategy — cordoning off the frontier between North and South Vietnam, he claimed, would have stemmed
the flow of men and materiel to fuel the insurgency.

It is difficult to assess such hypothetical scenarios. And in my view,
no discussion of war strategy should overlook the inherently self-

defeating national policy of "containing communism," which keeps us ever defensive (see Appendix). What may be most valuable about Summers' book, however, is the spirit in which it was written. As a representative of one of the institutions central to the war effort, he has declared publicly, "The buck stops here." He has demonstrated how to turn from defending our role in a bitter experience to using our mistakes as our greatest teachers.

Sondra and I began talking about living together. A short time later she went away for a few days to a professional conference for fellow English professors, leaving me alone to think. Mainly I thought about my battles with women, particularly the struggle to keep any one of them from getting to me. I realized that it wasn't a struggle I wanted anymore. In fact, women had already touched me deeply. Sondra had. My first wife had too.

I decided that if Sondra and I were going to live together, I would have to be truthful and say that she wasn't the only one I loved. So the evening she came back, while both of us stood in her small kitchen preparing dinner, I announced that I still loved my ex-wife. Sondra, who is ordinarily very eventempered and unflappable, picked up a quart container of yogurt and flung it at me. She yelled a series of nasty words, uncharacteristic of her, and started hitting me until I grabbed her fists. Then she broke away and ran out of the apartment.

During the hours that she roamed the streets of Manhattan's upper West Side, I asked myself what was so offensive about what I had said. My psychologist's training answered first. The problem was hers. Her father had just died, her next-door neighbor had just died, and she had broken up with a long-time lover shortly before we had started dating. In some way she felt that all of these men had broken her trust. So, I concluded, she expected all men to be untrustworthy in the same way and had unthinkingly included me.

These thoughts were depressingly familiar. I often had similar ideas about my first wife, and knew such interpretations would lead nowhere. So I began asking myself how I had contributed to bringing about Sondra's outburst. Once I raised that question, insights started to come. I hadn't made clear what I wanted to achieve by my confession. I had left that in doubt. In the background was my own history of broken relationships, a failed marriage during which I indulged in numerous infidelities, which Sondra knew about. And so what I hadn't said spoke loudest of all. I had been acting as though telling the truth meant blurting out whatever happened to be on my mind. Unless I made my intentions clear, she would suspect I meant to betray her as I had others.

When she came back to the apartment hours later, I told her what I had realized. Then I said that I loved her, that I wanted only her, that my dream was to have so strong a relationship with her that nothing needed to be hidden, not even how ample my loving is for others, and that for once I wanted to be so trustworthy that I would break all the precedents not only in my life but in hers as well. I knew my words rang true when the fight went out of her eyes. She told me what she had seen while walking outside — that her reaction came from thinking I wanted to push her away. She realized I didn't really want that. And she didn't want to keep reacting to me as if I was only repeating her bad experiences and mine.

It was clear that the only way to have a trusting relationship was to vow to be trustworthy and to keep my word. She said she would trust me as she had never trusted before. I said I would be trustworthy in the way I had always dreamed I would be. Soon after that I asked her to marry me. She said yes. One stanza of the poem I wrote on our engagement went like this:

> *To commit is not an act but more*
> *a vow to act — not once, but more and more,*
> *again and more, 'til often turns to always*
> *and repeated nows become forever.*

In 1970 George Leonard, who played a key role in launching the human potential movement during the late 1960s, wrote *The Transformation: A Guide to the Inevitable Changes in Humankind.* Though he drew partially on his personal experiences of transformation, the substance of Leonard's book derives from contemporary works by anthropologists, philosophers, and futurists who have been predicting vast cultural changes as global industrialization climaxes at the end of this century and the beginning of the next. Leonard discussed the economic, political, social, and cultural implications of this worldwide transformation. But bringing it about, he insisted, is up to each of us personally, a matter of the stance we take in our own lives:

Awareness *is* the transformation and there is no force that can stop it. Revolutions, riots, strikes and subversion are not required to bring the old order down. It is only necessary that enough people — having established the requisite discipline and order, having faced the pain of change — can bring themselves to accept the intrinsic delight of existence. The most radical act of this age is perhaps to experience four straight days of joy, without anxiety or guilt or regret. [The old] Civilization cannot survive very many such days.[29]

By the mid-1970s, what once seemed to be wild predictions such as these had become more plausible. Reviewing more than a decade of national surveys, Daniel Yankelovich found evidence of a vast cultural shift under way throughout the country.[30] A majority of American adults now hold a view that was formerly espoused only by the intellectual critics of industrial society during its earliest period in the nineteenth century. Respondents to survey interviews said they saw an imbalance in American life, with excessive emphasis on material values and insufficient concern for community, expressiveness, caring, and things holy. By the early 1980s, the shift had become even more pronounced. Almost half the population had moved from merely complaining about the imbalance to doing something about it, by searching for greater fulfillment in their lives.

Artists and writers who had become known for their outrageous assaults on traditional values a short time before were communicating a new and more reverent message. In 1979 William Barrett, formerly an editor of *Partisan Review*, wrote a book surveying, in personal and philosophical terms, some of the seminal thinkers of this century. His book culminates in a plea for the power of prayer:

There may be no more important task for our culture than to rediscover the sense of the mystics. . . . The way back may require from us a kind of discipline and patience that we had not suspected. . . . The mystic reclaims and redeems [the] instinctual source of life for us. We live from the same instinct that keeps the rat struggling in his trap. But who is to say that the struggle of the rat is not holy? Mysticism is instinct lifted to the level of faith and love. The mystic represents that point in evolution where consciousness, a perilous offshoot of the whole process, rejoins and affirms the great flood of life that has produced it.[31]

Transformation doesn't belong to the old left or the old right. Retired military officers are among these carrying the message in human potential and adult education workshops across the country. They are joined by people who once identified themselves as antiwar and antinuke, but who no longer see mere opposition to war as sufficient for global healing. Transformation has overtaken even the nuclear issue. Writing in the first issue of *Evolutionary Blues*, David Hoffman concluded in 1981 that if there is any solution to the nuclear stalemate, it lies beyond politics and economics. "It requires an evolutionary change of consciousness. You might call it an Awakening."[32]

Hoffman applauds the resurgence of activism on the nuclear issue, and the movies and films that depict the horror graphically, not because he wants to stir people's anger against the bomb, but because "Only by thoroughly acknowledging and imagining the 'unthinkable' consequences of nuclear war, can we hope to avoid it."

Hoffman speaks for a growing nonpartisan sentiment that no longer sees hawks in the Pentagon, the Soviets, or the arms manufacturers as the ultimate menace. There is no "them" pushing the world to the nuclear brink. It is a vast "us" — our history, psychology, and ways of going about our lives. "The war exists within all of us: in our fears, our frustrations, our greed, jealousy and intolerance. Mastering the bomb will require an awakening in our everyday lives."

Compared with this message, the antagonistic struggles against communism, war, and nuclear bombs seem shortsighted and bound to backfire. Within a healing perspective, with reverence for the whole, the crucial task is to create the grounds for worldwide healing, to create a world culture that simply renders war obsolete.

Forgiving others, taking vows to uplift ourselves, or giving our lives to service, to God, or to some other cosmic passion, are all ways to draw on a power that emerges as we pursue healing. In healing we open ourselves to the entirety of what is. In that opening we allow ourselves to be at one with a situation, or with life as a whole, and thereby cease to be preyed upon by anything in particular. At such times we say "I'm just being."

Simply being turns everything around. What was previously heavy becomes light. When we take it far enough, the turning cracks open our sense of the universe so we can contemplate intimately the consciousness in which the entire cosmos appears. This isn't consciousness that requires some new belief or knowledge of some theory or fact. Rather, it's the uncanny way of seeing that dawns when we let go, giving up our various obsessions with control and surrendering the urge to alter, manipulate, or explain whatever lies before us. It is like opening our eyes, relaxing the urge to squint and strain, letting ourselves be fully inspired by the presence of what's there.

This turning cannot be seen in the usual sense; it is an instantaneous reverberation with whatever we're contemplating. In such moments the ordinary becomes sublime and jumps back again. Lightning quick, the thing shoots out from nowhere, baring itself for that tiniest moment as naked truth before it retreats too fast for us to fix on anything at all. Only the trace is left, the knowing that our ordinary way of seeing is like a blank-eyed stare, dull and lifeless. And from then on we know we must keep refreshing our gaze in this way or else walk around blind.

When we take a healing view of our lives — that is, by simply being with ourselves — pain too can spring out as the bearer of some secret truth. Some long-lived cause for distress suddenly shifts and becomes a source of renewed confidence. In this way weaknesses become our strengths, mistakes our greatest teachers, wounds the new and sturdier foundation for carrying on. These are enlightening turns, for the burden of living falls away and darkness cedes to light.

Alan Watts referred to his own experience of such moments as announcing that "This is it!" an exclamation that bears this insight:

> Existence not only ceases to be a problem; the mind is so wonder-struck at the self-evident and self-sufficient fitness of things as they are, including what would ordinarily be thought the very worst, that it cannot find any word strong enough to express the perfection and beauty of the experience.[33]

After such a moment an altered approach to life becomes possible. But what occurs in the revealing moment itself? Responding to this question takes something other than ordinary words. Usually we speak in ways that assume unquestioningly that all things in the world are fragmented. Essentially what happens in moments when everything turns around is that we see, at least for an instant, the irreducible intimacy and togetherness of all that is. Moments like these turn living into a ceaseless opportunity for appreciation, shedding life of any sense of conflict or struggle.

In the clarity of such a moment we can observe presence itself as the distinctive quality of whatever's there. When we hear a sound, both the sound and its presence occur at once. A lamp across the room and its presence come into view instantaneously. In short, we see presence as fundamental to anything that is, and that presence has no source, as far as observation can tell, beyond itself.

To observe presence so clearly, we must open ourselves not to anything in particular but to being. We must be present ourselves, at which point we see everything as an eternal reflection of being, of what we are most essentially in that instant. In the light of such seeing, the thereness of all that is emerges freely, joyously, as awesome and wondrous, as shimmering openness.

Moments in which everything turns around are not yet common in our culture. Ordinarily we hold ourselves back from being fully with anything or anyone. Since we can always think of ways to improve on anyone's personality or on any set of circumstances, we don't think of a person or situation as deserving our full commitment. We place more importance on what we can imagine than on what is really there — in short, we go about our lives in a distracted state. Our common underlying attitude is "This isn't it!" to use a variation of Alan Watts's phrase. Rarely does anyone notice that what robs us of fulfillment is our distractedness from whatever's available, here, now, right in front of our nose.

Our most popular ideologies and religions differ only in the form of distractedness they espouse. On the liberal side, people reject the present in favor of an imagined future. On the conservative side, people reject all humanity as flawed and favor an imagined perfection in some great beyond. Conservatives and liberals inadvertently share with all other-worldly and fundamentalist approaches to spirituality a belief that salvation will come only through some medium greater than ourselves, in a time other than ours. All of this is distractedness.

This increasingly common critique of our culture was foreshadowed toward the end of the nineteenth century by Nietzsche, who recognized the pervasiveness of this rejection of the present. Nietzsche went so far as to state that our entire culture is grounded in nihilism, in its refusal to embrace reality as it is, rejecting this life, this world —

whatever is here now. But since what we *become* is finally only a further manifestation of what we are now, life lived in this way is a struggle against ourselves that has no source beyond our own self-rejection. Distractedness, then, is life's great plague. It is the ultimate antagonism, the grounds for all war and conflict, the posture in which human beings live by battling against being, resisting what is, hungering for the fulfillment that we alone make impossible.

The transformation that turns around our relationship with life lies in giving ourselves, knowingly and fully, to an existence that goes on only here and now. We shift to being available for life as it already is. Only when we unconditionally embrace what's there are we present. Only by being present are we able to contend with the challenges that await us.

What does it mean to "be present"? One way to answer is to look in a mirror. Most of us do this several times a day. Notice what you see. At first what's there may seem so familiar that you assume you've seen it all already. If you're like most people, you see your face, how your hair is brushed, and those little signs that are your particular way of determining whether you look good or bad on a given day. After so many years of looking at yourself this way, it's hard to see anything else.

So look again. See if *you* are there. What do you notice of this you? Perhaps you will begin to distinguish certain qualities of yours that are most familiar. Most people, in fact, first notice the features they wish they could change. Maybe you see the things you like about yourself, or you think others like or should like about you. Look once more and notice whether in being preoccupied with these opinions, good or bad, *you* are there.

Imagine now that another person is looking at you the way you're looking at yourself. How would that feel to you? Would such a look give you the feeling of being checked out or judged? Would you feel that the person was receptive to you or standoffish? Would you think that this is someone who is dedicated for life to your care and well being or who feels stuck with having to keep company with a person he or she resents?

Now notice the way your eyes meet the glance coming back from the mirror. What signals reverberate in this exchange? Is this a meeting that has a taken-for-granted quality? Or is there joy and excitement, as in saying hello to somebody special? Is the looking weighted down with attacks and counterattacks, or with jockeying for approval? Or do the eyes in the mirror radiate caring and respect? What's the relationship here, as this looking is going on? Is it one in which you can't wait to turn away? Or is it a welcoming embrace, a moment of recognition that nourishes the life reflecting on itself?

If what's present as you look is less than what you would like, ask yourself what would have to happen for what you'd like to be there. If the answer you come up with implies that you'd have to change yourself in any way, ask again. Ask if there's a way for you to be there fully for yourself as you are now. What would you have to see in order to recognize, embrace, and declare your love and devotion to the humanity that's there when you face yourself in the mirror?

It was by looking in a mirror that I discovered how much I take myself for granted, that the human presence in me has always been blocked from my own view. I've had moments of looking into another person's eyes, being so touched by the beauty of connecting with the presence available through them that tears came. But never had I connected that way with the presence in myself. I usually treat myself as a collection of characteristics or thoughts or feelings, and occasionally as some wider entity, but never before did I recognize that my own presence could be as deeply touching as any I've ever known. I've taken for granted the chilling, distancing blankness that comes with not being present for myself.

This confrontation brought me to ask my own forgiveness again, and to vow that whenever I look in the mirror, walk down the street, get up in the morning, and go to bed, I will open myself to the human presence who's there with me, and acknowledge the privilege of such company. And when I follow through on that promise, I notice that being there makes me more accessible to others. In moments of pure presence, whether I'm working or playing, a "me" isolated from them isn't even here. All of us are just being, together.

☆ 7 ☆

MASTERING EVERYDAY LIFE

[If] a soldier is strong enough, . . . insight . . . may help him gradually win a new relationship to his fellows and to the cosmos. . . . Such a soldier will discover his future mission in life to be as far removed as possible from the destructive work of war. . . . Atonement will become for him not an act of faith or a deed, but a life, a life devoted to strengthening the bonds between men and between man and nature. He will not be in any obvious way a reformer or a social worker or a preacher. But among his friends he will be known as extraordinarily gentle, sane, and wise.

J. GLENN GRAY[1]

If we treat people as though they were what they should be, we bring them whither they should be brought.

GOETHE[2]

HEALING ISN'T COMPLETE when the pain subsides. War has another hold on us, beyond the hurt. Ask veterans at random, "What's the most incredible thing that ever happened to you?" and you'll get a war story. Nothing beats it. In the words of a World War I veteran, war is the "one great lyric passage" in a man's life, or as Vietnam veteran Bill Broyles put it, "men love war."[3]

Most veterans, however, don't come right out and say that they love it. For many it's a dark secret they don't dare admit; for others it's cause for cynicism, the proof that there's no hope for mankind. And for some it's their ace in the hole, the thing they never mention but always hold over the guys who didn't go. The few who do say it know that they're violating one of our culture's great taboos. Nobody should love war. We're supposed to hate it, or at least regret it as a necessary evil. Saying that you love war is always offensive or upsetting to someone and makes everyone else take notice.

Like anything said for effect, the claim that people love war is partly true and partly misleading. What is true is that people love hot action, the chance to test themselves against the worst, to be part of events that sweep them into the center of history in the making. War not only blows people out of their minds but out of their skins — to ecstasy.

What is misleading about saying people love war is that almost nobody says it until their war is past. It only occurs to men to say it after they've been immersed in something else long enough to miss the earlier experience. This is a clue to the broader truth: Loving war does not stand on its own. It's only here for people who hate boredom more than they fear risk, for whom a life of insignificance is deadlier than the bloodiest horrors. Such men never just run off to war. They run away from ennui, from a life of not counting, of no action and slow death.

And so when the excitement of battle, the rich sentiments of mourning, and the preoccupation with lingering pain are gone, what's left? Is it all downhill from here? These are the questions men ask when they see their lives filled with everything they had hoped never to have to deal with — the "not much happening," "I don't count for much," and "one day after another of ordinary bullshit and then some more tomorrow" of everyday life.

Many veterans have a hard time with this life, basically because they decided long ago that they can't hack it or shouldn't have to. Sure they get married and settle down, but they do it halfheartedly, as though real living were off somewhere else. The problem may not surface until they realize they're too old to reenlist and too saddled with responsibilities to go AWOL from their lives.

What then? How do you deal with everyday life, not just to get through it but to thrive? Is there a way of being that delivers us from having to daydream about the adventures of war? Is there an alternative path to ecstasy?

The poet Nikos Kazantzakis asked such questions. He saw the challenge of the modern age as humanity's quest to outgrow war without losing its vibrance. Kazantzakis believed that we need a new myth to guide us through this transition, and felt that, of classical mythic heroes, only Homer's Odysseus was bold and spirited enough to be the protagonist of his modern epic of the human task on earth.[4] *The Odyssey: A Modern Sequel* will be a rude shock to anyone who hopes that human betterment will come through suppressing our raw and lusty striving. Kazantzakis's Odysseus is a cunning hero, a raucous, sly seducer of women, a mighty seeker after experience and truth.

The modern Odysseus has little taste for the tender, classical virtues of a calm and comfortable life. He is unlike most Western heroes, who are controlled and rational, modeled on the Apollonian ideal; nor is he like the Eastern sage who dissolves his ego into the infinite. "He prefers instead," Kazantzakis wrote, "to keep a sleepless vigil and to increase his strength by gazing into [the chaos]; yet he never abandons himself to chaos, for on the contrary, until the very last moment, when Death appears, he stands erect before chaos and looks upon it with undimmed eyes."[5]

He is the hero for a time of vast changes. "Our epoch," Kazantzakis said once, "seems to break the molds in political, economic, and social life, in thought and in action in order to achieve a new balance — a new classical age — on a higher plane; to create that which we have called a new Myth, and which might give a new and synchronized meaning to the world at last. Our age is a savage one; the Bull, the underground Dionysian powers, has been unleashed."[6]

Midway through Kazantzakis's epic, Odysseus comes down from the mountain after communing with God. He no sooner boasts that the Lord is at his side than he hears within him the voice of a mocking serpent: "You dunce, you nitwit, I'm surprised! . . . You're building mansions in the air," the snake accuses. There's no way around hard work, here on firm ground, with the concrete stuff of "wood, stones, trowels, men and clay." The sharp-tongued spirit reminds him that mere dreams don't heal, and souls are forged only from "blood, water, sweat, and tears." Enough of hot-air fantasies and musings on the infinite. "Come down to earth! Let's see what you are worth!"[7] At this point in his journey, the hero turns his energies toward building his ideal city.

According to the *I Ching*, the bringing of heaven to earth is an auspicious moment. When the creative, heavenly powers meet the receptive, earthly powers a blessing descends on all of life. "In the world of man it is a time of social harmony; those in high places show favor to the lowly, and the lowly and inferior in their turn are well disposed toward the highly placed. There is an end to all feuds."[8]

The notion of a heaven on earth is an age-old dream in the West as well. Whether in the form of the Old Testament prediction of a world-redeeming Messiah,[9] or St. John's revelation of a "holy city, new Jerusalem, coming down from God out of heaven,"[10] it is a blessed moment the devout have long awaited.

For the modern Odysseus there can be no waiting, for the struggle is already upon us. He sees not the salvation of man by God but an endless battle. It is God who needs salvation, and we who must do the saving. The modern Odysseus has a vision in which God announces himself as "Your Chief of Staff in War" and tells the hero that man is no longer a slave to God nor a plaything in his hands, or even a friend or trusted son, "but comrade and co-worker in the stubborn strife!" God tells the hero to learn to take orders, for "only that soul may be called free who follows and takes joy in goals greater than he." He also instructs Odysseus to learn to give orders, for "only that soul on earth who knows how to give harsh commands can be my mouth or fist."

The final commandment from this God is to follow his way, a "rough, rude, limitless ascent!" in which each comrade at arms must say, "No one but I can save the whole wide world! Where are we going? Shall we win? Don't ask! Fight on!"[11]

Many of Odysseus' followers are shattered when asked to confront so harsh a command. The hero comforts one by telling him not to worry: Hold on to the words that announce a new human destiny, of men who must save God, and the heavy words will turn to wings that help men soar.

Kazantzakis's epic was published in 1938, seven years before the atom bomb exploded at Hiroshima. But like many before him the poet knew that the only hero we can look to in an age when the human future is in doubt is one who thrives when nothing is assured.

As I studied the interviews with fellow veterans, I noticed a large minority who have adjusted to postwar life. They are generally satisfied with their lives, and most have steady jobs and families. Among them, I found an even more interesting subgroup, probably consisting of no more than 5 percent of all those who served, who have achieved all this and something more. These are the men who live for something beyond the pursuit of comfort, who make a contribution with their lives. For them, the challenges of the war were merely a warm-up for the tasks they see ahead.

My colleagues and I asked ourselves, What allows these men to surmount the obstacles of life so gracefully? What strategies and approaches have they developed for dealing with difficult situations? Whatever the answer, we knew that what these men had managed to do hadn't been automatic or easy. If we had interviewed them earlier in their lives, we would not have described them as thriving.

In recounting their past, most said they were "stuck" before the war, and looked to military service as a way to continue their holding pattern until they gained a clearer sense of direction.

Military life grated on all of them. None of them liked being in Vietnam. Virtually all said they were troubled by the killing. Some were disturbed by what they called the "no win" military strategy, and the blacks strongly resented the prejudice they saw and experienced. One said, "I would complain about the way the brothers were passed up for promotions and given all the shit details and that attitude kept me in trouble all the time." In general, the war raised troubling questions for everyone in this unusual group. As one former Marine observed, "Everybody there did some soul-searching."

After coming home, many of these men experienced difficulties of the sort I've described throughout this book. One reported, "You have to go through a kind of rehabilitation process when you come back. It took me a while to come out of it myself." Quite a few recalled having kept to themselves, shying away from other people. Yet today these men stand out in the way they speak of their work, their future, and the people around them.

These men all regarded their work as something meaningful and personally satisfying. Though none of the blacks we selected had gone further than high school before Vietnam, most of them graduated from college after the war and now hold managerial positions. With few exceptions, these veterans were enthusiastic about their jobs, saying that their work was "fantastic," or "very invigorating, really enjoy it," or "a good opportunity to see how the system works."

As for the future, these men spoke confidently without boasting. They readily acknowledged the difficulties of the past, yet claimed convincingly to have surmounted them. One spoke for the prevailing mood of this group. "I'm not as likely to criticize others for having a different point of view. I'm a warm person now, open to others and generous with my time, not necessarily with my money. But I give a lot and like to show my love toward the world." Another said, "I've reached a point where the things I had doubts about before — career, marriage, family, a house — have fallen into place, I guess through determination on my part. I feel good now." Still another reported, "I was more sheltered, naive and not as worldly as I've become since my experiences in the military and afterward."

As for life beyond their personal sphere, these men spoke openly and generously. One said, "I have hopes for a better world, of people helping each other." Another confessed, "I've got a need to be with people, to help them if I can." A third looked back on his life and concluded, "I've grown more strongly into the civilian community, know I belong there."

How have they done it? My research colleagues and I noticed that these men approach difficult situations as challenges. Some even said as much. "Basic training was tough; it was a challenge." Of Vietnam, another observed, "I was afraid, but I felt it would be a challenge. Whatever it was it would be a good experience."

These men also exhibit a combination of sensitivity and balance that is rare among veterans as a whole. They are not afraid to acknowledge fear. And to an unusual degree, they expressed empathy for the Vietnamese. "They were constantly menaced, having to support whoever was holding a gun to their heads." Other opinions run in the same vein. "The war was having a disastrous effect on their lifestyle," "We were a curse on them," "I felt sorry for them, not that they needed my pity."

Rather than being overwhelmed and immobilized by their compassion, these men sought constructive ways to express it. For example, one of the blacks said, "The Vietnamese didn't receive much respect from the American GI, and I found myself wanting to make up for it, treat them as human beings and not abuse them or their women." An officer recalled how he stayed centered in his tasks. "I just wanted to go home, but most importantly, I had two hundred men whose lives were in my hands. It wasn't a matter of righteousness for me, just survival and responsibility." A former Air Force sergeant described the school he set up to teach local Vietnamese children during his spare time.

Generally these men take pains to cultivate relationships with others on and off the job. They not only make above average incomes after having "worked their way up, " but form lasting personal connections, not just with an intimate partner but with groups of friends they stay in contact with for many years. In addition to work and family life, all participate in community, professional, or religious organizations. And no matter where they go, they find their way to positions of responsibility.

One can read many virtues into the lives of this unusual group. In reviewing what these veterans said about themselves, however, we noted that they mentioned two personal qualities most prominently. The first was self-discipline. One man said, "I got it more together after I came home — it was a matter of disciplining my mind. I knew what I wanted and how to go about getting it." Another attributed his self-mastery to changes that took place in the military. "One of the benefits I gained in the service was that I knew the value of what I was doing and therefore made a point of doing a good job. . . . The self-discipline and the organization was a great help to me."

The other attribute that stood out was the strength they gained from the relationship they formed with death. A black, born to a poor family, said, "When I left the military I think I was a more mature person, with a more stable outlook on life. More competence — before it was more bravado. It was like now I had an experience I had survived, and that helped me overcome a lot of the inner conflicts." Another man put it this way, "The most significant thing in the changes I went through was facing death, looking at it, saying I could die all right and that's it, wanting to make it count after this."

At the turn of the century, William James and Sigmund Freud declared that the historic challenge for humanity was to outgrow the mass fratricide of war. James was not a militarist, but unlike the pacifists of his time and ours, he did not simply condemn war. In his essay "The Moral Equivalent to War," which is more widely referred to than read, he argued that although he had no stomach for killing, some of the virtues associated with warfare are worth preserving, even in a culture in which war is obsolete.[12]

James was also practical. He thought that many people would be bored by what usually passes for peace, and considered it unlikely that we would banish war simply by making life more comfortable and tame — nor should we try, because the warrior virtues not only have dedicated partisans, but form the bedrock of any thriving culture. What community can flourish without the heartiness, courage, and dedication to service that people expect from their military heroes and leaders?

In the vast literature on the treatment of veterans, no author I know of has considered that James's prescription for humanity applies — at least in spirit — to the individual survivors of particular wars. Once we are relieved of the weight of previous war experiences, the appetites that made us ripe for war are revived. The Hemingway who wrote *A Farewell to Arms* became a champion of the Spanish Civil War less than a decade later. And with very few exceptions, the pacifists of the generation that survived World War I helped lead the crusade against Hitler. Many World War II veterans who came home disgusted with war became, soon enough, the antagonists in the moral crusade against communism and the struggle with the Soviet Union.

Prominent among these post–World War II cold warriors was Cord Meyer, Jr. A Yale graduate, he returned from serving as a Marine officer in the Pacific blinded in one eye, his twin brother killed, and committed to building a world that would abolish war. Soon after coming home, Meyer helped organize the American Veterans Committee, and spoke all around the country in support of the founding of the United Nations. Within a few years, however, he became so enraged at communist organizers at the UN and in domestic politics that he joined the CIA and ran the program to provide covert funds to anticommunist organizations around the world. After retiring he wrote a memoir recounting his change from champion of the United Nations to opponent of communism.[13]

Meyer, Hemingway, and hundreds of generations of old soldiers before them went on to fight another war. Was it that they never found an alternative path to ecstasy? William James insisted that the only way to create a sufficiently inspiring alternative was to acknowledge what men love about war. In James's view, the key to any "moral equivalent to war" is service. At several points in his life, James characterized himself as "tender-minded," but in his essay he gave this tough-minded advice:

"I do not believe that peace either ought to be or will be permanent on this globe, unless the states pacifically organized preserve some of the old elements of army-discipline. A permanently successful peace-economy cannot be a simple pleasure-economy. . . . We must make new energies and hardihoods continue the manliness to which the military mind so faithfully clings. Martial virtues must be the enduring cement; intrepidity, contempt of softness, surrender of private interest, obedience to command, must still remain the rock."[14]

James proposed an elaborate system of alternate service, in which young people would spend several years of early adulthood in demanding jobs. There "our gilded youths [would get] the childishness knocked out of them, and come back with healthier sympathies and soberer ideas. . . . They would have paid their blood-tax, done their own part . . . they would tread the earth more proudly, the women would value them more highly, they would be better fathers and teachers of the following generation."[15]

In our time, we would include women with the men, and declare harmony rather than war with nature as the basic collective task. But James's essential message is still apt. "The martial type of character can be bred without war. Strenuous honor and disinterestedness abound elsewhere. Priests and medical men are in a fashion educated to it, and we should all feel some degree of it imperative if we were conscious of our work as an obligatory service."[16]

James did not linger on a point that Freud emphasized during World War I, when he proposed that the confrontation with death lies at the heart of the enduring appeal of war.[17] Like Heidegger after him and like many generations of sages before, Freud asserted that life in peacetime is boring and unwholesome precisely because our culture makes existence a cocoon for avoiding unpleasant truths. We mourn when someone close to us dies, as if we ourselves have perished, because we believe that life is marred by death, rather than completed or enhanced by it. And so Freud contended that conventional existence is impoverished. "[Life] loses interest when the highest stake in the game of living, life itself, may not be risked."[18]

Freud linked war's attraction to the way it sweeps aside this conventional, numbing hedge on existence. In war, wrote Freud, "Death will no longer be denied; we are forced to believe in him. People really are dying, and now not one by one, but many at a time, often ten thousand in a single day. . . . Life has, in truth, become interesting again; it has regained its full significance."[19]

Freud was too literate not to have known about the lives of the saints. Though he did not point to it, there is congruence between his thoughts, occasioned by World War I, and one of the foremost principles of spiritual sages. In the time before secularism swept the

West, Thomas à Kempis wrote in *The Imitation of Christ*, his guide to the spiritual calling, that meditation on death is crucial to a life of inspired service. "Blessed are those who have the hour of death ever before their eyes, and who every day prepare themselves to die."[20]

If life's most stunning quality emerges only when we court great risk, making mortality our constant companion, what does this say of the search for a moral equivalent to war? It may be in vain. Or perhaps we will outgrow war, as individuals and then as a culture, only when we create alternative ways to live as though our lives are at stake. We will have to listen to the sages and learn to live each day at the sublime edge, without waiting for hostile fire to catapult us to the brink.

My work, one of the main events of my everyday life, is talking with other people about the preoccupations that fill theirs. Psychotherapy is my field of action. Responding to the people who come to me for aid is how I explore the way one person can have a life-enhancing impact on another.

Everything I've lived, seen, heard, and read can and does figure in this work. So for me, doing therapy is not too different from writing fiction. For each situation, I make up responses that are truthful only to the extent that they move other people to be more fully themselves.

Two admissions before I begin. First, in the following vignettes I portray myself as effective, and I usually am. But sometimes I'm not; in fact, I sometimes lapse into lecturing my clients, or confusing them, or trying to goad them one way or another. What saves them, and me, is a pained look on a client's face that alerts me more often than not that I shoved some life out of someone I'm trying to help.

Second, Artie Levy lives on in this work. I still traffic in secrets, probing in places where others don't dare to look. I conducted my first sessions when I trained spies in the war, and I'm still at it, only now I work for a different cause. Call it freedom and dignity. I still recruit and train people, one by one, working on the fringes of the battle perhaps, but with a good vantage point for seeing things far and wide.

My cover is that I do this work for a living, when in fact it fulfills my lust and craving. Is there ecstasy in psychotherapy, you ask? Might as well ask about sex. At its best, therapy is intercourse, pure joining, without the goo. It's no accident that Freud's first patients were hysterics, the old professional term for horny women. Freud invented an ac-

ceptable passion, an intimacy no less intense than an affair. The difference is that therapy offers what few affairs ever do: the virtual guarantee that both people emerge more loving, wise, and self-respecting.

Mastering everyday life doesn't mean changing what we do. It comes about through calling up a kind of peripheral vision, a way of seeing in which the routines of life appear as opportunities to serve.

Gilbert was an amateur prizefighter before he got his legs up in Vietnam. Now he runs an elevator in a building near my office, and lives in a tough section of Brooklyn with his wife and eight kids. Over the years, we've grown friendly. One day he dropped by.

"Today I need a five-minute session. Here's my question: How do you handle the depression after your mother or somebody close dies, and you keep thinking about her every day, and even when I go over to my buddy's house, the dishes he's got there are exactly like the ones my mom had. It really gets to you, you know."

He said that early in life she had become "senile" — his word for what mental health professionals call mentally ill. Still, he knew she was devoted to him — that had remained clear. It had meant a lot to him that no matter how spaced out she seemed, he knew she was pulling for him.

"Is she still pulling for you?" I asked.

"In my mind, I guess, if I think about it."

"Think about it," I said, inviting him to pause for a moment.

He stopped and took the question in. A moment later his expression shifted. "You know, it's not just my mother. Someone dies and you gotta think about life. When I dream about space it goes on and on. It never stops. But life has a wall at the end. That's what gets to me."

"You sure that that's what gets to you? None of us actually runs into the wall until it's all over. Could the hard part be what you think about it now?"

"I guess so. It's like I want to be able to look back and see that I really done something with my life. You know, when you're forty-five it's too late to start in."

"What's your gripe about what you've done so far?"

"Me? I'm doing fine. If I died tomorrow it'd be okay."

"Really? If that's true, then why are you upset?"

"Well, what gets to me is having a big family to raise, and lots of bad luck this year, with the house catching fire, and the kids getting in *trouble, the expenses and all that. And then the same old thing, day in, day out."*

"Well, anybody would be upset about so much to handle all at once. But is also sounds like your gripe is that the real thing isn't here yet. Your idea is that only when you get older will you know if it's turned out okay or not."

"Yeah, well I figure it'll be okay again when I can get back to doing some fishing. And then, I tell myself, look here, after a while the kids will all be grown, the pressure will ease off . . ."

"You sure you want to wait that long? Sounds like you're trying to lighten your load by promising yourself that one day it will ease up. And something in you isn't buying that routine. Right now is the problem. It's the load you're carrying right now."

"But I've got all these responsibilities! I can't ease off now."

"I'm not telling you to be irresponsible. I know you got lots to take care of, and that it's not easy. It just looks like you're carrying two loads — all your responsibilities plus the heavy idea that you won't really be living until you're doing something else. You're trying to relieve yourself by thinking there's some reward way off in the future, like promising a lollipop to a kid if he eats his spinach. That trick stops working as soon as you think about somebody who's dead, like your mother, because then you see that there's no lollipop that's going to make it all right at the end. That's why people say that life only goes on in the present. It's right now that you've got to live your life."

"I do that. I only live for today, and not worry about tomorrow."

"I'm not telling you to forget about tomorrow. Sometimes planning is important. You're complaining about missing out on fulfillment today."

"Yeah, it's no fun having to ride that elevator all day long, and then go home and deal with all that stuff back there. Same old thing every day. If you had to step into my shoes —"

"I'd have the same trouble you'd have if you stepped into mine."

He paused at that. So did I.

Then I continued. *"Look, you've got a choice. You can leave your family and work to go fishing, you can keep on the way it is now, or you can come up with another way to relate to it all that doesn't leave you feeling cheated."*

"I want the last."

"Fine. Look around you. Notice who took on the responsibilities

you've got. Notice who was there each time another one of your kids was conceived and born, and who has hung in there to be the kind of father you wanted them to have. And how about the people in your building? What do they think about the fact that you're the first person they see when they walk out of their apartments each morning?"

"A lot of them are glad. A lot of them are real friendly to me."

"That's probably no accident either. My guess is you stick with that job because you've made a whole world for yourself with those people."

I stopped a moment before continuing. "If you want fulfillment now, then it's right now that you need to give yourself a break. The fact is, you're in the same business as all the rest of us. There's not a single person who's spared the main task of life, which is handling the shit that comes along. You can either tell yourself that the real thing, the big juicy payoff, will come some day in the future, or get it straight with yourself. This is the payoff, right now. Handling the shit is what it's all about."

Gilbert smiled. Something had touched him. He straightened up and began speaking in an ironic tone, proud but wanting to show that he wasn't taking himself too seriously. "Who's that guy holding up the world? Atlas?"

"Yeah, Atlas."

"We're all him," he said. He grinned at me playfully, relieved and satisfied with himself. "Not bad," he said.

Psychotherapy itself isn't an alternative to war. The antidote to war, the essence of healing, lies in a way of being with others that flourishes in therapy and is possible outside therapy as well. The key to this way of being has to do with power. Healing draws on and manifests power no less than war does. But it is power expressed through empowerment rather than by domination.

This difference is worth lingering over. In his 1973 study of the relationship between war and power, Professor Geoffrey Blainey reviewed in detail the wars since 1700 and found that fighting doesn't break out for the reasons psychologists give for war's enduring appeal.[21] Leaders declare wars not out of nostalgia for the martial virtues but when, in their reading of events, they conclude that there is more to gain than to lose by taking up arms.

Blainey challenged the major theories that trace wars to various economic, social, psychological, and historical forces. He found that none of these explanations can account for the decisions by national leaders to go to war. Nor can they explain why all wars come to an end at some point. European nations have had alternating periods of war and peace in roughly equal measure. So whatever the prevailing conditions, they must influence both war making and peacemaking, leaving the various theories unable to account for either one.

Like the flawed theories of war, the prevailing theory of peace, Blainey argued, is based on imprecise thinking. After Napoleon's defeat in 1815, Europe was without a major war for an unprecedented several generations. "Those living in the three generations after Waterloo . . . noticed that international peace coincided with industrialism, steam engines, foreign travel, freer and stronger commerce and advancing knowledge. As they saw specific ways in which these changes could further peace, they concluded that the coincidence was causal."[22]

The view persists today among those who place their hopes for peace on promoting commercial and cultural exchange. They forget that most civil wars have broken out in areas sharing a common language and religion. And neither industrial and trade agreements nor rich cultural exchange has prevented the bloody disruption of peaceful alliances — not in the religious wars of Europe, in the American Civil War, in the two world wars of this century, in the communal violence among India's Hindus, Sikhs, and Moslems, in the Korean and Vietnam wars, or in the mass slaughter of Cambodians by their revolutionary compatriots.

As for the materialist theories of war that blame capitalists, dictators, and various social forces or pressure groups, Blainey concluded that these theories explain rivalries and tensions but not war itself. These enmities can exist for generations without armed conflict.

Blainey found one pervasive regularity in the decision making of warring governments. When the leaders of two or more nations differ in assessing their relative power, and the leaders nonetheless agree that they can gain more from fighting than from negotiation, then they will take up arms. When their assessments of relative power come into line, and the leaders agree that more will come from negotiating than from fighting, they begin seeking ways to make peace.

Blainey's view suggests that the basis of both war and peace is a worldwide preoccupation with power — the power of domination. Think for a moment and you'll notice that this preoccupation prevails not only in global affairs; it rules our everyday lives as well. Within families, offices, and between the major institutions of business and public life, much of our daily activity consists of making strategies to consolidate power — by winning allies and by resisting, outmaneuvering, and overpowering opponents.

In recognizing power struggles as the ground on which war erupts, Freud and others have argued that only a supranational authority, one that can wield power over national governments, can put an end to war.[23] The belief that we need a higher, international authority to forestall wars led to the creation of the League of Nations after World War I and the United Nations after World War II. In neither case, however, has the long-sought result been achieved.

Why? Has the shock of two world wars not been great enough? Does humanity need an even ruder awakening? Or could it be that the prescription is inadequate? Viewed from a perspective of healing, the idea that we will end war by erecting a still more dominant power is absurd. The creation of an even more threatening force in the world will only perpetuate our obsession with resisting and overpowering one another. The cure we need has to neutralize the basic obsession and transcend the condition of mutual threat by creating mutually beneficial expressions of power.

The word *power* comes from a Latin word that means to be potent or to be able. Being able doesn't mean thinking or doing anything so much as knowing that we *can* think and act. It is a matter of seeing the way clear to whatever objective we envisage. Once the way to go is in our sight, action can follow, more or less naturally.

What we commonly call power, efforts to consolidate control and resist or overpower opponents, is not an expression of power itself, but of power harnessed to a particular world view. This view of life focuses on what's wrong, missing, inadequate, or not yet right. Within this perspective we see parts and aspects and effects, and then look for causes and explanations to justify our way of seeing as the way things really are. This is the analytical approach, which still passes for high intelligence in our times. Analysis is a symbolic way to demonstrate power over whatever we take apart. It is the essential tool for creating a technology that advances the cause of domination: the manufacture of weaponry and other tools to manage what we see as threats to our way of life.

Analysis, or looking at things so as to exercise power and control, is ingrained so deeply that we mistake the picture it creates for the facts. In this piecemeal view, reality ultimately consists of isolated atoms, molecules, and cells, which can be molded into more complex objects and life forms. In addition to matter there is energy, either gravity or electromagnetic radiation in the form of light, x-rays, radio waves, and ordinary electrical current. These energies are forces that act on matter to produce various effects. Even the most complicated life forms are expected, in the piecemeal view, to react in predictable ways when certain forces are applied to them. The case of fundamentalist religion is another expression of the analytical. Even though God is regarded as the ultimate power, he is assumed to operate like the external forces of classical physics, pushing and pulling on us like a supergravity or superlight.

The technology developed by applying the piecemeal view has produced remarkable achievements — and just as remarkable catastrophes. Industrialization has brought appalling overcrowding and vast social dislocation to many of the world's major population centers, especially in less developed countries. Throughout the world, people are currently using this technology to annihilate whole species, deplete forests and other resources, destroy vast natural areas with acid rain, and kill one another with various environmental pollutants. On top of that we face the threat of a nuclear winter that would obliterate all of life. At best the current technological order is a mixed blessing that has arisen from our belief in a piecemeal view of things and from the exercise of power as domination — over nature, inconvenience, and each other.

Healing occurs through an alternative expression of power, one that creates empowerment. To empower means to enhance another's power, something that happens as others come to see themselves as competent, as not missing anything essential, as already intact. Bringing people to this view is possible only if we see them that way. Empowerment begins and ends with seeing others as already able and whole.

Seeing wholes is a distinct mode of perception. Wholes are sufficient in themselves. They precede parts, pieces, and aspects, and require no external principle to justify, account for, or explain them. Seeing wholes is essential for empowering others and for mastering life as I mean it here.

Some of the most exciting trends in contemporary science express a holistic rather than a piecemeal world view. One such trend consists of mounting discoveries that natural phenomena are not adequately accounted for by the play of external forces. When we are open to seeing it, a creative and self-organizing principle appears to be present even in the most elementary forms of physical and biological matter.[24]

Physicists have found that the highly directional nature of light cannot be accounted for by any force outside the light itself. Chemists have discovered that solutions of inorganic substances will, under certain conditions, undergo a reorganization into more complex substances in ways that are not explained by any known forces operating on the solutions. Biologists have documented the way single cells direct their own self-renewal, and fellow researchers are accumulating evidence that evolution occurs not only through random mutation but through a self-directing tendency that may operate within entire species. Ethologists and other students of animal behavior have observed that subhuman species can act creatively, in ways that cannot be predicted solely on the basis of past conditioning or inherited tendencies.

In other words, across many fields investigators are seeing relationships that accord with a healing world view. According to the perennial philosophy, the entire universe comes into being out of a creative possibility inherent in the universe itself.[25] This self-generating principle is the ground from which all manifestations or "parts" of the universe come into existence as well. Viewed from this perspective, self-generation, creation itself, is the greatest power in the universe. By comparison, examples of domination are merely local and paltry, as when acid corrodes a stone, or panthers prey on deer, or American ways dominate those of another culture. In its essence, power is manifest in making the potential actual, in bringing possibilities into being.

Throughout history, leaders who have sought power through domination and conquest have left their mark. But none has managed to gain so avid a following as those who have sought to manifest power by having others discover their own. Power turned to empowerment, the way of healing, enables others to master living. The ancient examples of Buddha and Jesus, and the contemporary examples of Schweitzer, Gandhi, and Martin Luther King, Jr., demonstrate the power that leads beyond war.

Empowering someone often takes little more than revealing their blindness to the potency they already have. A veteran who recently came to see me looked like a figure out of a time machine: a freaked-out hippie "beamed" from 1969 to 1984, complete with a drawn and skinny face, scruffy beard, long straggly hair, stooped shoulders, faded jeans, and rumpled work shirt. Paul told me that his troubles began in Vietnam, where he had been a company clerk in a chemical warfare outfit.

Things had gone smoothly until one day he found out that the stated policy of his unit was a cover. They weren't just spraying the roadsides to keep our guys safe from ambushes as they went on patrols. The unit's planes were making regular sweeps over the crops in the area. It was a deliberate effort to wipe out the local food supply, to deprive the local Vietcong by killing the crops they would buy or steal to feed their troops. The strategy was to let the peasants tend their rice right up to the last few days before harvest and then spray with defoliants. The pilots would come back roaring with laughter after seeing the farmers double up in their paddies — from the poison or just from the shock of watching months of work destroyed.

Paul became furious over the damage done to the local peasants. A conscientious and sensitive man, he believed in his country but wouldn't support this policy. He went to his company commander and asked for a transfer. Request denied. Then he wrote to higher-ups. Turned down again. Eventually he refused to go to work. His commander sent him to the nearest psychiatrist, a career officer who reacted in an unexpected way. He told Paul that he couldn't call him insane, that Paul seemed like one of the few straight-thinking people around, and that he himself was planning to get out as soon as he got back. He said the real craziness was the war.

Months later Paul was sent home with charges against him. The Army put him in solitary confinement, and then, while being transferred, Paul escaped. On the run, always trying to keep a low profile, he took odd jobs as a typist. He was often sick, always afraid, and very alarmed as the stories about Agent Orange began to appear in the news, since he had been exposed to it throughout his stay in Vietnam.

It was ten years before he met a woman he could get close to. They fell in love, married, and had a baby. The infant developed a strange infection. Paul feared that it was the Agent Orange, and his nervousness got worse. One night while waiting for results from a long series of hospital tests on the baby, his wife had a seizure. She went into a frenzied convulsion one evening at home. As Paul held her in his arms, fearing that she was breathing her last, he went into shock.

She survived and underwent surgery for a brain tumor. But after the operation, she was angry with him over his withdrawn reaction. She kept asking for a divorce, saying that she no longer wanted to live with a man who carried the burden of the war wherever he went. Paul began drinking heavily. His wife threatened to call the Army and turn him in if he didn't grant her the divorce. That's when he stepped up his inquiries about turning himself in. And that's when he came to see me.

"I've only got a few weeks before I'm turning myself in." He wanted me to help him prepare for whatever ordeal he had to face. I asked him if he was ready to let a few hours with me be the occasion for his turning his life around. At first he looked stunned and said he wasn't sure what to expect. So I asked him what it would be like if in the next few weeks we did something together that, by his own measure, was an overwhelming success. He said it would be a success if he could overcome his intense fears of going back.

I asked what he was going to do about his drinking. He mentioned Alcoholics Anonymous and asked me if I thought he should go. I gave the choice back to him by asking if that was what he wanted.

"If I've got the guts," he said.

"Do you? I mean, if stopping drinking is going to make the difference you say it will, will you go to AA and keep going as long as you need to?"

When I put it like that, he finally came to a straight answer. *"Okay,"* he said. *"Yes, I will."*

We went on from there. He said he mostly feared going back to the

Army, but he also feared that his marriage was falling apart. Wherever he looked he saw more stress and was afraid he couldn't take it. He kept asking me if I thought he could handle it.

"What if the main problem isn't the jail, or your wife, or the kid, or Agent Orange?" I asked him. "What if it isn't stress at all, but the idea you have of how little you can take?"

"What idea?" he asked.

I said that he seemed to think of himself as an emotional basket case and to be unaware that everything he'd told me was consistent with that idea. His story, I said, consisted of one calamity after another, with no awareness on his part of his own courage and persistence, particularly the outrageous act of taking on an entire national policy, even at the risk of landing in jail.

"That takes a lot," I said. "The only problem I hear is that you think you not only had to feel for the Vietnamese people, but hold on to your suffering to make sure your protest stayed legitimate. It's as if you think you've got to stay emotionally crippled or people won't believe you're sincere."

His expression eased when I finished. When he came back the next week, he had stopped drinking, begun an exercise program, and made notes of his fears, all of which concerned the military, referred to as "them" in ominous tones. I told him that he was forgetting that half a generation had gone by since he was in the Army. "Your guards," I said, "are likely to be a bunch of kids who were in grade school when we were over there, and if you mention 'Nam are likely to say, 'Who won that war, the Koreans?' " He laughed at that.

In our third and last session I told him to ask himself the question, "What still weighs on me?" and see what comes. Within seconds his eyes filled up. He said it was the strain between him and his wife. He wanted very much to get back with her, but found her anger and rejection of him impossible to handle. I asked him to pause again and to look more deeply, to ask himself what lay beneath all that. His response came quickly. "The night of her seizure. I went into shock. I felt I couldn't deal with it and freaked. I can't even remember what happened. Ever since then I can't deal with things with her."

I had him close his eyes and then guided him, step by step, through what took place. When I noticed droplets at the corners of his eyes, I told him it was okay to cry. When he reached the moment of recalling his terror that she was dying, he sobbed deeply.

Later I asked if there was any part of that experience he couldn't recall. No, he had found his way back to it, thoroughly. Was there any aspect of it he still felt he couldn't deal with? At first he said, "her dying," and we stayed with that. What would he do if she died? His answer came right away. "Take the best care of our baby I possibly can."

After a moment of silence, I asked him if he could forgive himself for freaking out that night. This time his response did not come right away. "I wish I hadn't let her down."

"Do you think you'll be more available for her now if you keep punishing yourself for that night?" I asked. He smiled in recognition. He saw this as another case of the old pattern. What kept him cut off and ineffective was his posing as a basket case.

"I not only can, I have to forgive myself and get on with things." We smiled together this time. Two months later he sent me a letter from prison:

> *Just a note to thank you. I returned to military "control" at Fort Dix. I was able to see my wife and daughter before that, and am happy to say that we've reconciled our differences, are working individually and collectively on our problems, and plan to live together again as a family as soon as the military is through dealing with me.*

In seeing things whole, we recognize power as the self-generating energy that brings the whole into being. Power in this sense is creative rather than mechanical. We attune ourselves to this power not through analytical devices like mathematics or conceptual models but through our aesthetic sense of what is most fitting or called for. To empower is to be creative, a matter of artistry.

Except for the last few centuries in the West, most cultures have expressed the intimate relation between power and creativity by placing art at the center of what was considered magic and holy. Only when the piecemeal view began to predominate was human creativity relegated to a secondary cultural role. A century ago, Friedrich Nietzsche predicted that a potent cultural transformation would occur when creativity is acknowledged as the greatest power in the universe.[26]

Nietzsche wrote that this transformation calls for an artistic approach to life, which is the only antidote potent enough to relieve our culture's mean-spiritedness, our obsession with revenge. Nietzsche linked the prevailing view of reality — the belief that our actions are determined by forces outside ourselves — with our deep indignation, our desire always to have someone or something to blame for the situations we face. For Nietzsche, who wished to "restore innocence" to the world, to "purify psychology, morality, history, nature, social institutions and sanctions, and even God" of the "filth" of this underlying vengefulness, the cure was the holistic vision. Healing comes with the recognition that there is "no place, no purpose, no meaning, on which we can shift the responsibility for our being . . . because nothing exists besides the whole."[27]

The restorative for world-rejecting and life-denying nihilism is art, which manifests creative power and celebrates existence by realizing the potential to create. The artist's great virtue is in creatively confronting the emptiness of a blank canvas or sheet of paper, a model for the way we can approach the stark challenges of life. That we die, that we are faced with annihilation, that everything is pervaded with meaninglessness are all opportunities for the artist to create sense and value.

Nietzsche loved the artist's lusty playfulness. He wrote that in primitive cultures human beings are transported to ecstasy through sexuality, intoxication, and cruelty. In higher cultures, ecstasy is achieved through the aesthetic state. For Nietzsche, beauty is the artistic ultimate, for "in beauty opposites are tamed." It is "the highest sign of power," for in beauty, what seems not to go together is nonetheless reconciled, and "violence is no longer needed . . . everything follows, obeys, so easily and so pleasantly — that is what delights the artist's will to power."[28]

In keeping with this view, Nietzsche proposed a naturally occurring hierarchy in the ways we seek power, evolving from lowly to more noble pursuits. Among the oppressed and enslaved, power is manifest in the fight for freedom. Those who are already free but not fully enfranchised strive for equal rights and justice. The "strongest, richest, most independent, most courageous" seek power in "*love* of mankind, of 'the people,' of the gospel, of truth, God." And so the progression he saw was "Freedom, justice, and love!!!"[29]

To be powerfully human, in the fullest sense, is to be a source of creation, an artist who lives creatively, giving expression to what he or she loves in the broadest spirit possible. "I agree more with the artists than with any philosopher," wrote Nietzsche.

> They have not lost the scent of life, they have loved the things of "this world" — they have loved their senses. . . . We should be grateful to the senses for their subtlety, plenitude, and power. . . . It is a sign that one has turned out well when, like Goethe, one clings with ever-greater pleasure and warmth to the "things of this world" — for in this way he holds firmly to the great conception of man, that man becomes the transfigurer of existence when he learns to transfigure himself.[30]

We empower ourselves by making choices, for in choosing a way to proceed, we are bound by nothing but our determination to follow this particular way. Choice is therefore creative; by choosing, we create a way of being in which we direct our own course. Much of healing, of empowering ourselves and others, involves seeing choices in situations in which there initially seem to be none.

John, a former infantryman who had been awarded a Purple Heart and Silver Star for valor and who now works as a plumber, called me recently. When he first returned from Vietnam, he began having nightmares and drinking heavily. Within months he landed in jail after trying to assault two policemen. While serving his time, he had a vision that God forgave him for killing dozens of people in the war, and he pledged himself to sobriety. After being released from jail, John became a regular member of Alcoholics Anonymous and began volunteer work at a mission in Harlem. On his own, he also went to a psychotherapist for seven years. He came to me because for the past year, after watching a TV program about the Vietnam War, his nightmares had resumed and were worse than ever, and his old therapist hadn't been able to help.

In response to my questions John revealed that in Vietnam he "loved killing gooks," and still has thoughts of "wasting people, for the fuck of it." He also made it clear that he was certain God forgave him, but he couldn't forgive himself and he didn't know why.

I said that he seemed to feel a need to prove himself, as if he believed he hadn't made the grade yet. He agreed. So I asked, "Is that the case you've got against yourself? You're unworthy, and an unworthy guy like you doesn't deserve forgiveness?"

"That's right. I don't think I deserve it," he chimed in.

I told him I saw two problems. One was that he was confusing for-

giveness with bribery, as if it were a reward for being good. In his vision of God forgiving him he had it straight: Forgiveness is not repayment for something you deserve, but a gift, like life or love. The second problem was that he seemed not to trust himself, as if he needed to be unforgiving and severe to keep himself in line.

"Yeah, I never know when I might blow," John said. "It all fits together."

"Ever consider that you might have a choice?" I asked.

"What choice?"

"Well, you can continue like that, and you no longer have to wonder where it will lead — nightmares, feeling distant from people, beating up on your girlfriend when you get so uptight you feel like bursting. Or you can stop playing the charade that maybe someday you'll turn into a good person if you keep treating yourself like a pile of crap."

"How can I just stop?" he asked.

"How did you stop drinking?" I asked back.

"Can I just stop it?"

"Can you? What do you think? What's possible for a guy who's been a faithful member of AA for over a decade, a plumber who would probably cheat himself before he'd cheat any of his customers, a guy who spends his vacation time volunteering at a mission in Harlem? Do you think a guy like that has to keep whipping himself to make sure he'll turn out okay in life?"

"If it's that easy, how come I haven't done it already?"

"I don't know. But one thing's for sure. If you cut the crap and stop thinking of yourself as a heavy, and use forgiveness to relieve yourself, you won't have an excuse anymore for being a prick when you don't feel like letting your girlfriend or somebody else get close. Once you give up the idea you're a mean sonofabitch who's beyond all help, you'll have to admit that you're already capable of functioning fully, now, like the decent human being you always hoped to be."

We covered that ground in a couple of hours, right before he went to work in Harlem for several weeks. After he came back he telephoned.

"I'm not sure what you said that did it, but it worked," John said. "Whenever things start coming back to me I just say, 'Look, I've been bothered by that stuff long enough, I don't have to pay anymore. There's work to do,' and I get on with it. I was just so used to thinking of myself *as a bad-ass underneath, like tough inside, and once I saw it I just had another way to go. People would say something and I'd start to close up, and right away I'd just tell myself to relax, let 'em in, I got nothing to prove anymore."*

Empowerment occurs through communication. In fact, all human communication provides opportunities for empowerment. Ordinarily, though, we don't recognize, let alone capitalize on, these opportunities, because we fail to appreciate the nature of what takes place as we speak.

Usually we think of the words we say, hear, read, and write as names for things — vehicles for transmitting and receiving information. In a sophisticated version of this perspective, one word can name many things, suggesting that people can say or hear words without being fully aware of their significance. This view is the basis of the most common rationale for psychotherapy. Therapy is taken to be a search for greater understanding of the metaphorical meanings of crucial thoughts and feelings. And since these meanings are communicated in words, talk is assumed to be the obvious medium for deciphering the metaphors.

This ordinary view of language fails to grasp the creative power of speaking and obscures the possibility of empowerment. An alternative was proposed by Martin Heidegger and Ludwig Wittgenstein. Wittgenstein pointed out that words are not just names, but actions with real effects,[31] and Heidegger demonstrated how our entire reality exists by virtue of language.[32] As human beings, we are born into relationships, families, communities, and societies, all of which are intricately structured as a result of many generations of the use of language. Speaking creates our cultural environment, and being human means carrying on this tradition. What we take reality to be is always an interpretation, a way of speaking.

This contemporary perspective is based on close observation of what occurs as we use words. Notice, for example, that things are there for us only by virtue of naming them. Before you refer to something by using a word or image, notice if in fact it is there for you. Notice that my writing the words *this book,* and then your reading them, make this book present, or there, for you. But an instant before you read *this book* it wasn't, at least not the way it is now. The thereness of things emerges with the speaking of them. Although things may "come to mind" when no word is spoken, what comes to mind in that sense is always something already spoken of. Only in creating something new is something there that wasn't before. But notice that even with something new, it is never *fully* here, for us or for anyone else, until we express it in some way — verbally, pictorially, or symbolically.

Each moment of speaking, or more generally, expressing ourselves so that something is now here, draws on the human power to create a reality. And when we speak, we also call up a relationship between us and what we speak of, a realm in which we and it exist together. For example, we are the creators of something new when we express it for the first time. When that something is a great oppressive presence in our lives, we evoke a relationship in which we appear as victims.

Insisting on the creative power of language places communication in a fresh light. To communicate, then, means to make common, to bring within our community. Rather than see ourselves as merely exchanging information, we can acknowledge that communicating engenders a shared view of things. In other words, speaking brings into being not only the relation between speaker and what is spoken of, but between speaker and listener. Speaking, using words, creates the connecting presence in which we, our reality, and those who share our world are "there."

What does this have to do with empowerment? People who are "disempowered" say they can't manage their lives. They use words to invoke a reality filled with burdensome relationships, responsibilities, tasks, desires, and obstacles, and portray themselves as overpowered by all they confront. They say they are unable to proceed; life has not endowed them adequately, or events have made them helpless. A new possibility dawns when someone in this state discovers that this feeling of heaviness is perpetuated by nothing more than their persistent, oppressive interpretation or way of speaking. When people cease to portray themselves as unable and claim instead that they are enabled to carry on, empowerment has taken place.

Empowerment thereby arises from a particular way of using language, one that considers talk as much more than the response to implied questions like, "What's on my mind?" or "What do I feel like blurting out?" or "What information do I have to relay to others?" Rather, empowering speech is a response to questions like, "What reality do I want to create here?" or "What relationship with the people and tasks in front of me do I want to bring into being?"

Grasping the creative power of speech is itself empowering. We come to see that what we say matters, that our ways of speaking are prophesies that call forth their own fulfillment, and that ultimately we have the say in how life is for us.

Empowerment doesn't mean "seeing the bright side" or "thinking positively." Often it's a matter of recognizing oneself as able to deal with a thoroughly bleak situation, even when the choices aren't in any way desirable.

When the situation is bleak, those who care for the person in pain may be just as much in need of empowerment as the one they're trying to help. Psychotherapists, for example, often disempower themselves by talking about their patients in the same way that their patients talk about themselves. If this goes on long enough, the therapist will feel unable to proceed, and in this state a wise one will turn to a colleague or supervisor for assistance.

A therapist who works at a nearby methadone clinic telephoned me for help in just such a situation. She told me about her client, a Vietnam veteran who is suicidal, isn't working, and feels terribly depressed. Her problem, she said, is that she didn't know what to do with him. He refused to go to the local VA hospital, claiming that nobody gets help there. So she was calling me to find out if anything was available to help Vietnam vets, if there was somewhere she could send him.

I asked her what made her think she had to send him someplace, since she already had been working with the man and had established a relationship. Evidently he trusted her to some degree or he wouldn't have confided in her so much already. Her answer was that she's a nurse, and she wasn't sure she could handle suicidal talk.

"Your client must think you can handle it or he wouldn't have bothered telling you," I said.

She answered that the vet does think she can help. She has seen him for years and is probably the only person in his life he speaks to.

Again she emphasized that her problem was not knowing what to do.

"*Why do anything?*" *I asked.*

"*Well, he might kill himself.*"

"*That's right, he might. It sounds like you'd miss him if he did that, but if he was dead set on it, do you think you or anybody else could stop him?*"

"*No, of course not. But he really needs help now, and I agree with him that it's all those things that happened back there in the war.*" *She explained that he says he's proud of what he did in the war, that the only problem was when he came home, when a whole gang of people at the airport yelled "Baby killer!" at him, and that he's been furious ever since.*

"*It sounds like he figures that if his life is a mess, all of us who didn't give him a better welcome ought to feel sorry. And so you've got to make a desperate phone call to try to save him.*"

She paused at the other end of the phone, muttered briefly, paused again, and said that I was giving her a whole different way of looking at things. "*You're telling me that he's just using suicide to get people to pay attention, like for being angry he wasn't treated better when he came home?*"

"*Maybe that's it. Maybe not. But if you say that to him he'll probably think you're scolding him. You can try it. But it might work just as well to acknowledge that if he's like a lot of vets, who spent some thrilling times facing death every day, he's just latched on to suicide as the most interesting substitute he's got right now. If someone's not interested in work or anything else, he can at least keep from being bored by spending his days wondering if he should live or die.*"

"*Do you think it'll work to tell him that?*"

"*I don't know. What do you think? You're the one who knows him.*"

"*It might. I'll have to see.*"

"*Good. From what I know, it's worth a lot to a guy if someone who cares about him says something straight. That might be better than sending him away, as if his problem is too tough for you to understand. Can you understand this guy?*"

"*Sure I can understand, but I wasn't sure I could do anything about it.*"

"*What do you have to do? Isn't it up to him?*"

"*Yeah, I forgot about that.*"

"Maybe he's really not sure he wants to live. Maybe he figures that forgiving the world for his lousy homecoming is more than he's willing to do. Maybe he really wants to kill himself. Or maybe he's into spicing his life up with the one thing he's got right now: thinking about death. Or maybe it's that he has two tons of leftover resentment from all the ways the world has done him wrong and he's not ready to let us off the hook. Either way, it's his choice, and you'll probably be doing him a favor if you remind him that he's the one who decides whether he lives or dies. At the very least, it will be hard for him to feel so helpless once you do."

Then I asked, *"Are you able to handle this now?"*

"I sure am."

How do you do it? How does one person empower another? Most people take these questions to mean, "What should I *think* about to make it happen?" or "What should I *do* to make it happen?" With regard to therapy in particular and healing in general, most discussions deal with theory and technique, the common ways to respond to questions of what to think and do. The problem, however, is that therapy and healing are performing arts. Unlike most dance, theater, and music, their purpose is to empower, not to entertain. But the underlying similarity is that discussions of theory and technique usually miss the point, which is "doing it" and not talking about it. For the artist, the creative core of the art is in the performance, and the key question is what it takes to perform masterfully.

A performance is masterful when the audience is moved. Something similar can be said about empowerment: Moving the other person is the key. You know you've connected only when the other person experiences a breakthrough, a sense of possibility where none existed previously. The person's concern may be a particular situation or it may be his or her whole life. But once the sense dawns that the situation is workable, people no longer feel unable to carry on. At some future point they may run afoul of a new situation that calls for yet another breakthrough. But when the needed shift occurs, they'll be on their way again.

In empowering others it's important to realize that breakthroughs take no time. Whatever leads up to and follows such moments may take a while; people may think and talk a great deal, and even suffer extensively beforehand. And afterward they may take still more time to translate the new sense of possibility into concrete actions to accomplish whatever's necessary. The moment of breakthrough, however, happens in an instant: What seemed impossible now appears workable. We are most available to empower others when we keep in mind that "making a silk purse from a sow's ear" or seeing that "shit makes good fertilizer" happens in an instant, and can occur at any time.

Bringing about this shift doesn't happen, however, by telling someone, "If you'd only see your sow's ear as a silk purse you'd be fine." Giving instructions in this way calls up a relationship in which the speaker knows something that the listener needs to heed in order to function adequately — as if the listener is not able to carry on without the speaker's wisdom. Similarly, reassuring people that they're fine or okay may also fail to empower, by further entrenching the speaker and listener in a relationship where the listener is assumed to be "one down" and needing to hear the speaker's pronouncements.

So what empowers? Nothing we do or say, if we regard empowerment as work that must be done or a place to get to, as if the other person were not already able and whole. What, then, is there to do? Essentially nothing. There is nothing more empowering than simply *seeing others as already equipped to handle their lives*. And when that way of seeing is genuine and real for us, and not merely a set of glib assertions, whatever we say or do naturally communicates, that is, creates a relationship in which the other is taken as a fully enfranchised partner in living.

People who cultivate this way of seeing can listen empathically to the most pained account of suffering without losing the sense that the situation is somehow workable. Empathy needn't blind us to a troubled person's capacities to surmount pain if he or she chooses. In the act of listening, people who empower others make the transforming leap themselves; they see what's being presented as workable, and the person confronting the situation as already competent to deal with it in *some* fashion. An empowering shift takes place when one creates ways to communicate this sense of possibility, that is, bringing others to see such possibility for themselves. Empowerment, then, is often a matter of leading by example.

Most of all, empowerment calls on us to be creative. Like any art, it is governed not by rules or methods but by aesthetics. We empower by seeing the beauty in another, speaking and gesturing in response to the natural music and choreography of any given exchange.

Almost every veteran I've seen in therapy has wanted help with intimate relationships. In his own way, each of these men has been deeply committed to individual survival and to the ethos of the lone adventurer who has to make it on his own. For such people, giving themselves to a relationship clashes with their long-standing refusal to let anyone get close enough to pose a threat.

Once these men get involved with a partner, the troubled relationship is not merely the vet's doing. If you look at the relationship as a whole, you'll notice that the intimate partner has certain commitments to controlling the other, to keep him at a comfortable distance. In a troubled relationship, both people struggle to overpower and resist being overpowered, though not usually in overt ways. With dramatic exceptions, most intimate relationships are more like two-man guerrilla warfare than pitched battles.

There are many strategies and techniques for counseling and treating couples. The effective ones reveal to the couple, in one way or another, their underlying commitment to express power by dominating or resisting the domination of the other. Then the couple can see how they prevent intimacy from flourishing between them. The choice always comes down to breaking up, staying together the way they are, or shifting their commitment to mutual empowerment.

To those couples who say they want to shift their commitment and seem to mean it, I usually suggest that they look at their relationship as if it were a mirror. In other words: to regard whatever quality the relationship has for them as a reflection of how they are being at any particular moment. This suggestion challenges the idea that a relationship should be fifty-fifty. In a healing perspective, both parties are 100 percent answerable for the way it is for them. If they look at their partner and don't see a person they feel privileged to be with, who feels loved and respected, they can know that it's probably because they're not treating the other that way.

As unsettling as this suggestion is for many people, the good news is that since each person has access to the whole 100 percent, neither one has to wait for the other's approval to bring generosity, care, and respect into the relationship. Being intimate with someone is as good a place as any to serve as if life were at stake. Here's a test of courage I suggest people try who like to think of themselves as brave: When you're absolutely certain that it's the other person's turn to initiate some openness, flexibility, and concern, assume that you're the one who's wrong.

This doesn't mean that partners always have to say nice things to each other. When the occasion warrants, lovers and spouses should call each other to account. The issue, then, is not what to say or how to say it, but what mode of relating you want to engender by the way you talk. Complaints like "How could you do this to me? I'm getting ripped off, and you're a jerk!" promote antagonism and further undermine the relationship. Firm requests that the other behave respectfully are more likely to be infectious, as in "I care too much about this relationship, and I know you do too, for you to go on like this. It's unbecoming, and I want you to stop now!"

Virtually all troubled couples view sexual problems as part of their difficulty. One of them will say that they ought to be having more sex. From a healing perspective, what they're missing is fulfillment, and they make it harder to achieve by thinking that more orgasms will provide it. They don't see that when sex is ecstatic it is never just the orgasm that does it. The ecstasy comes with giving oneself in a shared embrace. Although you can have orgasms alone or with *any* human being (some manage very well with animals), people seldom bother to do it with just anyone unless they can't be with someone they deeply love.

It's easier to have sex with a stranger than with a long-time partner who's hard to get along with. This is the excuse many people use to sleep around. But as long as they use the excuse, they don't discover that the ecstasy of relating is enhanced when one gives oneself where it's no longer easy.

Seeing clearly, being awake and present, isn't a steady state. Sooner or later we lapse into a blank stare, or blink, and reestablish a clean line of sight only when alerted that our vision has blurred. There seems to be no way to avoid this. Wakefulness grows only if we let ourselves be reminded ever more quickly when we're distracted, and welcome the reminders as empowering rather than annoying. The more willing we are to return to clear seeing, the less it takes to bring us back when we've wandered away. Perhaps all we need is another being, doing nothing more than reflecting back to us the presence we've lost sight of.

Sara is Sondra's and my first child, born the day after I finished an early draft of this book. I was there at her birth, coaching Sondra's breathing, bearing down on her belly for the final pushes, and stroking Sara during her first moments out in the air. Since I write and see clients in one of the rooms of our apartment, I've been on hand to hold, bathe, change, and rock Sara at various times each day, even though it's Sondra who spends most of the time with her.

I was primed by training, forethought, and the example of friends to be an attentive and active father. But nothing prepared me for the surprise I had one bleary-eyed morning a few weeks after Sara's birth. Sondra had left some milk for me to give Sara for her early morning feeding at five A.M. None of us was sleeping more than a few hours at a stretch in those weeks, and Sondra and I often felt worn thin. I lifted Sara out of her crib and poked a bottle in her mouth, almost as if I had been sleepwalking.

I began with the usual small talk, to amuse myself or anyone else who might be listening, saying that it was feeding time, not time to fuss or play. Although I didn't say it, what I meant was that the sooner we got this over with the sooner I could get back to bed. Sara was looking at me with a steady gaze, the kind you never get from a cat, dog, or horse, but only from another human being. And as we looked at each other, I began to observe that I was speaking to her as if the meaning behind my words made no difference. "You're really there, aren't you?" I said. "Even though you don't speak back, it matters just as much that I speak to you knowing that you're really there."

When I said that, tears of sadness came. I realized that I had let myself treat her as some thing to cuddle, play with, change, and bathe, without taking her into account. I could have been feeding a machine or doing any mechanical chore, going about it in a distracted state as if my way of looking at her didn't matter. It was as if I believed that because she was so young and couldn't talk, she wouldn't notice what my gestures communicated — that she was a burden to me.

Seeing all that woke me up and also brought a flash of relief. Already our relationship was self-correcting. Just by attuning myself I noticed mistakes I'd made, even thoroughly embarrassing ones. Ever since then, what I say and do with my daughter, and particularly the spirit in which I do it, matters as much as anything I've ever known.

In recent years many people have spoken and written about the New Man, who should be soft and tender, and should nurture his children. Some have begun to add manly strength to the picture, but they rarely say precisely what that means. For me, what is indispensable in being a parent, father or mother, is the "Count on me!" spirit of a soldier in battle, the willingness to lay down your life for a buddy who is rushing out under fire. Why not at home too? We should refine our notions of child neglect to take into account that anything less than giving yourself as if someone's life is on the line won't do.

People don't need to be therapists or do healing work professionally to learn how to empower others. We can all dedicate ourselves to serve, the one sure way to transform the duties and obligations of life from a burden to a dignified calling.

Recently I began giving workshops for teachers, managers, entrepreneurs, and health care professionals. The purpose is to enable them to use empowerment in their daily interactions — at home and at work, with colleagues, clients, friends, family, lovers, and spouses. Together we practice the art of seeing wholes and of putting that vision to work by assisting others in turning troubling situations into workable ones. In the last of our seven working sessions, we ask ourselves what it might mean to empower ourselves in the face of mortality.

In one of these concluding sessions, people noted that special powers accrue to the professional groups in our culture who confront death as part of their training — soldiers, priests, and physicians. Human beings seem to enhance their power, their sense of competence and wholeness, by looking steadfastly at the aspects of life that most people are afraid to face.

During one session on death, I led the group through a guided meditation for about half an hour. I asked them to close their eyes and picture their friends and family dying, then picture themselves living alone, falling ill, and then lying on their deathbeds reviewing their lives. I suggested that they ask themselves what they will have wanted to do with their lives when they actually reach that point. How will they have wanted to live?

Afterward many of them spoke. One or two who have already been through personal growth workshops said that they are already living the way they would wish from their deathbeds. For most, the exercise was new and disturbing, but strangely revealing and reassuring.

A woman named Jennifer said she realized that her deepest wish is to live lovingly and forgivingly. From the vantage point of her deathbed, all the things she gets petty about did not seem worth the trouble. Her one concern is that she will die without having changed the world as much as she would like. Someone then said with a sympathetic grin, "Well, you've managed to get this far without everybody who's wanted to change you having their way. Maybe the world will make it too in its muddlesome fashion." Jennifer smiled at that.

Wendy spoke next, saying that war seemed to be the great danger. But she added that since many people only become truly responsible for their lives when they start thinking about dying, maybe the whole world needs to be aware of its vulnerability before people will begin to care for all of life. Maybe our ability to obliterate the world, she concluded, will help humanity wake up.

Healing is prayerful. It means seeing ourselves as the pained, fallible, and confused beings we often are, and seeing that being as we are is all we need for living. This is vision, peering into the whole truth, seeing the holy.

None of this is new. What is unique about our time is that champions of healing are emerging in all guises, proclaiming common cause. Ecumenism has acquired new meaning in recent decades. Spiritual and intellectual leaders around the world are now reaching toward a consensus, one that respects diversity and grants validity to a wide variety of scientific, religious, philosophical, and political perspectives that for centuries vied with one another.

Healing advances through openness. This principle applies not only to world views and global perspectives, but to our physical well being. The holistic health movement proclaims the benefits of "opening up" physically so as to "let go" of physical tension. Medical facilities throughout the developed world include simplified forms of ancient meditative practices as part of biofeedback and stress-reduction training. These self-regulative techniques and deeper states of consciousness have long been known in the esoteric branches of all the great religions. Today they are hailed as practical aids in relieving a multitude of ailments brought on by inner strain.

A great visionary once declared that the fullest healing takes place through a wider perception that comes with a renewed sense of being alive. Jesus said, "Except a man be born again, he cannot see the kingdom of God" (John 3:1). What this means is clear only if we distinguish between terms of the spirit and the terms we apply to concrete things. Such a distinction may escape those who are not open to it, Jesus says to Nicodemus, ruler of the Jews. The Pharisee is impressed with Jesus and pays homage to his powers, but asks incredulously and in a very literal-minded way, "How can a man be born when he is old? can he enter the second time into his mother's womb, and be born?"

Jesus tells him it's all right that he doesn't understand, but not to expect further answers to clarify things for him. People who have not yet opened themselves to spiritual phenomena will simply not grasp references to the nonconcrete. Jesus proceeds, however, like a modern-day hypnotist who "uses psychology." After "predicting" that his listener won't understand, the great healer goes on to deliver his message.

Jesus says that people need only recognize their own divine nature. "For God so loved the world that he gave his only begotten Son, that whosoever believeth in him should not perish, but have everlasting life." The literal interpretion of this passage is that Jesus was setting himself up as the sole salvation for the world, that every human being must worship his historic personality as an exclusive, personal savior. But the injunction to distinguish between literal and spiritual meanings applies here as well.

As many "heretics" have insisted, the famous words carry a nonconcrete, thoroughly spiritual message — that each of us is a blessed offspring with the ability to redeem ourselves. Jesus taught that everyone is born into the lineage of cosmic creation, and that we may embrace as the source of our being the openness that gives birth to all that is. It is in that embrace that we enter into ecstatic, timeless harmony with creation as a whole.

How? What is the way? Essentially, Jesus says, it is by acknowledging that the way of truth is already available to us. We were sent into the world not to condemn it but to save it. We have only to turn toward the ultimate source of our being for the way of wholeness to open before us. This requires only that we move toward the light, and not hide in the darkness. What darkness? It is only the fear of the light, he says, our reluctance to recognize that we ourselves are the light. And so the darkness or evil in the world is nothing more than this failure to recognize, appreciate, and celebrate the magnificence that is our humanity.

Literalists seldom appreciate Jesus' claim that he was simply fulfilling the ancient teachings of his people. But an ecumenical reading of biblical texts can discern in his words an echo of the prophesy declared by the serpent of Eden. He tells Eve what will occur if she eats from the Tree of Knowledge. "For God doth know that in the day ye eat thereof, then your eyes shall be opened, and ye shall be as God, knowing good and evil" (Gen. 3:5). And when Moses comes down from Sinai, he passes on the covenant in which the voice of creation declares, "I have set before you life and death, blessing and cursing: therefore choose life, that both thou and thy seed may live" (Deut. 30:19).

The ultimate creative power emerges in us at the moment we see beyond the facades we show the world and all we disapprove of in ourselves and try to hide. When we open most fully to ourselves or to each other, what greets us is the nourishing life affirmation that reveals whatever is present as a manifesting of perfection. In this light, each of us is godlike, and we see that our most natural choice is to engage each task in life as servants of the whole, beings who have come into this world to create expressions of holiness.

☆ 8 ☆

TRANSFORMING WARRIORS

We are all one, we are all an imperiled essence. If at the far end of the world a spirit degenerates, it drags down our spirit into its own degradation. . . . This is why the salvation of the Universe is also our salvation, why solidarity among men is no longer a tenderhearted luxury but a deep necessity and self-preservation, as much a necessity as, in an army under fire, the salvation of your comrade-in-arms.

NIKOS KAZANTZAKIS[1]

The final belief is to believe in a fiction, which you know to be a fiction, there being nothing else. The exquisite truth is to know that it is a fiction and that you believe in it willingly.

WALLACE STEVENS[2]

HEALING FROM WAR doesn't mean pacifying or domesticating ourselves, or compromising our ability to defend ourselves or our country. It is not a matter of purging our warlike essence. This point would be well taken by many former soldiers who, hoping to make themselves good or kind or moral, resist what they see as their base natures. Efforts to banish our raucous energies only substitute an inner battle for the wars with others. The result is futile struggle rather than the well being and integrity of being whole.

Healing is inclusive, whereas whatever we battle against we exclude and despise. And so from a healing perspective, it is self-defeating to try to reject what we see as unworthy or threatening in ourselves or others. Healing occurs as we develop the openness, care, and vision to cast in a worthy light whatever appears before us. Healing asks us not to banish, domesticate, or pacify the warrior, but to honor and cherish him; not to exclude him from healing, but to welcome him to create and play his own unique role.

Inviting the warrior to take part in healing transforms this timeless spirit and makes available to us a power that would otherwise remain beyond our reach. "Transforming warriors" — a phrase that refers both to warriors engaged in transformation and to a way of being that transforms the warrior spirit — is essential to healing from war. What does transforming warriors consist of? What is its relevance to us now?

The Vietnam War was ultimately a blow to the American spirit. Although flickers of revival are apparent, as a people we have not finished with healing.

Vietnam did not, however, occur in a vacuum. America has experienced a bit of the worldwide epidemic that was already rampant before our veterans came back. In the wars and holocausts of the past century or so, we have killed scores of millions of our fellow beings, obliterated whole cities, uprooted entire peoples, wrenched tribes from traditional ways by placing them under national regimes, and yoked whole nations to empires and then to the spheres of superstates. We have warred mercilessly against nature, and for a generation we have threatened our world with apocalypse. No longer is the end of all life a theologian's eschatological nightmare, but a real world technological possibility no more removed than a presidential order.

People differ over when and how the blow was originally struck. Some say we lost our spirit after World War II, when Americans, the people of the dream, abandoned their spiritual calling to become the world's policeman.[3] Others point to the nineteenth century, when industrialization displaced the agrarian America our founders cherished, leaving a "land of opportunity" that thrived economically but became spiritually bankrupt.[4] Still others argue that true spirituality died in the Renaissance, when all of the Western world was secularized by the materialism that flourished with modern science.[5] Some trace the original error to Plato and Aristotle, who translated spiritual truths into doctrines that misled the masses into lumping together whatever is not physical, as if mind and spirit were one.[6] And some say that none of this would have happened without Saul or Tarsus, a persecutor of early Christians, who converted and took the name of Paul, the Apostle of Christ, and did more as a preacher to banish to obscurity the true teachings of Jesus than he did as a persecutor.[7]

The wise among us say that spirit is nothing to hold on to.[8] We are always losing it and always having to regain it. If we have suffered an epidemic loss of spirit, it is because whatever we had, in whatever form we had it, is no longer adequate to the new challenges of our age. And so we are faced with the task that always faces human beings: to embody what is holy in the terms of this historic moment, which presents us with tasks the world has never seen before. This is the proper context for speaking of healing in our time.

In the last decades of the twentieth century, people all over the world aspire to freedom and self-expression as never before. For the first time in history we have truly global markets, instant communications, and international organizations in business, science, and the arts, and even a fledgling parliament in the United Nations. However, the history now taught in our schools only rehearses various forms of provincialism. World history has yet to be written, world culture has yet to be created, and never have human beings posed such a threat to our natural environment and to one another.

The question is, What can we envisage to make healing from war a plausible prospect? What can convert the task from a do-gooder's hope to an objective for which the most dedicated, undaunted people on earth would give their lives?

What we need is an alternative service, one that frees warriorship from its enslavement to the cult of domination. We must give the warrior spirit within and among us a new cause, to achieve victory for life on earth by cultivating the power of empowerment.

One of the visionaries who has issued this call is Robert de Ropp, a biologist and author of several books on the development of consciousness. De Ropp makes the connection between spiritual power and warrior virtues with this prescription:

> We develop [this alternative] power through . . . the sacrifice of our favorite daydreams, our pet negative emotions, our habit of doing the easy rather than the difficult, our vanity and self-importance. This struggle is "the moral equivalent of war" — the Warrior's Way. We become, through this struggle, the creators of ourselves. We become food for a higher level of the cosmic process, "food for archangels." We enter the way of return, which is an uphill path and leads to that level that is rightly ours, [when we do not] waste our energies on inessentials. The kingdom of heaven is indeed within us, but we cannot reach that kingdom if we insist on living in squalid little hells of our own creating.[9]

De Ropp states openly what William James only hinted — that warriors have a crucial role to play in the struggle to outgrow war. We cannot hope to accomplish this without drawing on the energy that has fueled the greatest human projects — the warrior spirit, properly healed and called to a new mission.

☆

Transforming warriorship becomes possible by distinguishing clearly between warriorship and warfare. In the years after Vietnam, people began to say, "We've got to separate the warriors from the war," meaning, "Don't blame Vietnam vets for what happened in Vietnam." Although the slogan was useful in campaigning for veteran benefits, it doesn't reach far enough to bring about a thorough healing. Only when we recognize that warriorship and warfare have nothing necessarily in common can we call the warrior to action without first making enemies or fueling hostility.

Reviving the warrior spirit in this higher sense is what many troubled veterans need. They will come fully to life only when properly challenged, when moved by an inspiring vision. This is also true of professional warriors in our military. Many are resigned to the prospect of future wars, but virtually all regret their predictions. "At best a necessary evil," is what the most dedicated military planners say about the human ritual that has been the most heroic calling since the dawn of history. When war is debased, the warrior spirit can be uplifted only by a new cause to serve beyond war.

The same principle applies to whole nations and to the world. Communities that suffer an absence of spirit will be roused not by condemning, repressing, or banishing the most exuberant human energies, but by directing those energies to a dignifying and ennobling purpose. Thus the treatment of veterans, the recovery of national spirit, and the historic challenge of creating a global culture demand a common vision: the possibility of transforming warriors, of turning our appetite for power to the creation of empowerment.

How does one become a warrior? From what I know, warriorship is passed like a baton. Someone holds it out for another to grasp. I took it from my father. He bought me a pair of boxing gloves when I was four, and in those years he'd come home from work and ask me if my room would pass inspection. I knew what this meant from pictures around the house of his Navy days during World War II. One of them showed him reviewing new recruits during morning inspection. I had to pass inspection too if I wanted to stay up late and watch the Friday night fights on TV with him.

Another of the pictures showed my father shaking hands with his commanding officer, Gene Tunney, the famous prizefighter who was put in charge of organizing the Navy's physical fitness program. My father and several professional athletes were Tunney's wartime team. My father showed me the calisthenics they did then — I'm still really good at "cals." And he also taught me the spirit of training for war. "What if somebody gave you an order and people's lives depended on the way you followed it?" he'd ask.

He also taught me to play ball — baseball and especially football. He didn't talk much about his life, but from the time I was very young I knew one thing: He was a good athlete, good enough to teach physical education at the University of Pennsylvania in the 1930s and 1940s, but he never got to play football. His mother wouldn't let him. She had lost one son to a cerebral hemorrhage when he was twelve, and she wasn't about to lose another. The school I went to had football teams starting in fifth grade, and we competed with a half dozen other schools in the same league. My father loved to watch me play, and was so full of pride he could barely talk when I made Little All-American at age thirteen.

When I was a teenager, he and I stopped speaking. I was struggling to break away, and would sneak out of the house when I wasn't supposed to, smoke, and come home from dates with liquor on my breath. I was sullen toward him and he had no stomach for it. Neither of us seemed able to get through to the other for years — years that were hard for him at work. He had left teaching to go into sales, and wasn't making it big. It was only after a personal crisis that he went back to his first love, teaching kids.

After college, when I was in Europe for the summer, I wrote home asking my parents to support me for the following year while I stayed on in France and Germany. I said I needed to learn languages and study international relations, implying what I couldn't say outright, that I wanted to find myself. My father was the one who answered. "Follow your star," he wrote, as fine a blessing as anyone ever gave me.

We could talk again after that. The day I left for Vietnam I said to him, "Don't worry. I'm going to be one of the ones who come back." "I know," he said. When I did return we grew very close. He knew I knew something, and I knew he could see it in my eyes. On a Saturday afternoon soon after coming home I said something to him that I had never said straight to anyone else: "I love you." He would never cry, but he got teary when I said it. And he said it back.

A few years later he had a heart attack. While he was recuperating he prepared a talk on heart disease for all the faculty of his school. I helped him by getting some information from the library. Over the phone he and I would discuss his talk, the points he wanted to make about exercise, diet, stress, and what I thought he should add about psychological attitude. He recovered enough to go back to work, only to have a relapse a few weeks later. His heart was in bad shape, so the doctors decided to do a bypass operation. He died in surgery, which the doctors called "going down fighting."

I decided to give his talk for him. I went to his school on the appointed day and spoke to the whole faculty for an hour, the first time I ever gave a lecture to eighty people. I kept having the image of picking up my father's sword, after he had fallen, and charging on. He would've loved that. As my personal goodbye, I went through his belongings. I didn't want much — only his hair brushes, because they still smelled from him, and the sword he wore with his dress whites in Navy parades. Those were the years I was marching against the war, and I had no way to say why that sword was so important to me. Now I do. I'm a warrior's son, carrying the baton.

In earlier times, warriorship had an exalted meaning. According to medieval orders in both the West and East, the men of the nobility were trained as warriors and mastered codes of chivalry and honor. Throughout the world, the warrior-hero was one who gave his life to serve others, guided by a supreme intelligence. Homer's hero in *The Odyssey* was the "wiliest of men," whose mentor was Athena, the goddess of wisdom. The *Bhagavad Gita,* one of the ancient holy books of India, tells of the warrior-hero Arjuna, whose trembling in battle is calmed by direct teaching from the heavenly Lord Krishna.

Soldiers and veterans have no exclusive claim on the warrior spirit in this larger sense; the taste for action and enlightened service lives in everyone to some degree. Kazantzakis, the poet who served as a minister in his nation's government, wrote toward the end of his life: "The more I examine myself, the more I discover this psychological truth: that no one lifts his little finger to do the smallest task unless moved, however obscurely, by the conviction that he is contributing."[10]

For a decade and a half appreciation for the qualities of warriorship has seeped into our culture through the books of Carlos Castaneda.[11] Written as anthropological studies of native American culture, the narrator tells of his apprenticeship to Don Juan, a sorcerer in the Southwest. From his mentor, Castaneda learns the "higher knowledge" of living. Among the many requirements are these: to cultivate extraordinary respect for all beings including himself, to deal constantly with fear, to develop extreme vigilance and wakefulness, and to grow in self-confidence. Don Juan called a man of such knowledge a warrior.

The warrior of poetry and metaphor is a spiritual master who has nothing essentially to do with brutality or shedding blood. In *Tales of Power* Castaneda wrote: "The basic difference between an ordinary man and a warrior is that a warrior takes everything as a challenge while an ordinary man takes everything either as a blessing or a curse."[12] The difference is more than an altered attitude. The warrior's calling is to cultivate the ultimate human strength: the capacity for love and joy, honed in the face of adversity.

A warrior doesn't ask for an easy life. In Kazantzakis's epic, the modern Odysseus no sooner builds his ideal city than it is destroyed by volcanic fire and ash, his comrades scattered by dissension and death. Without flinching, the hero continues his quest. Eventually he sees that a strong man doesn't need fear or hope or deliverance in some great beyond. He bows to no idol and worships no distant being, but lives "To stare into the black eyes of the Abyss/with gallantry and joy as on one's native land." Kazantzakis explained the achievement of his hero's liberation. "Toward the end Odysseus' religion became unshakable, so that no idea or act could any longer tear it down — because, indeed, it was based on the Void; neither God, nor hope, nor fear, nor eternity. Every moment was itself deathless, and he had no need of any other deathlessness. He lived every moment intensely, with quality."[13]

Kazantzakis took his instruction in part from Nietzsche, who proclaimed a future time when everyone would share the insights formerly achieved only by the few and the great. Nietzsche remarked that the rare sages of every era who had attained this wisdom, seemingly by accident, actually held themselves answerable for the state of the world. It was Nietzsche who saw that freedom from illusion doesn't produce nihilists, but creators of a fulfilling human destiny:

"The exemplary life consists of love and humility; in a fullness of heart that does not exclude even the lowliest; in a formal repudiation of maintaining one's rights, of self-defense, of victory in the sense of personal triumph; in faith in blessedness here on earth, in spite of distress, opposition and death; in reconciliation; in the absence of anger; not wanting to be rewarded; not being obliged to anyone; the completest spiritual-intellectual independence; a very proud life beneath the will to a life of poverty and service."[14]

Nietzsche saw this healing as opening the possibility for a new order of being. "In the end there appears a man, a monster of energy, who demands a monster of a task."[15] And that task is nothing less than full responsibility for life, for healing the world.

It is not clear whether Castaneda read Nietzsche. But the great master of *Tales of Power* instructs his apprentice in similar tones. "Only if one loves this earth with unbending passion can one release one's sadness," says Don Juan. "A warrior is always joyful because his love is unalterable and his beloved, the earth, embraces him and bestows upon him inconceivable gifts. The sadness belongs only to those who hate the very thing that gives shelter to their beings."[16]

In his book, addressed to "The Saviors of God," Kazantzakis gave instructions to those who would be warriors in this higher sense. "Only he has been freed from the inferno of his ego who feels deep pangs of hunger when a child of his race has nothing to eat, who feels his heart throbbing with joy when a man and a woman of his race embrace and kiss one another. All these are limbs of your larger, visible body. You suffer and rejoice, scattered to the ends of the earth in a thousand bodies, blood of your blood. Fight on behalf of your larger body just as you fight on behalf of your smaller body. Fight that all of your bodies may become strong, lean, prepared, that their minds may become enlightened, that their flaming, manly and restless hearts may throb."[17]

"Transforming warriors" doesn't mean doing anything to anyone. It's not a matter of changing people from one form to another, as in putting bread dough in an oven until it's baked. Transforming warriors "resets the jewels of military virtue,"[18] to use Arnold Toynbee's phrase, regrounding warriorship so that a possibility is opened, just as revelation casts the world in fresh light. It is an alternative life service that brings the warrior virtues of courage and commitment to a new challenge. Instead of fighting as partisans we champion the whole — all that is, being itself.

This is not an instruction to strip people of their peculiarities and shortcomings. It is simply a choice to use ourselves, foibles and all, to serve healing. Setting aside the weaponry of the soldier, we turn ourselves to hone the vision of spiritual masters. This is not a vision in the sense of some lofty dream, but rather the clear-sightedness of looking beyond our illusions, to gaze directly in the face of what is.

Seeing of this order is transformative. It is the recognition that everything appears by virtue of the openness that allows it to be. In such moments of seeing there is no looker or object looked at, but only the seeing, which encompasses all that is there and brings the whole into view. Seeing things whole occurs only when one has taken a stance of "no position," of "nothing kept out," of "everything included." It is a stance that calls for courage and commitment of a magnitude beyond what is expected even from the bravest fighter.

The supreme challenge of this posture is that being open, holding "no position," means that one is vulnerable — not the vulnerability of one who is supersensitive and fearful, but the vulnerability of one who has nothing to hide, nothing to protect, and nothing to shield it with. The ancient sages grasped this possibility centuries ago. The Buddhists call it fearlessness. Embracing vulnerability is more clearly than ever a practical response in the age of nuclear weaponry.

Our worldwide obsession with defense has brought us to the point at which defensiveness threatens rather than makes us secure. And the only intelligent response, now as ever, is to enlighten ourselves to live in the face of the ultimate threat: that our own carelessness, pettiness, distractedness, or lack of generosity and forethought can, at any moment, destroy us. In a world of massive nuclear arsenals humanity has nowhere to hide, no way to defend against attack, and no way to preserve life other than to avoid attack and counter-attack.

In this context, taking "no position," although not partisan, is also not politically neutral. Seeing the situation whole reveals as absurd the widespread preoccupation with weaponry in our time. "Peace through strength" and "peace through disarmament" are mirror images of the same nearsightedness. We will have neither

peace nor security with more weapons or with less. Life is dangerous now, and always will be, because we are always capable of
blindness and of the vile deeds we commit when we fail to see clearly.
The only recourse we have is to cultivate clarity and exercise vigilance. In order to see that we have no other choice, we must give up
the ultimate illusion born of distractedness — hope of something
better — and embrace the present situation as if life depended on it.
For surely it does.

Warriors transformed in spirit have reappeared throughout history.
Twice in the Old Testament, in the books of Isaiah and Micah, appear the words, "They shall beat their swords into plowshares."[19]
Jesus championed this prophesy in his Sermon on the Mount, in
which he proclaimed, "Blessed are the peacemakers."[20] The war-
rior-knight inspired by spiritual service is found in the Arthurian
legend of Sir Galahad, the knight who searched for the Holy Grail.
    During the Middle Ages, soldiers returning to Europe from the
Crusades helped build the great Gothic cathedrals of Europe. The
Knights Templar, the secret order they founded, flourished briefly
before many of its members were persecuted and killed. They were
branded as heretics because they embraced a spiritual rather than
literal version of the Christ story. According to one historical interpretation, the Knights Templar went underground, surfacing again
in the Age of Enlightenment as founders of Freemasonry.[21]
    Spiritual warriorship is a common notion among Protestants, who
sing "Onward Christian Soldiers!" A similar inspiration took hold
in the Catholic church after the embarrassments of the Reformation,
when the church sponsored the Society of Jesus, known as the
Jesuits, to recruit "warriors for Christ." Their mission was to help
purify and strengthen the ailing church hierarchy. In the nineteenth
century, an innovative version of the "Christian soldier" spirit became the basis for a worldwide movement to redeem wayward souls
by recruiting them into the Salvation Army.
    Examples of transformed warriors also appear in the history of the
East. In the third century B.C., India had a mighty ruler named Asoka,
whose vast conquests consolidated virtually all of the subcontinent.
At the height of his last battle, Asoka came upon a river turned red
with the blood of the dead. In horror at what he had done, Asoka

surrendered his sword and dedicated himself to the principles of nonviolent coexistence. In the years that followed, he helped spread Buddhism, which had previously been a minor religious movement, throughout the Indian subcontinent.[22]

Japan provides a more contemporary example. In the sixteenth century, the rise to power of a particularly adept ruler, the first of the Tokugawa shoguns, brought an end to a long period of bloody civil wars. For more than two centuries after the Tokugawa ascendance, war was banished. The warrior class, known in the West as the samurai, still wore their swords, but large-scale fighting was forbidden. By this time, Japanese gunsmiths had begun making some of the world's finest weapons. But once the Tokugawa abolished war, the manufacture and use of firearms began to diminish and then ceased.[23]

During these two and a half centuries, the exacting training for war given to the children of the samurai class shifted in emphasis to preparation for an exemplary life of peace. The practices included in this peacetime training come down to us today as the Japanese martial arts. Previously the focus had been on the various combat techniques such as *kenjitsu* or sword fighting and *jujitsu* or hand-to-hand combat. When war was banished, these techniques served as vehicles for studying "the way of life," expressed by the Japanese word *do*, derived from the Chinese word that we write as *tao*. And so, *kenjitsu* became *kendo* and *jujitsu* became *judo*, and the most refined martial arts became a form of spiritual training.

During this time without war, the 5 percent of the population who were the warrior class became the nation's administrative elite. It was a time when the Japanese people were more productive, artistically creative, healthy, and prosperous than at any previous point in their history. In the texts that schoolchildren read, this period is often called a golden age.

This development in Japanese society, although sudden and relatively brief, had roots that ran deep in that culture. The Japanese word for warrior is *bushi*. The second syllable, *shi*, means man. The first syllable, *bu*, is usually translated into English as martial, or warlike. Beneath the common and literal translation, however, lies the original meaning. The Japanese (and Chinese) character for *bu* is formed by two parts, one representing "weapon" and one "stop."

The spirit of *bu* is thus to stop or neutralize the effect of weapons.[24]

In the last decades of the nineteenth century, the Japanese quickly remade their society into an industrialized world power. In 1905 Inazo Nitobe, a Westernized Japanese, published an influential book that attributes the Japanese feat to the influence that the warrior spirit exerts in Japanese culture.[25] Nitobe explained that *bushido*, the "way of the warrior," is inculcated in Japanese education. "Scratch a Japanese of the most advanced ideas," wrote Nitobe, "and he will show a samurai."

At the end of his book, Nitobe made this prediction for the future of this tradition: "Bushido as an independent code of ethics may vanish, but its power will not perish from the earth; its schools of martial prowess or civic honor may be demolished, but its light and glory will long survive their ruins. Like its symbolic flower [the chrysanthemum] after it is blown to the four winds, it will still bless mankind with the perfume with which it will enrich life."[26]

While traveling recently in Japan, I asked educated people I met, including Suichi Kato, a well-known social and literary critic, whether this was still true — that the dedication of the Japanese worker, the craftsmanship, and the tremendous energy of Japanese enterprise were modern reflections of the *bushido* tradition. Kato offered two cautionary remarks before answering. First, he said, I should not confuse the honor of *bushido* with the militarism that led to Japanese atrocities and violence before and during World War II. Second, he warned me against idealizing Japan, as so many Americans have done lately, for Japan has immense social and political problems. After these qualifying remarks, he then said, "Yes. In the heart, every Japanese wants to live as a samurai."

Transformed warriorship is not new to the American experience. The first European settlers who came to America in the early 1600s included various religious groups who had left their homes to build a new world. In Europe it was a time of social turmoil and change. Spiritual renewal was widespread, as followers of Luther, Calvin, and others carried the message of reform, a spirit that roused pilgrims to set out to create their various "New Jerusalems."

William Penn founded the most prosperous of the early colonies, which offered its principal city as the first capital of the new nation.

Penn's father had been a famous admiral, and it was on his account that the king of England had deeded property in the New World. Few American history books note that William Penn served in the British military before he came under the influence of George Fox, founder of the Religious Society of Friends, the Quakers.

Philadelphia Quakers later became known for their shrewd business practices, and in recent times, the nickname Keystone State has come to denote Pennsylvania's role in the industrialized Northeast. In 1683, however, Pennsylvania took shape from William Penn's bold vision to establish a "holy experiment" on his lands in the New World. Before he set sail from England, Penn mapped out a strategy that eventually made Pennsylvania the most tolerant and desirable of the original colonies, a melting pot of different nationalities and religions. Penn began by establishing relations with the native Americans on a basis that was unheard of in his time.

In the seventeenth century, native Americans were stranger and more threatening to the European settlers than any foreign group is to us today. They had bizarre religious practices, including the ingestion of urine and fecal matter. Their languages were unintelligible, and their indulgence in such barbarisms as scalping convinced most colonists that armed defense was the best strategy for dealing with them. Aware of colonial attitudes and of the famous massacres of colonists in Virginia and elsewhere, Penn was determined to make a treaty with the Indians that would establish a lasting and equitable peace.

And that is what he did. Both sides kept the terms of the treaty, which required unusual effort on Penn's part to resist British policies that called for armed defense. Although wars between settlers and natives were common throughout the other colonies, Pennsylvania lived in peace for as long as Penn's principles held — for several decades after his death in 1718. At that time, under the pressures of the French and Indian wars and of the mounting influence of non-Quaker immigrants who thought no Indian should hold land that a Christian wanted for himself, the Quakers were outvoted and resigned from the colonial government.

Many people proudly cite the tradition of religious tolerance in America without realizing that it was the Quakers who fought nonviolently in a life and death battle to achieve it. Initially tolerance was not practiced throughout colonial America. The original settlers of Boston were Puritans who adhered to strict Calvinist doctrines, and branded as heretics anyone who espoused more "free thinking" religious principles. A series of visits by Quakers campaigning for greater openness — we would call them nonviolent protesters — provoked the early Bostonians, who tried to banish the intruders. Many of the visitors were beaten bloody in public and a few were hanged before the English king was alerted to their plight. Spurred on by Quakers, the king issued the edict insuring religious freedom in the New World.[27]

Penn's "holy experiment" was the realization of a dream that men and women of vastly different backgrounds, beliefs, and ways of life could build a community where all would thrive. North Americans of every political stripe now revere this facet of our heritage. As the authors of a book-length listing of organizations dedicated to ending war conclude: "The United States is the world's first urban, industrialized, multi-racial, multi-ethnic society. Because a world society with similar features is in the making, the ability of democratic institutions in this country to process change without the violence of war remains an experiment of vital significance."[28]

Mohandas Gandhi is the best known contemporary example of a warrior's devotion to a cause beyond war. For almost half a century, Gandhi led the movement for India's independence from the British Empire. His approach for resolving conflict has been schematized in *Fighting with Gandhi*.[29] The Gandhian battler steadfastly engages his opponents, but without antagonism and without intending to violate the other's physical, mental, or spiritual well being. The fight then becomes more creative than destructive, a vehicle for former adversaries to achieve a satisfactory way to coexist.

In another book, Michael Nagler cites numerous examples of the effective use of alternatives to violence in daily life and among nations. Nagler repeatedly emphasizes the difference between the well-intentioned but ineffectual alternatives and those that have been highly successful. Of the latter, he points out, "It is sometimes overlooked, behind the glamour of Gandhi's personality and the drama of the Indian situation, that fifteen or twenty years of dogged, almost military discipline lay behind the conversion of ordinary Indian women and men into an irresistible flood of love that broke down the barriers of imperialism.''[30]

During the Boer War, Gandhi served enthusiastically as a sergeant in the British Medical Corps. He thrived on the discipline, daring, and challenge then as he did throughout his life. This warrior quality is often ignored by pacifists who admire Gandhi. Unfortunately many attempts to follow his example have broken down for lack of discipline, as did the South African resistance led by Albert Luthuli in the 1950s. Cohesion and steadfastness faltered there, and the horrid Sharpeville massacre put a stop to the movement.

Many young Americans practice transformed warriorship through training in martial arts. Although martial arts were virtually unknown two decades ago, there is hardly a child in America today who doesn't know someone studying in a *dojo* not far from where he or she lives.

The art I know from personal study is *aikido*, which was developed in the years after World War I by Morihei Uyeshiba, a Japanese master. He was determined to perfect a discipline in which the self-defeating nature of muscular force and physical domination is clearly revealed. In their place, the practitioner invokes the knowledge that "the only opponent is within" by perceiving the universe as an interconnected whole, in which disturbances initiated in one location send ripples that rebound everywhere. The most effective way to neutralize an attack is to discover how to make it benign without adding new aggression. This is not the pacifist's way of noninvolvement. It is a master strategist's way of responding effectively with the least effort.

Service to universal energy isn't just an idea, for included in the *aikido* practice is regular training in a powerful meditative state. Attention is focused on the midpoint of the body, two inches below the navel, in a way that invites awareness to radiate outward in all directions, to infinity. The challenge is not simply to relax but to cultivate this centered state in the midst of high-speed action.

Through this discipline students learn to distinguish between force and power. Force is muscular strength exerted against an intrusive resistance applied by another, whereas power arises from generating an energy field that surrounds the intrusion and allows one to redirect an opponent's thrust. To an *aikido* master there are no attacks, only invitations to dance.

Aikido serves as a metaphor for an enlightened way of responding to any threat. In the face of attack our biologically given options are either to fight or to run away. Reason adds the possibilities of doing nothing or trying to talk or trick our way out. The *aikido* alternative is the way of the enlightened warrior, who brings disturbances into harmony with the whole situation rather than trying to win by making another lose.

In a recent self-help book, Terry Dobson, a black belt practitioner of *aikido*, included many examples of everyday interpersonal challenges and various responses inspired by *aikido*.[31] He describes the practical philosophy behind this approach:

> Nature . . . is full of conflict. But, look around you. You won't find a scoreboard. Who, for example, is the winner in cell division? Who is the loser when wind and water clash to create an awe-inspiring wave? Are we winners or losers when gravity clamps down on us, forcing us to stay put? Face it: You've been sold a bill of goods. It's normal to want to win, but you've been led to believe that you must win or lose every conflict in life, and that just isn't so.[32]

The first step to mastery is to "stop seeing everything as a contest, which by definition must have a winner and a loser."[33]

Contemporary examples of transformed warriors are growing more numerous. One is the decorated British fighter pilot, actor, director, and producer Sir Richard Attenborough, who devoted twenty years to making a film of the life of Gandhi. In hopes of outlawing war, thousands of Attenborough's fellow veterans of 1945 worked to establish the United Nations. Successful in some of its efforts to promote social, economic, technological, and educational development around the world, the UN has so far failed in its principal mission. But if the human race survives, we will do so by following those who champion the cause of outgrowing war.

"For years I have believed that war should be abolished as an outmoded means of resolving disputes . . . and my abhorrence reached its height with the perfection of the atom bomb."[34] These words were not spoken by some tender heart, but by a warrior of the first rank, General Douglas MacArthur. The most progressive recommendation to date on the disposition of the atomic bomb — to put it "into the hands of those who will know how to strip its military casing and adapt it to the arts of peace" — was made in 1953 by another former general, President Dwight Eisenhower.[35] And one of the clearest statements of the challenge posed by the global conflict between the United States and the Soviet Union was made in 1957 by the "soldiers' general" of World War II, Omar Bradley: "It may be that the problems of accommodation in a world split by rival ideologies are more difficult than those with which we have struggled in the construction of ballistic missiles. But I believe, too, that if we apply to these human problems the energy, creativity, and the perseverance we have devoted to science, even problems of accommodation will yield to reason."[36]

California is the bellwether for cultural change in North America, the place where the "awareness movement" got its start and where martial arts are flourishing. At this writing, one authority estimates that there are now ten thousand *aikido* students in the San Francisco area alone.[37]

One man who has been influential in popularizing *aikido* and many other approaches to heightened awareness is George Leonard, a decorated fighter pilot in World War II. Leonard rose to national prominence as a writer for *Look* magazine in the 1950s and 1960s. Since then, he has led consciousness-training workshops around the country and written numerous articles and books celebrating the virtues of humor, intelligence, and passionate dedication to a humane world. Leonard, who received his black belt in *aikido* at age fifty, declares that ecstasy, truly joyful living, *is* possible for human beings to achieve — whenever we venture in body, mind, and spirit, beyond the cocoon-like limits of conventional approaches to life.

In an interview for this book, Leonard said, "We're living in a famine of feeling, and we desperately need some enterprise that's compelling enough so that we won't have to go to war, take drugs, or commit a crime in order to feel alive. People haven't acknowledged this compelling quality of war. And the pity of our conventional ways of living and organizing social existence foreclose that kind of exquisiteness. Traditionally, people have only been able to find it close to horror and killing. Only now that warfare is so unacceptable, we're going to have to make peace vivid. That's the transformation.

"My friend Leo Litwak saw this back in the late 1960s. He's a close friend, my age. His father was a labor leader, and Leo was a medic in World War II, followed Patton's troops all across Europe, the worst campaigns, a real miracle that he lived through it. He still says that the smell of a cup of coffee in the middle of Germany is far more real and vivid than anything else in his early life. It's really striking that a man like that says that only one other experience is so real. It was an encounter group at Esalen, an adventure in being alive and awake. Leo wrote about this 'joy' in a long piece in the Sunday magazine of the *New York Times* in late 1967.

"To top that kind of thing, you have to live as a warrior. That doesn't mean killing and being shot at. You can do it washing dishes, as long as you know what it means to challenge yourself, to be really awake. . . . The world is in a great historic struggle over this question of war and peace. Some of us see that it can't be solved by condemning war, but only by creating a more vivid and more vital way to live without shooting."

The warrior within us surfaces most clearly when all else fails — something I learned while writing this book. After working on it for two years I showed what I had to a publisher, who revealed his opinion by not returning any of my phone calls. I asked a free-lance editor to comment on what I had written so far. She wrote something like, "You talk about 'warriorship' but don't show us how you got there. What is it like to be committed to openness? What's it like for you? You're writing as if you're afraid to let the reader see who you are."

Her remarks hit home. I felt like someone who couldn't talk, except that instead of being choked in my throat the message was stuck somewhere deeper inside. I mentioned my dilemma to friends. "How's the book?" they'd ask. I'd say, "The real stuff isn't coming through yet." One of them, an actress, said, "Maybe it would help to open yourself more, the way we do in the theater." She told me about a weekend workshop for actors that was open to professionals in other fields. I decided to take it.

The only requirement was that each participant come prepared to say some lines from the stage, so the director could coach the delivery.

I wrote a page summarizing the message I wanted the book to convey. At the beginning of the workshop, the director asked each of the twenty of us there what we had come for. I said that I wanted passionately to write about healing from war, but everything I turned out seemed flat, like someone on stage who read lines mechanically instead of bringing them to life.

"We'll see," said the director.

We warmed up by doing "theater exercises" — acting out anger, sadness, happiness, fear, lust, coolness, love. Then came the time for individual coaching. The director chose me to lead off. First he asked me to say the lines I had prepared. I went through them once, beginning with the line, "I woke up in Vietnam and saw that war is the deadliest disease on earth . . ."

The director then asked me to say it all again, only this time in a whisper. "Caring people blame militarists, arms manufacturers, and politicians for keeping the war system in place, but our moral outrage is weak," I said.

He didn't comment. Then he said, "Do it again, only this time shout it as loudly as you can."

"OUR FITFUL WARS AGAINST WAR ONLY PERPETUATE CONFLICT AND MAKE THOSE WE ATTACK MORE COMMITTED TO MISTRUST. WE NEED AN ALTERNATIVE STRATEGY TO REALIZE THE AGE-OLD DREAM OF A HUMAN FAMILY THAT NO LONGER RESOLVES DIFFERENCES THROUGH FRATRICIDE . . ." I was straining my voice and I hoped the director would let me stop.

"Not enough," he said. "Do it again."

"TO CREATE A GLOBAL CULTURE WILL TAKE UNPARALLELED ENERGY, DETERMINATION AND COMMITMENT. WHERE WILL WE FIND IT? ONLY IN THE HEARTS OF OUR SUPPOSED ENEMY. THE WARRIOR SPIRIT MUST BECOME OUR ALLY — THE WILLINGNESS TO SERVE AND THE READINESS TO ACT . . ."

This time I thought I had done it, but the director only looked at me blankly. Then he said, "Do it again, only this time shout loud and punch at the air with your fists, as hard and as fast as you can."

"ONLY THE DEDICATION OF WARRIORS CAN MAKE REAL THE VISION OF THE PROPHETS. WE MUST TRANSFORM THE RESOLUTENESS TO KILL ON COMMAND TO THE COURAGE TO LOVE WITHOUT LIMIT . . ."

I began to worry that he'd never let me stop. Exerting myself under

the stage lights was making me sweat. My vision blurred from the drop-
lets that fell in my eyes each time I punched. My shirt was sticking to
my skin and restricting my movements. My throat was getting hoarse
and my muscles were so tired I could barely lift my arms.

"Do it again," the director said.

Wearily I continued, "So let's send out the call —" but stopped in
the middle this time. My head was spinning with thoughts of how sick
this was going to make me, how I'd be too tired to see patients the
next day and too hoarse to talk with anyone.

"No passion to communicate, huh, Arthur?" the director asked.

I hung my head and started walking off stage.

"You know where the difficulty lies now?" he asked.

I was too embarrassed to answer. To myself I said, "Yeah, it's guts.
It always comes down to guts."

Just as I was about to walk down the stairs and take my seat, I stopped.
Instead, I turned around and walked back into the lights. I began
shrieking this time, pounding the air with my fists, and my fellow par-
ticipants were standing up and cheering as I went at it with all I had
left. Toward the end I nearly dropped but I made an extra effort to say
the final words clearly:

"Recruiting has begun for the most glorious campaign in history.
Humanity calls for the bravest souls to lead the charge — to proclaim
humanity sovereign on earth, to open hearts afraid to care, to celebrate
the adventure of life, and to cure ourselves of war."

When I finished that time the director said, "That's it. You can sit
down now." After that I knew I could write the book. I could let it all
out because I saw that a warrior doesn't have to be above defeat. The
crucial part is handling failure, picking himself up each time he falls,
and carrying on.

Warriorship as I mean it here — the commitment to look at and
beyond ourselves and address what needs to be done in the
spirit of service — is not just an idea. In our time, an expanding
subculture is already rallying to the call for "warriors without war,"
to use the phrase coined by José Arguelles. It is an effort that has
spawned many inspiring leaders. Here are a few who have touched
my life.

• The Frenchman Robert Muller was a World War II resistance fighter in the anti-Nazi underground who later became the protégé of U Thant. Today Muller is the chief visionary and prophet at the United Nations. In his speeches around the world and in his daily meetings with people, as well as in his two books,[38] Muller calls for new global studies and awareness, especially for a spiritual awakening that will enable people the world over to realize their common destiny.

• Chogyam Trungpa, a Tibetan meditation master who has established teaching centers in many cities of the United States and Canada, has developed a nonreligious training that applies the virtues of enlightened warriors to everyday living. Like Japan, Tibet was a warrior kingdom until the Middle Ages, when Buddhism became ascendant. In Trungpa's teaching, these ancient warrior traditions, transformed through higher consciousness, constitute "basic human wisdom that can help to solve the world's problems."[39]

• The foremost chronicler of contemporary scientific, educational, medical, social, and psychological breakthroughs in North America is Marilyn Ferguson, whose book, *The Aquarian Conspiracy: Personal and Social Transformation in the 1980s,* has been translated into many languages. One of Ferguson's convictions is that professional soldiers have a crucial role to play in working out the global security arrangements that will make warfare obsolete. She remarks that none of the audiences to her talks respond as enthusiastically to that message as the groups of professional soldiers who invite her to speak.

• In recent years, one of Ferguson's close associates has been retired U.S. Army Intelligence Officer LTC James Channon. Channon traces his personal transformation to a day in Vietnam when, as the leader of a platoon of airborne infantry, he escaped death three times. Since then he taught communications skills for seven years at the U.S. Army War College. Before retiring from his postwar job there, Channon composed an elaborate fantasy, with drawings and maxims, and published it in the form of a mock training manual for "warrior monks" dedicated to world service.[40] The theme is captured in his central pledge: "My allegiance goes beyond duty, honor and country . . . to PEOPLE and PLANET." Thousands of copies of his manual have been circulated throughout the U.S. Army officer corps.

In an interview for this book, Channon said, "The military in this country could go either way. There's the old guard, still, and they're strong, and if they prevail, they could lead us to arm outer space. But there are enough dedicated soldiers who have committed themselves to higher principles that we could see the American Army pioneer the idea of global service. Eighty of our best generals have already been trained in the most advanced consciousness principles of the New Age. The Army had a special Task Force Delta that for three years spent 4.5 million dollars on eighty projects to experiment with human potential on the battlefield and off. You name it, they did it: body-mind coordination, attention to diet, self-regulating and meditative techniques taught in the best workshops from Esalen to the East Coast growth centers. Lots of these changes grew out of a confrontation in 1974, when the junior officers at the Army's Command and General Staff School laid our failures in Vietnam at the feet of twenty generals and asked what they were going to do about the way they were running things."

• A former president of Antioch College, Robert Fuller dates his activism on war and peace issues to a visit he made to Vietnam during the war years. After that experience, Fuller realized that the campaign to banish war by condemning it would never succeed, and that the inspiring core of warrior service needs to be preserved and redirected. In his articles talks, and workshops around the world, Fuller calls for "a better game than war."[41] He leads the Mo Tzu Project, named for an ancient Chinese activist who brought a similar message to the warlords of his day. Fuller and his associates are involved in Track II Diplomacy, a forum in which private citizens explore the possibilities for breakthroughs in international relations wherever official diplomacy is stymied.

• While leading an infantry charge as a young Marine lieutenant in Vietnam, Robert O. Muller was shot and paralyzed for life. After a subsequent period of profound questioning and doubt about the war, Muller regained his desire to serve and initiated Vietnam Veterans of America (VVA), the first new veterans' organization in a generation to be federally chartered. Muller has dedicated himself not only to serving veterans but to applying the lessons of the war. "Healing, that's my cause," he said to me in an interview. In the face of governmental stalemate, VVA has taken the initiative toward opening talks with the Vietnamese government. Muller knows that veterans in particular, and the country as a whole, will not heal from the war until we stop acting like sore losers and reestablish relations with our former enemies. Braving scathing attacks by more traditionally minded people, Muller led a small team of his associates on a series of recent visits to Vietnam. Their purpose was to begin talks with Vietnamese leaders on the effects of Agent Orange, a final accounting of Americans missing in action, and humanitarian exchanges between our two peoples.

• John Marks served with the State Department in Vietnam. After coming home, Marks turned first to writing, publishing two books that challenged our intelligence and foreign policy establishment to learn from its mistakes.[42] After undergoing a personal transformation, Marks set out to empower people on both sides of the hawk-versus-dove debate over national security, so that those who advocate "peace through strength" and those who espouse "peace through disarmament" could together forge a new, more viable national consensus. Working in Washington, D.C., Marks established an organization called Search for Common Ground. Among his various programs, Marks has offered weekend workshops where Pentagon analysts and retired generals have joined peace organizers in a rigorous, Socratic inquiry to discover fresh approaches on which they can agree.

• A soft-spoken, athletic former antiwar protester, David Gershon "grew up" in the consciousness movement of the late 1960s and 1970s, then became a workshop leader himself. With his wife, Gail Straub, he founded a program called The Empowerment Workshop, a weekend training designed to help people break out of restrictive patterns in their work and personal lives. Through this work, Gershon came into contact with scores of young people seeking to make their way in small businesses and imaginative entrepreneurial activities. He noticed the enthusiasm of the most dedicated and successful, and decided to enunciate that spirit in a way that would make it more widely accessible. The result is a new series of workshops on "entrepreneurship as a warrior's path," which aid participants in facing uncertainty and risk with integrity and steadfastness. Gershon has joined Channon and others to help organize the "First Earth Run," scheduled for 1986, which will coordinate runners from many nations to pass a torch around the world to celebrate our common humanity.

Citing examples doesn't prove that a trend will or must prevail. The point is simply that the inspiration to transform the warrior spirit is available and already being drawn on by those who choose to do so.

Until such time that warfare is, in fact, obsolete, the warriors in our military should be prepared for whatever missions we devise for them. In fact, it is not simply a visionary project but a practical necessity for us to nourish the warrior spirit there. A recent study of U.S. defense policies concluded that our preparedness suffers on just this score: We are failing to assert the primacy of the warrior spirit within the defense establishment.

The author of the study came to his conclusion after undergoing a transformation different in content but similar in spirit to the experience of many veterans. A journalist and former speech writer for President Jimmy Carter, James Fallows, made an enduring contribution to healing the domestic social rifts of the Vietnam War years through his widely read article, "What Did You Do in the Class War, Daddy?"[43] As a student at Harvard College during the war, Fallows starved himself to such a low weight that he was disqualified for military service. Writing of the day he was rejected as physically unfit, he said, "I was overcome by a wave of relief, which for the first time revealed to me how great my terror had been, and by the beginning of the sense of shame which remains with me to this day."

The point of Fallows's article was that "the Vietnam draft was unfair racially, economically, educationally. By every one of those measures, the [new] volunteer Army is less representative still." The conclusion he draws is that "such a selective bearing of the burden has destructive spiritual effects in a nation based on the democratic creed [and] its practical implications can be quite as grave."

Fallows took on the task of spelling out those practical consequences in his 1981 book, *The National Defense*. His aim was to bring "the facts" about defense into public debate, and to strip away the nonfactual basis of much of the post-Vietnam controversy over national defense. He argued that the American military is structurally flawed; it has become overloaded by unnecessarily expensive, complex, and unreliable technology. It is ruled by an increasingly managerial ethos, which, as the best private enterprises found long ago, undermines the personal touch, the morale, and the inspired performances necessary for large organizations to thrive.

After interviewing experts in and out of the Pentagon and studying budgets and performance records, Fallows concluded that "for at least the last twenty years, American defense has been very greatly shaped by the economist's pattern of thought, and those of the manager, the technologist, and the armchair nuclear analyst. The warrior's perspective has counted for little, perhaps because there is less and less connection between the military culture and the most influential parts of the civilian world."[44] It is this loss of contact with the warrior spirit, even within the military itself, that Fallows sees as an enduring weakness in American society.

Shortsighted policies that favor machinery over well-trained, spirited men and women draw support from various political and economic forces. Arms manufacturers have most to gain from winning defense contracts to build weapons that cost billions and take years to design and manufacture. Political clout comes from unions that represent workers in these companies, from large corporate contributions to election campaigns, and from politicians in the states where the manufacturers are located. Amitai Etzioni cites these forces in calling attention to the decline in combat readiness in the Army and Air Force during the years 1981–1984, the period of the most costly peacetime military build-up in our history.[45]

Soldiers, sailors, and Marines have nobody lobbying for them, no campaign to nourish the warrior spirit of those who, in a crisis, will need it most. And no such campaign will be possible until we recognize the value of cultivating warriorship — whether to forestall wars, to win them, or to create a condition in which they no longer occur.

The warriorship we need for deterrence and in times of crisis is not, however, a monopoly of those who bear arms. Dr. Gene Sharp of Harvard's Center for International Affairs has documented the "forgotten history" of hundreds of successful nonviolent responses to armed aggression.[46] Sharp has shown that when large numbers of ordinary citizens are empowered to act with clarity, resolve, and cohesiveness, nonviolent displays of courage and commitment can be effective foils to military force. The American Revolution, for example, was virtually won before the Continental Army ever fired a shot, through nonviolent protests like the famed Boston Tea Party. Sharp argues that the armed battles of the Revolutionary War itself postponed rather than hastened our independence. The recent experience of the Solidarity movement in Poland is an even more stunning example. In a few short years, Solidarity put a bigger dent in Soviet totalitarianism than the billions of dollars spent by the Pentagon.

Sharp has called for a radical expansion of our notion of defense to include the possibility of planning widespread civilian participation. "Spreading power out to all segments of society [is] the best weapon against foreign aggression, dictatorship or totalitarian governments."[47] In a proposal that has won support from both traditional hawks and doves, Sharp has asked for feasibility studies of civilian-based defense for individual countries and a ten-year crash program to educate people and their governments to the superior alternatives to fighting fire with fire.

War will cease only when the peoples of the world surrender a measure of national sovereignty. At present, any proposal to relinquish war-making powers would be rejected as too radical by most people. Before world opinion grants our common humanity higher priority than the "freedom" to do violence, a change will need to occur. What change? What will it take?

Some say that it will never happen. Others say that it will take a catastrophe horrible enough to shock the entire world. Still others claim it will take an awakening of a sufficient core of humankind to usher in a successor culture. Many other answers are also possible. The point is, it is how we answer that matters. Choosing where we want to end up introduces purposefulness into otherwise haphazard living. And so I offer some aspects of what I foresee, not as a source of hope or as predictions to lull us into a false sense of security, but as work that needs to be done.

National Character. We will need enormous trust in order to empower our leaders to surrender sovereignty in our name. We must challenge the illusion that our well being and our place in the world depend on being able to resort to violence. And we will need to trust our leaders, and the leaders of other nations, to act wisely with the nonviolent powers left to them.

In the United States and elsewhere, generating such trust will require a major evolution of national character. At present, North Americans commonly express their love for freedom as a lack of confidence in authority. The prevailing wisdom is to find fault with our system, to justify saying, "There's good reason not to trust our leaders! See what a mess they're making of things!" We haven't yet seen that such "common sense" is only an excuse for rationalizing our inaction. Empowering our leaders, rather than habitually demeaning them, will only come as we deepen our dedication to service — their service to us and our service to one another.

Only through increasing participation by citizens who care enough to act, and have sufficient integrity to act wisely, will we create conditions for leaders to emerge who warrant our trust.

National Interest. The task of world healing implies a new common sense and a new set of "self-evident truths." One such truth is that power is most widely and reliably demonstrated not by imposing our will but by empowering others; the most potent leader, therefore, is one who most thoroughly serves those who follow. This is as true for countries as it is for individuals. Rather than equate our national power with our economy, military force, large population, or natural resources, we need to recognize that our supreme potential for world leadership lies in our ability to serve humanity. Our broadest national interest is to live by our most cherished principles, with the vision that wise men nourished for millennia before adventurers, spiritual seekers, and misfits from all continents came here and embarked on the greatest social experiment in history, creating, as our national seal claims, "a new order of the ages" — "out of many, one."

We have no monopoly on this vision; it belongs to the world. It is ours to share, which makes us fundamentally a visionary and missionary people, on humanity's mission. Our calling is to demonstrate that diverse peoples can govern themselves, nourish their distinctiveness, and share the fruits with the entire world. Living this vision must become our national project for the new millennium.

Education. For the past few centuries, knowledge and its transmission have been organized by the aggressive principle of divide and conquer. The materialist credo worships analysis, and is dedicated to an illusory quest for the ultimate pieces, particles, and causes out of the willful urge to dominate nature, our bodies, and other people.

Educating world citizens to become participants in fulfillment is a healing task and requires a holistic science. We need to initiate young people into a lifelong dedication to openness, to the art of attending to wholes, to the wisdom of recognizing interdependence, relationship, infinity, and eternity as ever-present foundations for our lives.

We must school ourselves in creating a technology with an ecological purpose not to control but to serve life. And we need to cultivate the love of wisdom, the philosopher's discipline of fundamental inquiry. Citizens educated to view life whole will ask, "What does it mean to be a human being?" and invoke that question repeatedly as the context that gives direction to their lives. We must adopt a more ambitious standard for literacy so that education aids every person in discovering his or her voice — so that each thinks, speaks, and acts in a way that reflects a life dedicated to the human community.

Spirituality. Rather than promise salvation in an imagined beyond, world healing calls for a heaven on earth, now, in this life. Rather than prescribe rules for living or impose dogma and creeds, we must encourage all people to awaken their capacity to see clearly, to find their way in life for themselves. A nonsectarian spirituality teaches that this ability is available to all, not just to our heroes, priests, and saints.

As part of everyday life, ordinary citizens must learn to practice living with the consciousness of death, an awareness that will make shooting wars, the cultural vehicle for transporting large numbers of people to an exalted state, unnecessary. We must practice forgiveness and acknowledge it as our spiritual birthright, available for everyone to give and receive, at any and every moment. The spread of this practice, of living the dying life, will call people throughout the world to bring forth a generosity and grace that once were the exclusive privilege of the spiritually elect.

Ideology. We need to recognize the limits of ideology so we don't abuse it. In our public dialogues we must acknowledge that ideologies proliferate and change, and that people will always differ in ideology as well as in temperament and personal taste. As we distinguish more thoroughly between absolute and relative truth, enlightened use of ideology may then be possible. Absolute truth cannot be reduced to any single form or formulation. No statement of it can be more than provisional, which means that no claim to truth can ever be more than partially or relatively certain.

The seductiveness of dogma will wither only when people are empowered to think for themselves. This kind of profound thinking enables us to appreciate the usefulness of each ideological perspective without falling into the trap of regarding views other than our own as "enemies." Left, right, hawk, dove, collectivist, and individualist will be heard as important voices in our social chorus. However centralized or decentralized the administration of a given community and nation, the variation in ideological perspective must be valued as the fertile ground for creative thought.

Politics. We must subordinate all political structures to naturally occurring wholes — the person, relationship, family, community, culture, and the whole of life. Hierarchical and representational systems must be used as provisional tools only. Supreme allegiance must be to life, to the earth, and to the creative source — called by whatever name — from which everything springs.

People who recognize that power accrues to those who empower others are naturally concerned with the welfare of others. Relationships, families, communities, and cultures thereby become opportunities for creating empowerment through our contributions. For those who see that serving others ultimately serves them, mutual support becomes a way of life. Spreading this recognition will generate a communal ethos that will reinvigorate local settings, and find ultimate expression in our celebration of the "global village."

Individuals will always differ in status and personal resources. But stimulating the appetite for spiritual power will bring about a widened interest in sharing material wealth, thereby reducing the disparity between rich and poor.

We must make deliberate use of the network, the one form of social organization that enables each person to be the center of communication to the whole. Asking "How should we organize the world?" must no longer be merely a theoretical question or the practical concern of an elite group. Each world citizen must be seen as capable of drawing creatively on the overlapping networks that comprise his or her social life. Lifelong tasks will consist of organizing, communicating with, and taking part in projects with one's family, co-workers, friends, friends of friends, and the people clustered around one's various interests.

Communication technologies must be used to provide each person access to everyone else and to all human knowledge. Such developments hold the promise that anyone who is sufficiently determined, regardless of political boundaries, can participate in worldwide projects. To realize this promise, we must open these boundaries and create ways to encourage people everywhere to take part in shaping world events. Human destiny is of vital concern to everyone, and to fulfill that destiny means that everyone must be empowered to play his or her part.

Aesthetics. Art must no longer be detached from life and viewed as a vocation of the unusually gifted alone. Life needs to be recognized as the natural poetry and dance. World sounds — animal noises, the wind, and the whirring of time — should become hailed as our essential music. Diversity must be embraced as the source of richness and vibrance, and every individual invited to value creative inspiration and expression as well as worldly action and achievement.

The most desired human traits will always vary from place to place. But leaders everywhere must realize a common goal: to point the way by cultivating their uniqueness while drawing on the uniqueness of others to create what neither could achieve alone. In place of tastes and standards dictated by a cultural elite, the aesthetics of world healing must encourage a profusion of new forms — new modes of expression — in unprecedented combinations, and a resurgence of the appreciation for craftsmanship among ordinary citizens.

Economics. A holistic economics needs to embrace the workings of mind and spirit, and to transcend the classical principles, which apply only to exchanges affecting physical needs. Instead of an exclusive preoccupation with supply and demand, based on the exchange of scarce materials for limited amounts of money, an economics of empowerment must use the interactions that engender healing as its primary model. A new economic wisdom will emerge from studying the ways of healing, in which provider and recipient are both nourished fully.

In an economy of empowerment, everyone is potentially a provider and recipient of healing. All service transactions, in an increasingly service-oriented economy, can then draw inspiration from this model. Lawyers, teachers, financial advisers, politicians, artists, performers, sales personnel, managers, health professionals, technicians, scientists, and consultants of all sorts must come to see their vocations as a healing service to other people. Value can then be determined by how aptly a service opens possibilities for those who avail themselves of it, and by the extent to which a service embodies caring —the most precious, though most plentiful resource of all.

Eros. Love must be seen as the most sublime, the most nourishing, and potentially the most abundant natural resource on earth. Likes and dislikes, tastes and preferences will develop as always, but need to be subordinated to a more encompassing principle: Love is one, and when one truly loves another, one loves all.

Elementary school pupils should be given occasions to learn that the ultimate source of all neurosis, self-torment, and violence is the doubt that one is loved. This doubt, the great blight on humankind, will dissolve only through the universal recognition that each of us is the manifestation of love, that each of us comes into being as an expression of the oneness that is the love of all by all.

Sexual frustration and promiscuity will diminish only as people develop a counterpart to the wisdom of the deathbed: the integrity of the love bed. Not reducible to codes of conduct, rules, or strictures, the integrity of the love bed will guide us in respectful and creative experimentation, in which each person can find an evolving way to express caring in intimate ways with others. The age-old struggle between repression and license will end as singles, couples, old, and young discover an honorable and responsible freedom to explore the endless possibilities for erotic joining.

When loving is understood to have everything to do with our being, and only incidentally with our genitals, the erotic principle for world healing will empower us to make universal love, not war.

Between now and the time when masses of people no longer dismiss such visions as strange, seeing the possibility for inspired action is vision enough. A prominent example of one such action was the building of the Vietnam Veterans Memorial in Washington, D.C., an act that has already touched millions of lives.

The idea for the memorial came from Jan Scruggs, a former corporal in the 199th Light Infantry Brigade, who came back wounded from his tour in Vietnam, and went on to graduate study in psychology and to counsel fellow vets. In 1976, while testifying before Congress in support of a national outreach program for Vietnam veterans, Scruggs mentioned the need for a memorial as a tangible sign that the country cared. In 1979 he stopped waiting for someone else to pick up the idea and found a few others who shared his dream. Together they worked over the following three and a half years to make the dream real.[48]

Insisting that the monument be "reflective and contemplative" and "make no political statement about the war," the organizers were determined that this memorial be an effort to heal. The program distributed on the day the monument was dedicated quoted the groundbreaking ceremony, when the names of the dead were read aloud. "The pain, the reality, and the brokenness were there for all to see.

And the barriers to learning and the need for reconciliation were there for all to see as well." The goal was not to bury the past, but to dig beyond the various forms of ideological prejudice to reach the sources of life's renewal.

It was chilly in Washington on the dedication day, November 13, 1982. A crowd of thousands listened to eulogies for the dead, words of comfort for the grieved, and hopeful talk of reconciliation and new beginnings for the country as a whole. For more than a decade, many veterans had hoped for such a national event, one that would punctuate our lives, consecrate the dead, and acknowledge past service.

I was there, watching the faces. There were many, many guys my age, a chorus of clear and steady gazes. The Marine band played "This Is My Country, Land That I Love." I sang along, then looked around again. There was strength in the many teary eyes, a crowd of men who had the depth of spirit to let their hearts be touched. Such handsome men, I thought, and from the sobs in my throat I realized how profoundly I loved these people.

It was an old sentiment, one I'd felt for years as the bond to some dark brotherhood, linking haunted spirits. With the dedication a corner turned, and the connections came into clearer light, making our presence the boldest statement of the day. The gist appeared on makeshift signs carried by some in the parade, signs that read TOGETHER AGAIN. *Former infantrymen, officers, pilots, sailors, Marines, and clerks were joined once more in a common purpose. They were men in business suits, jungle fatigues, casual dress, jeans, and love beads from the 1960s. Together again. It also meant that many of us were more whole and sound, and willing to turn out. "Yes, count on me, I'll be there," thousands had said and followed through.*

A small group of dedicated ex-soldiers accomplished this feat of having a memorial built and a National Salute to Vietnam Veterans held on the day it was dedicated. The chairman of the group, John Wheeler III, a West Point graduate, was an Army captain in Vietnam who came home feeling "alone and in need of repair" and spent his first year back in an Episcopal seminary. After work on the memorial was done, Wheeler wrote a book about the future of the Vietnam generation and about the opportunity to turn the pain and conflict we've suffered into renewed strength. He reflected on his time at the seminary, the work he did to build a memorial at West Point and then in Washington, his time

*writing, and the projects he envisaged for the years to come. All of it,
he wrote, is a "prayer for healing."*[49]

*Each year millions of visitors now confront the memorial's granite
walls and scan the names of every soldier who died. Each person finds
his or her own meaning. But the experience of being touched will be
common to many. Veterans who once felt they were the only ones who
cared can know now that the grief is shared. Remembering is no longer
our job alone. And the faith that each person matters has now been
carved in stone. For those who served and who wish to set down the
burdens of the troubled vet, the way is now easier. For those who didn't
go, who have felt separated from the war and its veterans by age, ideology, privilege, fear, or self-righteousness, it's not too late. With a
public monument accessible to everyone, we announce that anyone
can be witness to the suffering of at least the American side of the war.*

What of the larger task? Who will carry healing to the veterans of
life? No single set of proposals will be adequate. Healing is everyone's birthright and responsibility. Only together will we create a
culture that supersedes the cycles of battle and retreat — not through
our fear of war but through mastering a superior way to live.

The seed of this culture is the determination within individuals,
and then small groups and communities, to devote our lives to the
greatest vision of all time: not to wait for a savior one day to deliver
us; not to wait for a government to pass truly just laws; not to wait
for a revolution to right the wrongs of a cruel world; and not to
mount a crusade to overpower some distant source of evil beyond
ourselves. Each of us, singly and with all the others, is answerable
for creating joy through the way our lives unfold, here and now.
And once this purpose becomes primary, we can turn to the endless
job of bringing well being to others, justice and integrity to our government, and instituting constructive programs for change here and
elsewhere. When inspired in this way, we don't have to wait for the
final outcome before we're nourished. There is no finer way to live
or die.

The campaign for world healing already has among its champions
men who've been burned and bled in prior service, who've wrenched
their guts, poured out their hearts, and honed their vision through
war itself. It is time to formalize a new grand alliance, between those

who care enough to dream and those who dare enough to act. Only through mutual empowerment will we leave behind the cult of domination. And when the monuments are built to honor the achievements of that glorious campaign, many of us who learned to love life in the face of cruelty and death will be there to sing once again.

Appendix
Suggestions for Healing Action

Healing is a way of being that is expressed most clearly in action. What sort of action? By whom? When? Where? How? There are no stock prescriptions, only the answers that each of us comes up with, situation by situation. Guidelines are nonetheless useful, and one is that healing comes to light only by sharing it, which means acting in ways that empower others, at home, at work, or in our wider communities — local, national, and international.

To provide a few illustrations of what it would mean to bring empowerment to these broader spheres, I offer some suggestions regarding four activities I've touched on throughout the book: psychotherapy; services provided by the Veterans Administration; programs offered by veterans' organizations; and the relations between the United States and foreign governments.

Empowering Psychotherapy

Psychotherapy is the most widely practiced secular approach to healing in our culture. As an institution, however, therapy suffers from low public esteem and professional schisms. Doctrinal disputes over theory and technique are almost as baffling for practicing professionals as they are for the public.

One way to empower therapists and help heal therapy as an institution is to make the therapeutic setting more public, by inviting clients and colleagues of different persuasions to look on. Although professional expertise is required to provide healing on a reliable

basis, anyone can tell whether he or she is in the presence of healing. Observers don't have to agree on methods to know when something valuable has taken place for a person seeking help. This openness will increase people's respect for therapists and put the emphasis
in our profession where it belongs — on achieving results that are
readily observable and meaningful for our patients and clients.[1]

A Purpose for the Veterans Administration

The VA has many functions but no dignifying, overarching purpose. It distributes pensions, disability payments, educational benefits, and administers a national medical system consisting of
hundreds of hospitals, outreach centers, and mental hygiene clinics.
Of all federal agencies, only the Department of Defense has a larger
budget. The accepted view is that the VA does what any other social
service and medical system does, except that it does it for veterans,
who hold on to their own particular system through powerful veterans' lobbies. This view demeans the VA, robs the people who work
for it of inspiration, and leaves many veterans to feel and be treated
as if they were freeloaders on the government.

The VA does have a special role to play in our society, but its
purpose has not yet been clearly articulated, adopted, and acted upon:
*to promote healing from war among those who have been most directly af-
fected.* Proclaiming this purpose, and following through with actions
that accord with it, would transform the VA, opening vast new possibilities for inspired and effective performance. Among the benefits
that would ensue are these:

First, the variety of mental health treatments now given throughout the VA system would have a unifying purpose. At present, the
VA employs all the standard practices for treating mental disorders.
As it is, however, people working in the VA do not have a way to
conceive, let alone study and refine, what distinctive responses are
called for by the difficulties veterans bring to treatment. A diagnosis
of "post-traumatic stress" doesn't answer the question, "What should
we do for this guy?" When the purpose of treatment is to promote
healing from war, the distinctiveness of the therapy required by veterans will finally be clear.[2] This new clarity will make it possible to
train therapists, study their performance, and refine the treatments

with more rigor and precision. When that happens, what I have written on healing from war will be recognized as merely the beginning of a new and largely uncharted area of inquiry.

Second, when the VA itself adopts and communicates a suitable vision for its work, people employed by the VA will be encouraged to bring visions of their own to their work. At present, only the extraordinary few come to work each day inspired. For most it is just a job — dispensing money and services — and the atmosphere at VA facilities usually reflects this lack of purpose. Virtually everyone who takes a position serving others would *like* to approach their work with a sense of mission or calling. But only by promulgating a clear vision itself can an institution support its employees in doing the same. Until such a change comes about, periodic "employee training seminars" will lift spirits for a brief time, but fail to empower the staff to sustain that uplift on their own. Only when the VA's purpose is declared and acted upon will its vast staff have both a vision that will inspire their work together, and a basis for calling their own institution to account.

Third, adopting healing from war as its explicit direction would clarify how the VA can transform the spirit in which benefits and pensions are given and received. In the light of healing, warriorship is transformed, so that the spirit of service is renewed for causes beyond war. For transformed warriors, service is its own reward. Nothing is owed for what happened in the past. Treatments, aid to further education, and pensions for the disabled would be offered to enable veterans to continue to serve, in new ways, in the present. Veterans would no longer need to justify their receiving benefits with the rationale of "They owe me!" and VA employees would no longer look down on their clients as freeloaders. Veterans would not have to try to prove they are helpless in order to qualify for assistance. The new rationale for treatment, benefits, and services would be respect, not pity or sympathy or obligation, for it is in the country's interest to enable any veteran, no matter how handicapped, to continue a life of service. And those in need of special assistance in order to do so should have what is possible to give to them, within the budgets set by Congress.

This shift in purpose could transform the way disability claims are made and adjudicated, by making the transaction mutually dignifying for both provider and recipient. Veterans and the VA would no longer need to be adversaries, arguing over whose fault it is that a man comes for assistance — the military or the man's premilitary mind and body. Like no-fault car insurance and no-fault divorce, no-fault VA services are long overdue and will become possible when VA programs are reconceived as the means to empower veterans to give themselves to what they most care about.

Translating this vision into action would be a vast undertaking, requiring the participation of many people who work for and in support of the VA. Before such a change could even be contemplated, however, assent would have to come from the veterans' organizations, which appeal in the public's name to the congressional committees that oversee VA operations. And so, the initiative in promoting healing from war will have to begin with veterans themselves.

Veterans Groups as Genuine Service Organizations

For most veterans, belonging to a service organization stems from deep inspiration. Once you've risked your life with people who are ready to do the same, you unleash for a lifetime an energy that cries out to be expressed. One way veterans do it is by banding together and "being with the guys." They want to preserve the best of their war — their bond as blood brothers — and they want to advance that spirit among their countrymen.

Most veterans' groups, however, limit their ability to honor service by failing to distinguish between fighting the last war and giving themselves to serve here and now. The problem takes the form of deeply entrenched defensiveness. Generally veterans are either defending the attitude they took into their war or defending the conclusion they brought home with them. Either way, they're more committed to maintaining old battle lines than to opening their eyes and hearts to see what needs their commitment, courage, and care right now.

The remedy will come only when veterans' groups make healing from their war a top priority, to free their members from any sense of debt to the past — of what we owe the dead — so that they can give themselves cleanly to serving what's alive.[3] Only when this purpose is uppermost will these groups begin to distinguish their resignation, resentment, and indignation from the empowering expressions of a warrior's commitment. And only then will their leaders be prepared to transform their own tendencies toward emotional avoidance, blame, self-pity, and self-punishment into ways to communicate effectively the message that's in their hearts, which is how much they care.

A veterans' group dedicated to healing could contribute powerfully to a revival of the national spirit by taking actions such as the following:

First, a veterans' organization could lead the way in transforming the relationship between the veterans' lobby and the VA. At present, veterans' groups fluctuate between being cronies and adversaries of the VA. The veterans' agenda is "to get what's coming," which means that when it comes, the vets and the VA are buddies, and when it doesn't, they're antagonists. Shifting the organizational agenda from "getting" to "giving" would shift the relationship with the VA as well. An appropriately inspired veterans' organization could become a partner of the VA, sharing a purpose for which each plays its unique role. The veterans' group would retain its capacity for constructive criticism of the VA's shortcomings. But the dialogue could then take place in a mutually empowering context — with neither party needing to talk down, or to portray the other as a bad guy or victim.

Second, a veterans' organization dedicated to healing could provide services and support to a host of veterans who will not be helped by the VA or any other agency. The majority of Vietnam veterans rightly do not see themselves as mental patients or as candidates for even the innovative counseling program established by the VA. Yet for many, life has a dull edge, and they lack the training and support necessary to free themselves from the sense of burden from what they've lived through. A veterans' group could encourage its members to take part in workshops, trainings, and spiritual disciplines of their choice. The organization could sponsor weekend seminars, and have its scouts explore whatever services are available locally. In the past, there was a smaller-scale version of what I'm suggesting: veterans' self-help projects spread across the country in the early 1970s and continued to function as Vietnam Veterans of America lobbied for a national outreach program through the VA; then the

Disabled American Veterans initiated such an effort on its own. But something more is needed now, for healing from war cannot be done without a wholehearted commitment. Individuals can promote healing only when they're on the way themselves, and the same is true for an organization. Unless it makes healing its central purpose, whatever a group does in the name of healing will always fall short.

Third, a veterans' organization whose purpose is to promote healing could widen the opportunities for the entire country to follow. Veterans have the capacity to lead a campaign for national healing, because nobody has as much at stake in how the war is remembered as veterans do. Most nonveterans know this and are therefore reluctant to move too fast on any action that might offend the memory, meaning the veterans' memory. Once veterans make healing their goal, they can unleash a nationwide flood of healing, simply by no longer holding the country in an emotional straitjacket.

At present, America's post-Vietnam "syndrome" plagues people who want to forget about the war as much as those who want to remember it at all cost. People don't liberate themselves from the past by acting as if it didn't happen, anymore than they do by becoming obsessed about it. The truth about the much touted "lessons of Vietnam" is that in some situations they will apply and in others they won't. But we will be free to distinguish one kind of situation from another only when we are no longer compelled either to link whatever happens now with Vietnam or to deny that any such parallel can be drawn. This will take healing from the war, thoroughly and completely, and those who already have an overwhelming interest in leading the way are veterans themselves.

Empowering People: A New National Policy

Psychologists have made various contributions to those who conduct international relations. Largely, these have been suggestions of alternative ways to interpret behavior and motives in the international arena, on the level of the "digging inside" described in chapter four.[4] More recently, psychological experts have been giving advice on conflict resolution, by drawing attention to the ever-present possibilities for turning situations around, an approach that applies the kinds of insights described in chapter six.[5] This is the approach

taken by advocates of the new National Peace Institute, the successful campaign for which was directed by a graduate of the U.S. Naval
Academy, Mike Mapes.

Interpreting motives and resolving conflict are ways to respond to
difficult situations after they arise. A more ample opportunity opens
through empowerment.[6] In seeking to empower others, that is, by
acting with greater dignity and grace than is customary among world
powers, Americans could take the initiative and set a new global
precedent. Instead of restricting ourselves to the age-old power game,
which limits our options to dominating or resisting dominion by
others, we can turn our relations with others into opportunities for
the mutual benefit of empowerment, long before ordinary annoy-
ances become acute conflicts needing resolution.

In our best moments, American efforts abroad have demonstrated
this approach. Particularly after the two world wars, we sought to
empower people in other nations to provide for themselves and to
manage their own affairs. *What we have not yet done is to declare empowerment as the primary purpose of U.S. policy in the world.*[7] We have
yet to proclaim officially that we have set aside the self-defeating
illusion that "protecting our interests" could somehow take prece-
dence over empowerment. Bringing American policy more fully to
reflect this purpose is a way to heal the affliction of our national
spirit.

In the foreign policy sphere, we are currently burdened not merely
by our defeat in Vietnam, and by the image of ourselves as world
policeman that developed in the post–World War II era, but also by
a conflict between hawks and doves. While vast and important differences separate these two camps, they have one overriding commitment in common: Both insist on dividing the world into right
and wrong, our side and theirs. This basic strategy, of focusing on
opponents and trying either to overpower or resist them, is ineffective for bringing about a condition in the world that enhances life.

What is the alternative? How can we transform the divisiveness
that hampers our ability to act effectively to advance the ideals of
freedom and dignity that both hawks and doves favor? The most
effective U.S. foreign policies are ones based on consensus, a compromise that avoids the excesses of either extreme. The last great
compromise between hawk and dove positions is the policy called

containment. During the Korean War, when hawks wanted to coun-
terattack against China and doves wanted not to be involved at all,
the compromise became: contain them, keep them within set
boundaries. Except for a brief period of détente in the early 1970s,
the containment policy has prevailed since the late 1940s.[8]

From a healing perspective, the main shortcoming of the containment policy is that it erects a compromise between hawks and doves
by appealing to their common commitment to divisiveness, which
is their common weakness and not their common strength. Containment is a defensive policy, defined by what we oppose rather than
by what we stand for. A truly viable alternative would draw on the
strength of both sides: their love — love of country among hawks
and love of humankind among doves. A healing alternative to containment would allow us to draw on both loves: to cultivate what
we love as distinctly American as our way to express our love for
the world we call home.

Many, many obstacles would have to be surmounted before such
a policy could be shaped and adopted. People may be more likely to
consider such an alternative, however, when they recall that we have
already initiated such broad-spirited policies in the past, most out-
standingly in our use of diplomatic and economic resources in post–
World War II Europe and Japan. Notice that on these occasions our
efforts were masterminded by great generals who had turned their
efforts to a cause beyond war. In the case of Europe, under the Mar-
shall plan, named for the American general who was secretary of
state at the time, we laid the groundwork for our former enemies
and allies to rebuild and cooperate as never before. In Japan, Douglas MacArthur used his authority as commander of occupation forces
to break the power monopoly of Japanese industrialists and militarists. Trusting that the best people Japan had to offer would govern
best, if given the chance, MacArthur sought out such people and
encouraged them to redistribute income so as to elevate the poor,
grant women the vote, open education to all, and bring representatives of labor into a dialogue with Japanese management. In the first
few years after the war, nobody in Japan applauded the American
presence more than the most progressive thinkers and activists.

We are no longer in a position to duplicate these triumphs. But
the spirit of what we did then could serve as inspiration for renewed

American activism. *Empowerment is the clear alternative to both domination and resistance, to both the hawk and dove versions of divisiveness. A* policy of empowerment offers the opportunity for a historic realignment of domestic and foreign relations.

Empowering people in foreign countries will not happen, however, until we elevate the status of foreign relations and the institutions that conduct them. This means we must empower the people, agencies, and institutions that conduct our relations abroad. *A policy of empowerment has to begin at home.* Here are some ways to begin implementing such a policy:

• Declare the new national policy in the same spirit that the Peace Corps was announced by John F. Kennedy, the last U.S. President with an inspiring vision that touched people throughout the world.

• Stop appointing as ambassadors to foreign countries the political cronies of new Presidents, and appoint instead the most skilled senior diplomats who speak the local language and have knowledge and experience in that area. We cannot hope to empower local leaders until we empower our most able and dignified representatives to act in our name.

• Grant new initiatives for the formulation of policy to the State Department, at the ambassadorial level. The President should authorize these ambassadors to work with local political leaders, and to draw not only on U.S. military attachés and representatives from our intelligence agencies, Commerce Department, and U.S. businesses abroad, but also on the most esteemed local leaders in business, education, science, government, and the arts. The goal would be to shape policy options for the greatest mutual interest of our people and theirs. As we did in our post–World War II foreign policy triumphs, we need to empower representatives to think broadly and deeply about each local situation and to draw on the diversity of local leaders in ways that centralized decision makers back in the United States cannot.

• Declare a new era of governmental entrepreneurship, empowering American officials abroad to be creative and energetic in brokering mutually beneficial projects that combine American private sector resources and community and business needs in Third World countries. Government-to-government loans and transfers will never be ample enough, nor can they be as empowering to as many citizens as people-to-people arrangements that foster mutual interests. Employees in the CIA and other intelligence agencies already operate creatively and independently "on the ground." We must now give similar powers to employees of the departments of State, Commerce, and Treasury to "make things happen" — to help private initiative integrate Third World peoples into the world economy.

• Make the post of U.S. Ambassador to the United Nations an honor to which only our most accomplished senior diplomats are appointed. The abysmal state of our relationship with the UN is not something to complain about, but to correct. There should be a bipartisan consensus that once an able U.S. representative is in place, he or she will not be replaced merely for partisan reasons, so as to give that person ample time to cultivate relationships and expertise.

• Elevate the study of foreign languages and cultures in our schools, and use economic incentives to encourage colleges and universities to work out exchange programs, particularly with schools in non-European countries, where students most need exposure to us and we to them.

• Institute a two-year obligatory national service for all young people within six years after graduating high school. A national conservation corps should be added to the Peace Corps and Vista and as an alternative to the military. The purpose of these services should be consistent with a national policy of empowerment: to enable each person in early adulthood to begin making a meaningful contribution through some form of national participation. Initial training and ongoing management in all services should have at least one crucial feature in common: support for the consistent application, by both permanent cadre and two-year participants, of the principles of empowerment.

• Establish and fund a new National Institute for Human Empowerment. We already have national institutes that encourage and fund research and action projects in natural and social science, space, medicine, education, mental health, drug and alcohol abuse, humanities, and the arts. Although the State Department, CIA, and Department of Defense already fund a limited amount of nongovernmental work on international relations, we need to broaden our approach so that many more scholars, activists, inventors, researchers, and ordinary citizens can participate in creating ideas, techniques, and programs for empowering people here at home and abroad. This will enhance the training and education of policy makers and diplomats, who can call on a wider range of knowledge and innovative ideas.

• Direct the new national institute to pioneer ways for government to draw on the services and support provided voluntarily by private citizens, including those who are already contributing to our relations abroad through what is now called Track II, or unofficial, diplomacy. Most of these efforts are currently focused on relations with the Soviet Union. But in the near future, we should look to citizen participation to foster our relations with countries all over the world.

As for our struggle with totalitarianism, the way to demonstrate to the world that a superior alternative exists to governing people with top-heavy, dictatorial bureaucracies is to put such an alternative on international display. In other words, if we are going to compete with Leninist states, why concentrate on the manufacture of weaponry, on which ground the Soviets are almost as strong as we? Why not compete in areas where we are strongest and where humanity has the most to gain from the way we and the Soviets put each other to the test? Why not initiate the most flexible, enlightened, and efficient relations with developing nations that the world has ever seen? Why not shatter all precedents by making the most thoroughly decentralized and therefore responsive effort to enhance the infrastructure-building efforts of Third World nations? Why not provide economic incentives and administrative aid to private enterprises to assist U.S. representatives, local governments, and their citizenry, encouraging the widest possible participation and cooperation among people at home and abroad? And if the Soviets retool their policy making to follow suit, so much the better for everyone.

A policy of empowerment would not be a panacea. Many pitfalls and risks would attend it, principally the rising expectations among the least advantaged majority of the world population. No matter what we do, however, strains between the rich and poor of the world are inevitable. The crucial question is how best to deal with them. If we want to create a world that is more to our liking, the choice is clear: to accept the risks of promoting a world polity, through bilateral and multilateral initiatives in economic, educational, and diplomatic realms. The way for us is to act beyond our borders according to our cherished principles of freedom and dignity for all.

A national policy of empowerment should include reconciliation with our former enemies in Indochina. Two decades' experience should be enough to remind us that the Vietnamese will prevail, on their own if they have to. It is not because they need us that we should reestablish relations. No doubt our medical, economic, and educational aid would be appreciated. But the greatest benefit from reconciliation would be to the American spirit. Living with bitterness is not good for anyone. It is particularly devastating for a people who pride themselves on generosity.

We don't have to approve of the Vietnamese repression of their ethnic minorities, their mistreatment of political opponents, and their occupation of Cambodia in order to have official relations. We didn't need to approve of similar repression and mistreatment in China or of the Chinese cultural genocide in Tibet in order to reestablish relations with the People's Republic.

On this score, it is again useful to recall what we did after World War II. Within a few years after Japan attacked us and Germany committed the worst national crime in history, we had the grace to treat the Japanese and the Germans with official respect. When we began our ill-advised intervention in Vietnam, the people of Indochina were focused on fighting among themselves. More than a decade after withdrawing our forces, however, we have not yet had the breadth of spirit to persist in negotiations with the Vietnamese so as to follow our earlier precedent. The fact that we have not yet had a final accounting of our missing and prisoners of war, and will not have one until after such a reconciliation, should be sufficient incentive for those among us who don't care about generosity, but do care about MIAs and POWs.

In a world where many heads of state are still tempted to use violence, we must have a policy of defense. But it should be a secondary purpose of our foreign policy, and not, as our national budget presently suggests, the primary aim. Furthermore, our defense policies will support an inspired national purpose only when we give our military establishment, those who have dedicated their lives to serve as warriors, a proper mission. This mission would add one crucial facet to all defense planning: Develop, in coordination with the State Department, detailed strategies for transforming each of our current adversaries into partners in the quest to make warfare obsolete.

Twenty years of bitter enmity between the People's Republic of China and the United States dissolved in a matter of months, after relatively few exchanges between Nixon, Kissinger, Chou, and Mao.

Projecting how to bring about such nonviolent transformations in our relations with the Soviet Union, Libya, Iran, Albania, Cuba, Nicaragua and other such adversary nations should be part of national strategic thinking.

We will experience our greatness again as a people when we undertake a project that calls us to serve interests far greater than our own. We can no longer rely on vast conflicts like World War I and World War II to provide an occasion to go to the aid of other nations in distress; in the nuclear age we must avoid worldwide violence at all costs. The choice we face is either to languish in the pursuit of "national interest" and global rivalry with the Soviet Union or deliberately to create conditions that call us to demonstrate unselfishness as never before.

It is time to set aside our nostalgia for an American century, a world dominated by American business, American military might, and American popular culture. It is time to proclaim a human century as prologue to a new millennium, and to assert truly inspired leadership by placing ourselves and our national institutions in service to humanity, both here at home and abroad.

Acknowledgments

Many people contributed to this writing. The influence of my mentors will be obvious to anyone who knows the work of Robert Lifton, Eugene Gendlin, and Robert Shaw. I have taken on Lifton's concern for bringing healing to history, Gendlin's care for rejoining psychology with its roots in philosophy, and Shaw's dedication to the practice of "black belt" psychotherapy, in which therapists have a deep, lasting impact in the briefest exchanges. I have tried to honor their example and encouragement here, not by echoing their voices but by expressing my own.

For initiating me into various aspects of healing work through their practices, I thank Bob Chapra, Moshe Feldenkreis, Ben Lapkin, Ethel Lombardi, Charlotte Selver, Bernie Weitzman, Hannah Woods, and students of Chogyam Trungpa and Tarthan Tulku.

Much of the work I draw on here became possible when the National Council of Churches and the Center for Policy Research responded to a request for support, a decade before national healing became mentionable in public. In the years since, many people, including dedicated public servants in the House, Senate, Veterans Administration, and three federal administrations — under Presidents Ford, Carter, and Reagan — made certain that the most bitter national experience of the century would benefit from open inquiry through the Vietnam Era Research Project. I thank the dozens of workers who took part in that research, and in particular my principal co-investigators: Charles Kadushin, Robert Laufer, George Rothbart, and Lee Sloan.

Dozens of men gave their heart and guts to form the original veteran rap groups. The ones whose voices were still distinct to me as I wrote about them a decade later include: Jan Barry, Harry Behret, Bob Bliss, Harvey Block, Ed Damato, Joe Hirsch, Dave Krause, Bob McLane, Jim Noonan, Per-Olof Odman, Marty Pessin, Steve Rose, Steve Seid, Al Singerman, Jack Smith, and Joe Treglio. Many of us will long be indebted to two unusually dedicated professional colleagues, Chaim Shatan and Florence Pincus.

Throughout the writing, I drew strength from the growing number of people dedicated to healing from the war. My gratitude goes out to the Gold Star mothers and to all the veterans' groups, professional lobbyists, and others who helped mobilize this community. I am especially indebted to the VA's Outreach program to Vietnam Veterans, the Vietnam Veterans Memorial Fund, and the Vietnam Veterans Leadership Program.

Both my agent, Barney Karpfinger, and editor, Larry Kessenich, contributed enormously to this book by seeing something of value here when it was barely more than a promise. As for the writing, Judith Rodgers steered me through repeated drafts and then made line-by-line suggestions for sharper phrasing. I couldn't hope for a better writing coach. I also thank Larry Cooper for his copy editing, Manuela Soares, who read and reread the later drafts and offered many valuable suggestions, and Judith Yellin, who gave useful editorial advice early on.

For devoted friendship, collegiality, suggestions, and readings of early drafts, I thank Bob Flax, Ann Pollinger Haas, and Roslyn Wolff. Many other friends listened or read drafts or otherwise encouraged me along the way: Fred Abatamarco, Goldie Alfasi, Harry Behret, Rick Bellingham, Diane and Ross Burkhardt, Jim Channon, Jack Cirie, Sue Eisenstat, Alison Fisch, Vic Gioscia, H. Hamilton Gregory, Bill Hay, Marcia Landau, Josh Mailman, John Marks, Elizabeth Cowan Neeld, John Poppy, John Siffert, Al Singerman, Jeff Wilcox, and Jennifer Wortham.

Several groups of people made it possible for me to experience and observe healing on a broad scale: the Centers Network and its founder, Werner Erhard; the Ki Society and Sensei Imaizumi; fellow practitioners of the Contextual Approach to psychotherapy, in particular Roslyn Wolff, a devoted colleague and friend, and Bob Flax, master therapist, teacher and blood brother; and the healing community that meets under the circle in the sky.

There's no support like a supportive family, the people who keep revealing to me what it means to be related. Thanks especially to Richard Perl for his comments on various drafts, Ruth Fox for her unceasing expressions of appreciation, and Bebe Egendorf for the devotion that only a mother can offer.

Nobody has given more amply of her trust, love, and intelligence than my partner in life, friend, advocate, lover and wife, Sondra Perl. And for the grace and meaning she has added to our life and work, I thank our daughter Sara.

The one who has been most prominent for me throughout the writing is you, the reader. It was only after I could sense your presence that this work became possible. And so, without seeing your face or knowing your name, I have you to thank for the privilege it has been to write this book.

Notes

Introduction

1. Arthur Egendorf, Charles Kadushin, Robert S. Laufer, George Rothbart, and Lee Sloan, *Legacies of Vietnam: Comparative Adjustment of Veterans and Their Peers* (Washington: U.S. Government Printing Office, 1981). For further corroboration, see Josefina J. Card, *Lives after Vietnam: The Personal Impact of Military Service* (Lexington, Mass.: D. C. Heath, 1983).
2. For a summary of these findings, discussed with reference to major themes in the professional literature, see Arthur Egendorf, "The Postwar Healing of Vietnam Veterans: Recent Research," in *Hospital and Community Psychiatry* 33 (November 1982), pp. 901–7.
3. The classic article is James Fallows, "What Did You Do in the Class War, Daddy?" originally published in *Washington Monthly* (October 1975), and reprinted in A. D. Horne, ed., *The Wounded Generation: America After Vietnam* (Englewood Cliffs, N.J.: Prentice-Hall, 1981). Another article that stirred considerable debate is Christopher Buckley, "Viet Guilt," *Esquire* (August 1983). For Buckley's summary of the responses he received, see his "Still Thinking About Vietnam," *Washington Post,* December 19, 1983, op-ed page. For the confessions of a nonveteran who now counsels troubled ex-soldiers, see Edward Tick, "Apocalypse Continued," *New York Times Magazine,* January 13, 1985.
4. See Henry Kissinger, *Years of Upheaval* (Boston: Little, Brown, 1982), especially pp. 235–46. This theme is echoed by many, including one of Kissinger's successors from the opposite party. See Zbigniew Brzezinski, *Power and Principle: Memoirs of the National Security Advisor, 1977–1981* (New York: Farrar, Straus and Giroux, 1983).
5. This difference is reflected in countless op-ed articles in the nation's newspapers. Two of the many veterans, now authors, who have portrayed their contrasting views in memoirs and novels are Philip Caputo, *A Rumor of War* (New York: Holt, Rinehart and Winston, 1977); and James Webb, *Fields of Fire* (Englewood Cliffs, N.J.: Prentice-Hall, 1978). Myra MacPherson has aired the two positions at great length in *Long*

Time Passing: Vietnam and the Haunted Generation (Garden City, N.Y.: Doubleday, 1984). A useful summary of the issues is in Horne, ed., *The Wounded Generation.* The one book that raises the possibility of reconciliation is John Wheeler, *Touched with Fire: The Future of the Vietnam Generation* (New York: Avon Books, 1985).

6. Cultivating a perspective on what is "unitary and all-encompassing" is the purpose of all healing traditions, an assertion developed in an anthology by Aldous Huxley, *The Perennial Philosophy* (New York: Harper & Row, 1945), and reissued in paperback in 1970. The statement in this part of the introduction is an abbreviated summary of a rigorously developed exposition in Arthur Egendorf, "Human Development and Ultimate Reality: the Perceptual Grounds for Transformation," in R. H. Moon and S. Randall, eds., *Dimensions of Thought: Current Explorations in Time, Space, and Knowledge,* vol. 2 (Berkeley, Cal.: Dharma Publishing, 1980).

7. Questions like these often initiate the kind of inquiry that lies at the heart of most psychotherapeutic encounters. One well-known therapist and philosopher has sought to teach this method of inquiry with simple instructions. See Eugene T. Gendlin, *Focusing,* 2d ed. (New York: Bantam Books, 1981).

8. A brief sample from a vast literature: Kenneth Boulding, *The Meaning of the 20th Century: The Great Transition* (New York: Harper & Row, 1965); George B. Leonard, *The Transformation: A Guide to the Inevitable Changes in Human Kind* (New York: Dell, 1972); R. Buckminster Fuller, *Critical Path* (New York: St. Martin's Press, 1981); Alvin Toffler, *The Third Wave* (New York: Bantam, 1981).

9. Robert Jay Lifton, *Home from the War: Vietnam Veterans: Neither Victims nor Executioners* (New York: Simon & Schuster, 1973), p. 442.

Chapter 1: Coming Back

1. Willard Waller, *The Veteran Comes Back* (New York: Dryden Press, 1944), p. 119.

2. The classic history of this period is Bernard Fall's *Two Vietnams* (New York: Praeger, 1963). See also Henry Kissinger, *The White House Years* (Boston: Little, Brown, 1979), especially chapters 8, 12, 23, 24, 25, 27, 31–34; Stanley Karnow, *Vietnam: A History* (New York: Viking Press, 1983); and Michael MacLear, *The Ten Thousand Day War: Vietnam, 1945–1975* (New York: Avon Books, 1981).

3. These are the estimates now cited by the director of the Readjustment Counseling Service in the Veterans Administration. See Arthur S. Blank, Jr., "Apocalypse Terminable and Interminable: Operation Outreach for Vietnam Veterans," in *Hospital and Community Psychiatry* 33 (November 1982), pp. 901–7.

4. These are rough estimates. See *Report to the U.S. Senate Committee on the*

Judiciary (Washington: U.S. Government Printing Office, 1974), January 27, 1974.

5. "Viet Nam: Destruction — War Damage," a pamphlet mailed on request by the Vietnamese Mission to the United Nations, 1982.

6. Ibid.

7. Ibid.

8. Most studies cite 1967 as the watershed year when majority opinion turned and favored withdrawal. See Myra MacPherson, *Long Time Passing: Vietnam and the Haunted Generation* (Garden City, N.Y.: Doubleday, 1984), p. 27. For an analysis of public attitudes toward the war five years after its official end, see Louis Harris and Associates, Inc., *Myths and Realities: A Study of Attitudes Toward Vietnam Era Veterans* (July 1980), especially chapter 3 (a study conducted for the Veterans Administration).

9. Ernest Hemingway, "Soldier's Home," quoted in Willard Waller, *The Veteran Comes Back* (New York: Dryden Press, 1944), p. 134.

10. Erich Maria Remarque, *The Long Road Back* (Boston: Little, Brown, 1931), quoted in Waller, *The Veteran Comes Back*, p. 135.

11. Waller, *The Veteran Comes Back*, pp. 14–15.

12. B. Drummond Ayres, Jr., "The Vietnam Veteran: Silent, Perplexed, Unnoticed," *New York Times* (November 8, 1970), reprinted in *The Vietnam Veteran in Contemporary Society: Collected Materials Pertaining to the Young Veterans*, (Washington: Veterans Administration, 1972), part IV.

13. Murray Polner, *No Victory Parades: The Return of the Vietnam Veteran* (New York: Holt, Rinehart and Winston, 1971).

14. Louis Harris and Associates, Inc., "A Study of the Problems Facing Vietnam Era Veterans: Their Readjustment to Civilian Life" (October 1971), conducted for the Veterans Administration.

15. This figure was initially given as a rough estimate by the Veterans Administration in 1973 and later substantiated by survey research. See Arthur Egendorf, Charles Kadushin, Robert S. Laufer, George Rothbart, and Lee Sloan, *Legacies of Vietnam: Comparative Adjustment of Veterans and Their Peers* (Washington: U.S. Government Printing Office, 1981), pp. 476–7; and Josefina J. Card, *Lives after Vietnam: The Personal Impact of Military Service* (Lexington, Mass.: D. C. Heath, 1983), p. 113.

16. Egendorf et al., *Legacies of Vietnam*, pp. 476–77; Card, *Lives after Vietnam*, p. 113.

17. Egendorf et al., *Legacies of Vietnam*, pp. 711 and 745.

18. The data on handgun deaths are given on a mailing from the National Coalition to Ban Handguns, 100 Maryland Avenue, Washington, D.C. The data on highway deaths are available from the National Safety Council, Statistics Department, Chicago, Ill.

19. Erik H. Erikson, *Identity: Youth and Crisis* (New York: W. W. Norton, 1968), pp. 66–69.

20. "Synchronicity" is an ancient alternative to mechanical notions of causality and has become more widely embraced in the twentieth century

through the efforts of Jungian scholars and therapists. See Carl G. Jung, "Forerunners of the Idea of Synchronicity," reprinted in *Psyche and Symbol: A Selection from the Writings of C. G. Jung* (Garden City, N.Y.: Doubleday Anchor, 1958), pp. 243–82. For an elaboration of a synchronous interpretation of art and history, see José A. Arguelles, *The Transformative Vision: Reflections on the Nature and History of Human Expression* (Boulder, Colo.: Shambhala Publications, 1975). The idea of historical synchronicity lends structure to Gore Vidal's novel about the fifth century B.C., *Creation* (New York: Random House, 1981). It is also an idea that is beginning to gain currency among scientists. See Erich Jantsch, *The Self-Organizing Universe: Scientific and Human Implications of the Emerging Paradigm of Evolution* (Oxford: Pergamon Press, 1980), p. 304.

21. Joseph Campbell, *The Hero with a Thousand Faces,* 2d ed. (Princeton: Princeton University Press, 1968); and *The Masks of God,* 4 vols. (New York: Viking Press): *Primitive Mythology,* 1959; *Oriental Mythology,* 1962; *Occidental Mythology,* 1964; *Creative Mythology,* 1964.

22. Campbell, *Hero with a Thousand Faces,* p. 218.

23. Richard Wilhelm, trans., *The I Ching, or Book of Changes,* 3d ed., rendered into English by C. F. Baynes (Princeton: Princeton University Press, 1967), p. 99.

Chapter 2: Retracing Steps

1. J. Glenn Gray, *The Warriors: Reflections on Men in Battle* (New York: Harper & Row, 1970), p. 24.

2. Homer, *The Odyssey,* trans. R. Fitzgerald (Garden City, N.Y.: Doubleday Anchor, 1961), pp. 101–2.

3. Sigmund Freud, "On Psychotherapy," in Philip Rieff, ed., *Freud: Therapy and Technique* (New York: Collier Books, 1963), pp. 63–76.

4. A relatively recent summary of his views and recommendations appears in Carl Rogers, *On Personal Power: Inner Strength and Its Revolutionary Impact* (New York: Dell, 1977).

5. Arthur Egendorf, Charles Kadushin, Robert S. Laufer, George Rothbart, and Lee Sloan, *Legacies of Vietnam: Comparative Adjustment of Veterans and Their Peers* (Washington: U.S. Government Printing Office, 1981), Table 1.05, p. 385.

6. Ibid., Table 1.04, p. 384.

7. Louis Harris and Associates, Inc., *Myths and Realities: A Study of Attitudes Toward Vietnam Era Veterans* (July 1980), p. 11.

8. Michael Herr, *Dispatches* (New York: Alfred A. Knopf, 1978), p. 63.

9. Ibid., pp. 63–64.

10. *Diagnostic and Statistical Manual of Mental Disorders,* 3d ed. (DSM-III) (Washington: American Psychiatric Association, 1980), p. 236.

11. Roy R. Grinker and John P. Spiegel, *Men Under Stress* (Philadelphia: Blakiston, 1945), p. 353.

12. This list is an updated version of one given in Richard J. Barnet, *Roots of War: The Men and Institutions Behind U.S. Foreign Policy* (New York: Penguin Books, 1971), pp. 3–4.

13. Norman Podhoretz, *Why We Were in Vietnam* (New York: Simon & Schuster, 1982).

14. Barnet, *Roots of War*, p. 5.

15. José Arguelles, *The Transformative Vision: Reflections on the Nature and History of Human Expression* (Boulder, Colo.: Shambhala Productions, 1975), p. 249.

16. Barnet, *Roots of War*, p. 30.

17. Ibid., p. 32.

18. Ibid., p. 164.

19. Lewis Mumford, *The Myth of the Machine: Technics and Human Development* (New York: Harcourt, Brace & World, 1966), especially chapter 10.

20. *Diagnostic and Statistical Manual* (DSM-III), p. 236.

21. Carl G. Jung, *Psychological Reflections: A New Anthology of His Writings, 1905–1961*, ed. J. Jacobi (Princeton: Princeton University Press, 1953), p. 96; originally published as "The State of Psychotherapy Today" (1927/1931), and included in *The Collected Works: Civilization in Transition*, vol. 10.

Chapter 3: Getting Involved

1. Willard Waller, *The Veteran Comes Back* (New York: Dryden Press, 1944), p. 159.

2. Dixon Wecter, *When Johnny Comes Marching Home* (Boston: Houghton Mifflin, 1944), pp. 555–56.

3. J. Glenn Gray, *The Warriors: Reflections on Men in Battle* (New York: Harper & Row, 1970), pp. 23–24.

4. Homer, *The Odyssey*, trans. R. Fitzgerald (Garden City, N.Y.: Doubleday Anchor, 1961), p. 252.

5. Compare the subjects of the early volumes of Freud's collected works (hysteria, dreams, sexuality, jokes, and individual case studies) with the subjects of the more substantial postwar works (group psychology, religion, and "civilization and its discontents").

6. Ernest Jones, *The Life and Work of Sigmund Freud*, ed. L. Trilling and S. Marcus (New York: Basic Books, 1961), pp. 335–54.

7. Sigmund Freud, "Reflections upon War and Death" (1915), in Philip Rieff, ed., *Freud: Character and Culture* (New York: Collier Books, 1963), p. 112.

8. Sandor Ferenczi, Karl Abraham, Ernst Simmel, and Ernest Jones, *Psychoanalysis and the War Neuroses* (London and New York: International Psychoanalytical Press, 1921).

9. Erik H. Erikson, *Identity: Youth and Crisis* (New York: W. W. Norton, 1968), p. 69.

10. Robert Jay Lifton, *Death in Life: Survivors of Hiroshima* (New York: Random House, 1967), especially Chapter 12.
11. Testimony before Subcommittee on Veterans Affairs, U.S. Senate, January 27, 1970, reprinted in *The Vietnam Veteran in Contemporary Society: Collected Materials Pertaining to Young Veterans* (Washington: Veterans Administration, 1972), part IV.
12. Robert J. Lifton, *Home from the War: Vietnam Veterans: Neither Victims nor Executioners* (New York: Simon & Schuster, 1973), p. 69.
13. Waller, *The Veteran Comes Back*, p. 5.
14. Ibid., see prologue for more details.
15. John Talbott, *The War Without a Name: France in Algeria, 1954–1962* (New York: Alfred A. Knopf, 1980).
16. John Kerry and Vietnam Veterans Against the War, *The New Soldier*, ed. David Thorne and George Butler (New York: Collier Books, 1971), pp. 8–10.
17. Ibid., pp. 172–73.
18. Louis Harris and Associates, Inc., *Myths and Realities: A Study of Attitudes Toward Vietnam Era Veterans* (July 1980), p. 121.
19. Myra MacPherson, *Long Time Passing: Vietnam and the Haunted Generation* (Garden City, N.Y.: Doubleday, 1984), p. 55.
20. Personal communication, Office of Vietnam Veterans of America, Washington, D.C., March 1985.
21. Louis Harris and Associates, Inc., *Myths and Realities*, pp. 132–48.
22. Ibid., pp. 121–31.
23. This story is like many I've heard over the years. To provide readers with a written source they can consult, I've taken this and the following few examples from Kerry et al., *The New Soldier*, p. 42.
24. Ibid., p. 52.
25. Ibid., p. 48.
26. Ibid., p. 56.
27. Richard J. Barnet, *Roots of War: The Men and Institutions Behind U.S. Foreign Policy* (New York: Penguin Books, 1971), p. 48.
28. Ibid., p. 59.
29. Ibid., pp. 59–60.
30. William Corson, *The Betrayal* (New York: W. W. Norton, 1968), quoted in Cincinnatus, *Self-Destruction* (New York: W. W. Norton, 1981), p. 244.
31. Cincinnatus, *Self-Destruction*, p. 23.
32. G. A. Geyer, "Military Soul-Searching," *Washington Post*, June 20, 1977, quoted in ibid., p. 58.
33. Dave Richard Palmer, *Readings in Current Military History* (West Point: Department of Military Art and Engineering, 1969), quoted in Cincinnatus, *Self-Destruction*, p. 60.
34. Cincinnatus, *Self-Destruction*, p. 83.
35. Anthony B. Herbert, *Soldier* (New York: Dell, 1973), quoted in ibid., p. 85.

36. Douglas Kinnard, *The War Managers* (Hanover, N.H.: University Press of New England, 1977), quoted in Cincinnatus, *Self-Destruction*, pp. 46–47.
37. Cincinnatus, *Self-Destruction*, p. 47.
38. Sun Tzu, *The Art of War*, trans. S. B. Griffith (London: Oxford University Press, 1963).
39. Karl von Clausewitz, *On War*, as quoted by B. H. Liddell Hart in Sun Tzu, *Art of War*, page v.
40. Sun Tzu, *Art of War*, p. 73.
41. Sir John Duncan, quoted by B. H. Liddell Hart in ibid., p. vii.
42. Sun Tzu, *Art of War*, p. 64.
43. Chang Yu commentary in ibid., p. 64.
44. Neil Sheehan, Hedrick Smith, E. W. Kenworthy, and Fox Butterfield, *The Pentagon Papers, As Published by the New York Times* (New York: Bantam Books, 1971).

Chapter 4: Digging Inside

1. J. Glenn Gray, *The Warriors: Reflections on Men in Battle* (New York: Harper & Row, 1970), pp. 206–7.
2. Kurt Vonnegut, Jr., *Cat's Cradle* (New York: Delacorte Press, 1963), p. 124.
3. E. E. Cummings, "Introduction," in *New Poems* (1938), reprinted in *Complete Poems: 1913–1962* (New York: Harcourt Brace Jovanovich, 1980), p. 462.
4. The German original is *Wo Es war, soll Ich werden*, which means, "Where it was, I shall become," or, less literally, "In place of it-ness, I-ness will prevail." For a discussion of the way the standard English translation has obscured the relation between psychoanalytic procedure and the study of reflection in nineteenth century German thought, see Jurgen Habermas, *Knowledge and Human Interests*, trans. J. J. Shapiro (Boston: Beacon Press, 1971), to chapter 10, p. 344, footnote 31.
5. G. Papini, "A Visit to Freud," reprinted in *Review of Existential Psychology and Psychiatry* 9 (1969), pp. 130–34.
6. Ibid.
7. F. Ungar, ed., and H. Norden, trans., *Goethe's World View: Presented in His Reflections and Maxims* (New York: F. Ungar Publishing, 1963), p. 79.
8. John 8:32.
9. I draw here on numerous philosophical reformulations of psychotherapeutic inquiry. The most accessible work of this kind I know is Herbert Fingarette, *The Self in Transformation: Psychoanalysis, Philosophy and the Life of the Spirit* (New York: Harper & Row, 1965). Philosophers of both the Continental and analytic schools have had their say about these matters. For a collection of such perspectives, see Richard Wollheim, ed., *Philosophers on Freud: New Evaluations* (New York: Jason Aronson, 1977). My own reinterpretations of psychotherapy are more influenced

by the Continental tradition, embodied in such works as Habermas, *Knowledge and Human Interests;* and Paul Ricoeur, *Freud and Philosophy: An Essay on Interpretation,* trans. D. Savage (New Haven: Yale University Press, 1970). The one systematic work I find most valuable was written by a German psychiatrist who spent decades studying with Martin Heidegger. See Medard Boss, *Existential Foundations of Medicine and Psychology,* trans. S. Conway and A. Cleaves (New York: Jason Aronson, 1979).

10. Alfred Adler, "Individual Psychology, Its Assumptions and Its Results," in Clara Thompson, ed., *An Outline of Psychoanalysis,* rev. ed., (New York: Random House, 1955), pp. 292–93.

11. D. C. Douglas and G. W. Greenaway, ed., *English Historical Documents, 1042–1189* (New York: Oxford University Press, 1968), pp. 606–7. I thank Professor Charles Wood of Dartmouth University for bringing this document to my attention.

12. Leo Tolstoy, *My Religion,* quoted in M. Green, *Tolstoy and Gandhi, Men of Peace: A Biography* (New York: Basic Books, 1983), p. 194.

13. Leo Tolstoy, "Church and State," quoted in Green, *Tolstoy and Gandhi,* p. 194.

14. Ernest Hemingway, quoted in John Kerry and Vietnam Veterans Against the War, *The New Soldier,* ed. David Thorne and George Butler (New York: Collier Books, 1971), p. 167.

15. John Donne, "Meditation XVII," *Devotions upon Emergent Occasions* (1623), reprinted in *The Norton Anthology of English Literature,* vol. 1, rev. ed. (New York: W. W. Norton, 1968), p. 917.

Chapter 5: Reaching Bottom

1. Joseph Campbell, *The Hero with a Thousand Faces,* 2d ed. (Princeton: Princeton University Press, 1968), p. 391.

2. *King Richard II,* act V, scene V, lines 30–43.

3. Friedrich Nietzsche, "What Is the Meaning of Ascetic Ideals?" (Aphorism 28) in *Toward a Genealogy of Morals* (1887), reprinted in Walter Kaufmann, ed., *The Portable Nietzsche* (New York: Viking Press, 1968), p. 453.

4. Viktor E. Frankl, *Man's Search for Meaning: An Introduction to Logotherapy,* a revised version of *From Death Camp to Existentialism,* trans. I. Lasch (Boston: Beacon Press, 1962).

5. Louis Harris and Associates, Inc., *Myths and Realities: A Study of Attitudes Toward Vietnam Era Veterans* (July 1980), pp. 108–9.

6. Arthur Egendorf, "One Vietnam Veteran: A Study of Continuity and Change," Yeshiva University, 1977. University Microfilms, Ann Arbor, Michigan, Order #77-20,284 (241 pages).

7. Aaron Hershkowitz, "A Phenomenological Approach to a Theory of Motives," *Annals of the New York Academy of Sciences* 340 (1980), pp. 16–44.

8. Homer, *The Odyssey,* trans. R. Fitzgerald (Garden City, N.Y.: Doubleday Anchor, 1961), p. 212.

9. Ibid.
10. Nikos Kazantzakis, *The Odyssey: A Modern Sequel*, trans. K. Friar (New York: Simon & Schuster, 1958).
11. Nikos Kazantzakis, *The Saviors of God: Spiritual Exercises*, trans. K. Friar (New York: Simon & Schuster, 1960), pp. 51–52.
12. For a compilation and discussion of survey data and other indications of a "hollowing of America," a whittling down of community, see Amitai Etzioni, *An Immodest Agenda: Rebuilding America Before the Twenty-First Century* (New York: McGraw-Hill, 1983).
13. Lewis Mumford states the point this way: "Pugnacity and rapacity and slaughter for food are biological traits, at least among the carnivores: but war is a cultural institution" (Lewis Mumford, *The Myth of the Machine: Technics and Human Development* [New York: Harcourt, Brace & World, 1966], p. 216). For a further inquiry into the evidence on the cultural origins of war, see Ken Wilbur, *Up from Eden: A Transpersonal View of Human Evolution* (Garden City, N.Y.: Doubleday Anchor, 1981), chapter 8.
14. Professor Bernard Weitzman, Department of Psychology, New School for Social Research, New York City.
15. This was a revelation for me, but the idea itself has an ancient history. See Aldous Huxley, *The Perennial Philosophy* (New York: Harper & Row, 1945), especially chapter 3, "Personality, Sanctity, Divine Incarnation." The development peculiar to our time is that this ancient, esoteric notion is becoming more accessible to greater numbers of people. For a historical model of the way the consciousness of the many slowly catches up with the developments of the consciousness of an extraordinary few, see Ken Wilbur, *Up from Eden: A Transpersonal View of Human Evolution* (Garden City, N.Y.: Doubleday Anchor, 1981). One of the better known scholarly studies of the way contemporary mass consciousness is being shaped by the insights of the past century's existential thinkers is Ernest Becker's *The Denial of Death* (New York: Macmillan, 1973). As many critics have pointed out, Becker's book is unnecessarily dreary, dualistic, and uninformed by principles of enlightenment. Wilbur offers one corrective by referring to Eastern sources. For another approach, showing how such great lights as Goethe, Hegel, Nietzsche, and Heidegger provided the basis for Freud, Jung, and Adler to develop a psychology for our own "unmasking," see Walter Kaufmann, *Discovering the Mind* (New York: McGraw-Hill, 1980), vol. 1–3.
16. Many, many books, courses, trainings, and workshops offer instruction in meditative techniques. My two favorite works are Shunryu Suzuki, *Zen Mind, Beginner's Mind: Informal Talks on Zen Meditation and Practice* (New York: John Weatherhill, 1970); and Tarthang Tulku, *Gesture of Balance: A Guide to Awareness, Self-Healing, and Meditation* (Emeryville, Cal.: Dharma Publishing, 1977).
17. This idea is explored in Martin Heidegger, *Discourse on Thinking: A Translation of Gelassenheit* (1959), trans. J. M. Anderson and E. H. Freund

(New York: Harper & Row, 1966). The rest of this section draws on readings of Heidegger's earlier and later works, principally *Being and Time* (1927), trans. J. Macquarrie and E. Robinson (New York: Harper & Row, 1962); and *What Is Called Thinking?* (1952), trans. J. Glenn Gray (New York: Harper & Row, 1968). See especially lectures 8–10 of part I of the latter book for Heidegger's reflections on the link between the absence of profound thinking in our culture and war. The discussion of dread and nothingness comes from "What Is Metaphysics?" (1929), in *Existence and Being,* ed. Werner Brock (Chicago: Henry Regnery, 1949).

Chapter 6: Turning It Around

1. Robert Oppenheimer, "Preface," in D. Pire, *Building Peace,* trans. G. M. Ogg (London: Transworld Publishers, 1967), p. 12.
2. Alan Watts, *This Is It, and Other Essays on Zen and Spiritual Experience* (New York: Random House, 1960), p. 36.
3. J. Glenn Gray, *The Warriors: Reflections on Men in Battle* (New York: Harper & Row, 1970).
4. Ibid., pp. 233–34.
5. Ibid., pp. 232–33.
6. Ibid., p. 220.
7. This point recurs throughout Jung's works, but it is already prominent in the first book he published after breaking with Freud. See Carl G. Jung, *Symbols of Transformation: An Analysis of the Prelude to a Case of Schizophrenia* (1912), vol. 5 of *The Collected Works,* trans. R. F. C. Hull, rev. ed. (Princeton: Princeton University Press, 1956).
8. Nikos Kazantzakis, *The Odyssey: A Modern Sequel,* trans. K. Friar (New York: Simon & Schuster, 1958), p. 1.
9. Ibid., p. 443.
10. Friedrich Nietzsche, *The Gay Science* (1882), in Walter Kaufmann, ed., *The Portable Nietzsche* (New York: Viking Press, 1968), p. 95.
11. The *est* training was available in several dozen cities in North America, Europe, the Middle East, and southern Asia from 1971 through the end of 1984, when it was "retired" by Werner Erhard & Associates. In 1985 a different and more explicitly philosophical endeavor called "The Forum" became the principal training vehicle of the Erhard organization. A vast literature grew up around the *est* training, much of it narrowly polemical, filled with praise or condemnation. Only one study, to my knowledge — an intellectual biography of Erhard written by a well known philosopher — has attempted to integrate interviews with Erhard, an experience of the training itself, empirical research, and an exploration of the personal and philosophical influences that led Erhard to this work. See W. W. Bartley 3d, *Werner Erhard: The Transformation of a Man, the Founding of est* (New York: Clarkson Potter, 1978). My purpose in this

section is not to criticize or praise *est* but to reveal key aspects of the role it has played in my own healing.

12. For an analysis of the influence these men had on the origins of the "human potential movement" of recent decades, see Walter Truett Anderson, *The Upstart Spring: Esalen and the American Awakening* (Reading, Mass.: Addison-Wesley, 1983).

13. This is the theme of a recent novel by Michael Murphy, one of the founders of the Esalen Institute and a leading figure of the "human potential movement." See *An End to Ordinary History* (Los Angeles: J. P. Tarcher, 1982).

14. José Arguelles, *The Transformative Vision: Reflections on the Nature and History of Human Expression,* (Boulder, Colo.: Shambhala Publications, 1975), p. 168.

15. William James, *The Varieties of Religious Experience: A Study in Human Nature* (New York: Mentor Books, 1958). "One may say that the whole development of Christianity in inwardness has consisted in little more than the greater and greater emphasis attached to this crisis of self-surrender [which represents] progress towards the idea of an immediate spiritual help, experienced by the individual in his forlornness and standing in no essential need of doctrinal apparatus or propitiatory machinery" (pp. 172–73).

16. Anderson, *Upstart Spring.*

17. James Moffett, "Underground Spirituality," unpublished manuscript. Moffett is best known as the author of *Teaching the Universe of Discourse* (Boston: Houghton Mifflin, 1968); and, with Betty Jane Wagner, *Student-Centered Language Arts and Reading, K–13: A Handbook for Teachers,* 2d ed. (Boston: Houghton Mifflin, 1976).

18. Quoted in Arguelles, *Transformative Vision,* p. 143.

19. Ibid., pp. 143–44.

20. Ken Wilbur, ed., *Quantum Questions: Mystical Writings of the World's Great Physicists* (Boulder, Colo.: Shambhala Publications, 1984).

21. Ken Wilbur, *Up from Eden: A Transpersonal View of Human Evolution,* (Garden City, N.Y.: Doubleday Anchor, 1981), p. 4.

22. Ibid., p. 6.

23. Abraham Maslow, *Toward a Psychology of Being,* 2d ed., (New York: Van Nostrand Reinhold, 1968), pp. iii–iv.

24. Rick Eilert, *For Self and Country: A True Story by Rick Eilert* (New York: William Morrow, 1983).

25. Ibid., p. 262.

26. Max Cleland, *Strong at the Broken Places: A Personal Story* (Lincoln, Va.: Chosen Books, 1980).

27. Ibid., p. 145.

28. Harry G. Summers, Jr., *On Strategy: A Critical Analysis of the Vietnam War* (Novato, Cal.: Presidio Press, 1982).

29. George B. Leonard, *The Transformation: A Guide to the Inevitable Changes in Humankind* (New York: Dell, 1972), p. 238.

30. Daniel Yankelovich, *New Rules: Searching for Self-Fulfillment in a World Turned Upside Down* (New York: Random House, 1981).
31. William Barrett, *The Illusion of Technique: A Search for Meaning in a Technological Civilization,* (Garden City: Doubleday/Anchor, 1979), pp. 319–20.
32. David Hoffman, "In the Time We Have Left," in *Evolutionary Blues: An Interhelp Quarterly* 1 (summer/fall 1981), Ten Directions Foundation, San Francisco.
33. Alan Watts, *This Is It, and Other Essays on Zen and Spiritual Experience* (New York: Random House, 1960), p. 18.

Chapter 7: Mastering Everyday Life

1. J. Glenn Gray, *The Warriors: Reflections on Men in Battle,* (New York: Harper & Row, 1970), p. 211.
2. F. Ungar, ed., and H. Norden, trans., *Goethe's World View: Presented in His Reflections and Maxims* (New York: F. Ungar Publishing, 1963), p. 79.
3. Dixon Wecter, *When Johnny Comes Marching Home* (Boston: Houghton Mifflin, 1944), pp. 555–56. Compare with General Robert E. Lee's famous line: "It is well that war is so terrible — we should grow too fond of it" (D. S. Freeman, *R. E. Lee,* vol. 2 [New York: Scribner's, 1933], p. 462). "Why Men Love War" is the title of an essay by William Broyles in *Esquire,* November 1984.
4. Kimon Friar, "Introduction," in Nikos Kazantzakis, *The Saviors of God: Spiritual Exercises* (New York: Simon & Schuster, 1960), p. 25.
5. Nikos Kazantzakis, *The Odyssey: A Modern Sequel,* trans. K. Friar (New York: Simon & Schuster, 1958), p. xviii.
6. Ibid., p. xix.
7. Nikos Kazantzakis, *The Odyssey: A Modern Sequel,* trans. K. Friar (New York: Simon & Schuster, 1958), p. 447.
8. Richard Wilhelm, trans., *The I Ching, or Book of Changes,* 3d ed., rendered into English by C. F. Baynes (Princeton: Princeton University Press, 1967), p. 48.
9. Isaiah 11 and 53.
10. The Revelation of St. John the Divine, 21:2.
11. Kazantzakis, *Odyssey: A Modern Sequel,* p. 470.
12. William James, "The Moral Equivalent to War" (1910), in W. F. Irmscher, ed., *Man and Warfare* (Boston: Little, Brown, 1963).
13. Cord Meyer, *Facing Reality: From World Federalism to the CIA* (New York: Harper & Row, 1980).
14. James, "Moral Equivalent to War," p. 73.
15. Ibid., p. 74.
16. Ibid., p. 75.
17. Sigmund Freud, "Reflections upon War and Death" (1915), in Philip

Rieff, ed., *Freud: Character and Culture* (New York: Collier Books, 1963), p. 112.

18. Ibid., p. 123.

19. Ibid., p. 124.

20. Thomas à Kempis, "Of the Remembrance of Death," in *The Imitation of Christ* (1427), trans. R. Whitford (Garden City, N.Y.: Doubleday, 1955), p. 63.

21. Geoffrey Blainey, *The Causes of War* (New York: Macmillan, 1973).

22. Ibid., p. 29.

23. "Wars will only be prevented with certainty if mankind unites in setting up a central authority to which the right of giving judgement upon all conflicts of interest shall be handed over" (Sigmund Freud, "Why War?" [1932], letter to Albert Einstein, reprinted in Philip Rieff, ed., *Freud: Character and Culture* [New York: Collier Books, 1963], p. 139).

24. All of the examples in this section are discussed in Erich Jantsch, *The Self-Organizing Universe: Scientific and Human Implications of the Emerging Paradigm of Evolution* (Oxford: Pergamon Press, 1980), p. 304.

25. Aldous Huxley, *The Perennial Philosophy* (New York: Harper & Row, 1945).

26. He wrote often of a "higher kind of man" who, to lay hold of "the destinies of the earth" would "work as artists upon 'man' himself. . . . The time is coming when politics will have a different meaning" (Friedrich Nietzsche, *The Will to Power*, trans. Walter Kaufmann and R. J. Hollingdale [New York: Random House, 1967], p. 504. See also the aphorism that begins, "Art and nothing but art!" on p. 452). *Will to Power* is a controversial work, which remained unpublished until after Nietzsche's death. See Philippa Foot, "The Brave Immoralist," *New York Review of Books* (May 1, 1980), pp. 35–44. Foot's and others' arguments, however, cannot deny the compelling influence of Nietzsche's posthumous volume. See Walter Kaufmann's Introduction to *Will to Power* and the volume by Martin Heidegger, *Nietzsche, Volume I: The Will to Power as Art*, trans. David Farrell Krell (New York: Harper & Row, 1979).

27. Nietzsche, *Will to Power*, pp. 402–3.

28. Ibid., p. 422.

29. Ibid., p. 407.

30. Ibid., p. 434.

31. I hope philosophers will excuse the simplification. Wittgenstein spoke and wrote about "language games" in *Philosophical Investigations*, trans. G. E. M. Anscombe (New York: Macmillan, 1953). This line of thought was pushed another step in J. L Austin, *How to Do Things With Words* (Cambridge: Harvard University Press, 1962). For a more freewheeling development of a related perspective, see the works of Kenneth Burke, especially *Language as Symbolic Action: Essays on Life, Literature, and Method* (Berkeley and Los Angeles: University of California Press, 1968).

32. "Man speaks. . . . We are always speaking, even when we . . . are not particularly listening or speaking but are attending to some work or

taking a rest. . . . We are continually speaking in one way or another.
. . . Only speech enables man to be the living being he is" (Martin
Heidegger, "Language," in *Poetry, Language, Thought*, trans. Albert
Hofstadter [New York: Harper & Row, 1971], p. 189).

Chapter 8: Transforming Warriors

1. Nikos Kazantzakis, *The Odyssey: A Modern Sequel*, trans. K. Friar (New
   York: Simon & Schuster, 1958), p. 115.
2. Wallace Stevens, *Opus Posthumous: Poems, Plays, Prose*, ed. S. F. Morse
   (New York: Random House, 1982), p. 163.
3. Richard J. Barnet, *Roots of War: The Men and Institutions Behind U.S. Foreign Policy* (New York: Penguin Books, 1971), makes clear that he dates
   the great soiling of American policy to World War II: "Bureaucratic
   homicide is the monster child of technology and expansionism. . . .
   Americans . . . have been engaged in this form of bureaucratic homicide for almost thirty years, since the decision in 1942 to bomb Germany
   into submission. A milestone was the fire raid on Tokyo in 1944, when
   fire bombs incinerated one hundred eighty thousand residents of the
   city" (p. 15).
4. Henry David Thoreau, *Walden, or a Life in the Woods and Civil Disobedience*
   (New York: New American Library, 1960), and Walt Whitman, "Democratic Vistas," in *The Portable Walt Whitman*, ed. Mark van Doren (New
   York: Viking Press, 1945), are two of the more familiar writings in which
   the transcendentalist vision points beyond the rapidly industrializing
   young republic to a more spiritually vital nation.
5. This is the refrain in José Arguelles, *The Transformative Vision: Reflections
   on the Nature and History of Human Expression* (Boulder, Colo.: Shambhala
   Publications, 1975).
6. Occasionally this argument crops up in Robert Pirsig, *Zen and the Art of
   Motorcycle Maintenance* (New York: William Morrow, 1974).
7. Against the so-called Christian anti-Semites of his time, Nietzsche wrote
   that the "little superlative Jews" so worthy of being denounced were
   not to be found among the prophets or among the likes of Moses and
   Solomon, but in the New Testament, among the disciples, and particularly in the likes of Paul. See *The Antichrist*, in Walter Kaufmann, ed.,
   The Portable Nietzsche (New York: Viking Press, 1968), p. 567.
8. Ralph Waldo Emerson's "Politics," in *Emerson's Essays* (New York: Harper & Row, 1951), conveys this spirit, although the statement in the text
   is my formulation, not Emerson's.
9. Robert S. de Ropp, *Warrior's Way: The Challenging Life Games* (New York:
   Dell, 1979), p. 297.
10. Nikos Kazantzakis, *Report to Greco* (New York: Bantam Books, 1966), pp.
    278–79.
11. Carlos Castaneda, *The Teachings of Don Juan: A Yaqui Way of Knowledge;*

A Separate Reality: Further Conversations with Don Juan; Journey to Ixtlan: The Lessons of Don Juan; Tales of Power; and *The Second Ring of Power* (New York: Simon & Schuster, 1974–1977), pocket book editions.

12. Castaneda, *Tales of Power*, p. 109.
13. Nikos Kazantzakis, *The Saviors of God: Spiritual Exercises*, trans. K. Friar (New York: Simon & Schuster, 1960), p. 36.
14. Martin Heidegger, *Nietzsche, Volume I: The Will to Power as Art*, trans. David Farrell Krell (New York: Harper & Row, 1979), p. 102.
15. Ibid., p. 518.
16. Castaneda, *Tales of Power*, p. 285.
17. Nikos Kazantzakis, *Saviors of God*, p. 73.
18. " 'The military virtues' are virtues none the less for being jewels set in blood and iron; but the value lies in the jewels themselves and not in their horrible setting; and it is flying in the face of all experience to jump to the conclusion that the only place where we can ever hope to find these precious things is the slaughterhouse where they have happened to make their first epiphany to human eyes" (Arnold J. Toynbee, "Militarism and the Military Virtues," reprinted in W. F. Irmsche, ed., *Man and Warfare* [Boston: Little, Brown, 1963], p. 139).
19. Isaiah 2:4; Micah 4:3.
20. Matthew 5:9.
21. This is the claim made by various Masonic orders themselves, and credible enough for one scholar who is highly critical of such secret societies to take the Masons at their word. See Nesta H. Webster, *Secret Societies and Subversive Movements* (Christian Book Club of America, 1924), now available in paperback.
22. This is a story I heard repeatedly from guides while traveling in India. Reference to Asoka's role in spreading Buddhism appears in David Snellgrove and Hugh Richardson, *A Cultural History of Tibet* (Boulder, Colo.: Prajna Press, 1980), p. 66.
23. Noel Perrin, *Giving Up the Gun: Japan's Reversion to the Sword, 1543–1879* (Boulder, Colo.: Shambhala Publications, 1980).
24. This etymology was provided by the Japanese sociologist Chumin Miyakawa in a personal communication, August 1982.
25. Inazo Nitobe, *Bushido: The Soul of Japan*, rev. ed. (Rutland, Vt. and Tokyo: Charles E. Tuttle, 1969).
26. Ibid., p. 192.
27. I gleaned much of this information from my eight years as a student in the school Penn founded in 1689, the William Penn Charter School in Philadelphia. For a more detailed account of this history, see Rufus Mott Jones, *The Quakers in the American Colonies* (London: Macmillan and Company, 1911).
28. Robert S. Woito, *To End War: A New Approach to International Conflict* (New York: Pilgrim Press, 1982), p. 509.
29. Mark Juergensmeyer, *Fighting with Gandhi* (San Francisco: Harper & Row, 1984).

30. Michael N. Nagler, *America Without Violence: Why Violence Persists and How You Can Stop It* (Covelo, Cal.: Island Press, 1982), p. 153.

31. Terry Dobson and Victor Miller, *Giving In to Get Your Way: The Attack-Tics System for Winning Your Everyday Battles* (New York: Delacorte Press, 1978).

32. Ibid., p. 8.

33. Ibid.

34. Douglas MacArthur, quoted in William Manchester, *American Caesar: Douglas MacArthur 1880–1964* (New York: Dell, 1978), p. 589.

35. Dwight D. Eisenhower, "Atoms for Peace" speech, December 8, 1953, quoted in James Reston, "The Book of History," *New York Times,* December 7, 1983, p. A31.

36. Omar Bradley, November 5, 1957 speech, Washington D.C., quoted in James Reston's column, *New York Times,* April 10, 1981.

37. George Leonard, personal communication, January 22, 1984.

38. Robert Muller, *Most of All, They Taught Me Happiness: Years of War, Moments of Peace, and Lessons in Living from Extraordinary People* (Garden City, N.Y.: Doubleday, 1978); *New Genesis: Shaping a Global Spirituality* (Garden City, N.Y.: Doubleday, 1978).

39. Chogyam Trungpa, *Shambala: The Sacred Path of the Warrior* (Boulder, Colo.: Shambhala Publications, 1984).

40. James Channon, *Operations Manual: Evolutionary Tactics of the "First Earth Battalion,"* Privately distributed by Channon, 73 Madrone, Fairfax, Cal.

41. Robert Fuller, "A Better Game Than War," excerpted in "The Mo Tzu Strategy: Our Enemies, Our Selves?" *New Age Journal,* January 1984, p. 45.

42. John Marks, *The CIA and the Cult of Intelligence* (New York: Knopf, 1974); *The Search for the "Manchurian Candidate": The CIA and Mind Control* (New York: McGraw-Hill, 1980).

43. James Fallows, "What Did You Do in the Class War, Daddy?" originally published in *Washington Monthly* (October 1975), and reprinted in A. D. Horne, ed., *The Wounded Generation: America after Vietnam* (Englewood Cliffs, N.J.: Prentice-Hall, 1981).

44. James Fallows, *National Defense* (New York: Random House, 1981).

45. Amitai Etzioni, "Military Industry's Threat to National Security," *New York Times,* op-ed page, April 6, 1984.

46. Gene Sharp, *The Politics of Nonviolent Action,* vols. 1–3 (Boston: Porter Sargent, 1973).

47. Gene Sharp, "A Political Analyst Offers a Workable Alternative to War," *The Tarrytown Letter* 45, January 1985, p. 3.

48. The story is told in Jan C. Scruggs and Joel L. Swerdlow, *To Heal a Nation: The Vietnam Veterans Memorial* (New York: Harper & Row, 1985).

49. John Wheeler, *Touched with Fire: The Future of the Vietnam Generation* (New York: Avon Books, 1985), p. 10.

Appendix: Suggestions for Healing Action

1. The best known family therapists routinely conduct therapy sessions in front of audiences, and supervise fellow therapists "live" while they work with clients. Unfortunately, such openness is still the exception in the training settings where most therapists learn their craft. One notable exception is the Contextual Psychotherapy Institute, Berkeley, Cal., which has branches in major cities in the United States. The Contextual Approach is named for its emphasis on what lies beyond theory and technique: the context that the therapist establishes in each moment of interaction through the posture or stance he or she takes toward the patient.

2. This is a key point. I insist on the phrase "healing from war" not to quibble with semantics, but to distinguish clearly what I'm saying from the terms that have begun to creep into clinical practice with veterans, such as "veterans' recovery" or "the need to integrate the experience" or "work through the trauma." Over the years I've invoked such terms myself in the struggle to be understood. The problem is that these terms hedge on the truth. What we confront with veterans is the experience of war. War is what demands a response. Shifting attention to some more easily grasped issue, with streamlined concepts imported from other areas of clinical theory and practice (e.g., "stress"), strips away the personal, historical, and spiritual dimensions of what it is that so many of us, veterans and those who care for veterans, have had to deal with.

   Many veterans' advocates with fine motives have avoided the issues raised by war itself in the interests of gaining acceptance for their work by the established authorities in mental health, government, and law. At crucial junctures, we have formulated the problems and remedies in terms that people who don't work with veterans will accept. This accommodation, although seemingly desirable in some lights, has imposed a limitation that we must remedy: reducing veteran trauma to something other than the human dilemma of contending with war in our time obscures the very problem, deludes us into groping after easy fixes, and blinds us to what is really required as a response.

   Men whose lives have been wrenched through war are preoccupied with *war* and suffer from their personal experience of war itself. It is war that we must address, not some streamlined notion that fits just as well for some other category of disaster. And once we admit the whole of war itself, then the response must be equal to the challenge. War is the tearing apart, battling to the death, of two sides that call the other enemy. The only adequate response is to unleash in us the power to create healing from war, the vast challenge I've outlined in this book. It's not the words "healing from war" that I care about. What's crucial is that we see the challenge clearly, rise to it, and go all the way.

3. There are probably a number of veteran groups who have already con-

templated or brought about this shift for themselves. The one I know personally is the Veterans Ensemble Theatre Company in New York City, whose founder, Thomas Bird, speaks of using theater to promote healing.

4. As an example, see William D. Davidson and Joseph V. Montville, "Foreign Policy According to Freud," *Foreign Policy* (Winter 1981–82), pp. 145–77. Davidson and Montville exemplify an approach that first reached prominence with Sigmund Freud's *Civilization and Its Discontents* (New York: W. W. Norton, 1963). For a summary of the "psychoanalytic literature on war," see Franco Fornari, *The Psychoanalysis of War* (Bloomington: Indiana University Press, 1975). A classic pamphlet representing this approach is *Psychiatric Aspects of the Prevention of Nuclear War* (Washington, D.C.: Committee on Social Issues, Group for the Advancement of Psychiatry, 1964).

5. The most practical, down-to-earth example of this approach is Roger Fisher and William Ury, *Getting to Yes: Negotiating Agreement Without Giving In* (Boston: Houghton Mifflin, 1981).

6. Empowerment, as I mean the term, is not a matter of interpretation (the Freudian revision of foreign policy thinking) or of a set of procedures for working out agreements (the conflict resolution approach). It grows out of a way of being. The word *empower* has been used occasionally in discussions of domestic policy; see Peter L. Berger and Richard John Neuhaus, *To Empower People: The Role of Mediating Structures in Public Policy* (Washington, D.C.: American Enterprise Institute, 1977). The concept of empowerment is even more uncommon in discussions of foreign policy.

7. Two recent works that hint at the possibility of a policy of empowerment are Robert C. Johansen, *The National Interest and the Human Interest: An Analysis of U.S. Foreign Policy* (Princeton: Princeton University Press, 1980); and Guy Gran, *Development by People: Citizen Construction of a Just World* (New York: Praeger, 1983). Most such "world order" contributions stem from exemplary motives. Even the progressive works, however, fail to embrace empowerment directly, for they are marked by a limitation that is even more endemic among conservative proposals for contending with conflict: a view of reality that does not fully admit the creative role of the viewer. For a far-reaching, but difficult discussion of this point, see Norman K. Swazo, "The 'Ontological' Meaning of the World-Order Movement," *Alternatives: A Journal of World Policy* 10 (fall 1984), pp. 267–96, World Policy Institute, New York.

8. For a review of this history, see Stephen E. Ambrose, *Rise to Globalism: American Foreign Policy since 1938*, 3d rev. ed. (New York: Penguin Books, 1983).

Index

Abraham, Karl, 303
Acheson, Dean, 99
Activism, veteran, 89, 93–97; by
Vietnam veterans, 96–97, 98
Activity, as healing, 107–8
Adler, Alfred, 128, 306
Agent Orange, 21, 270, 271
Aikido, 263–64, 265
Alcoholics Anonymous, 140, 227,
231
Alcorn, Robert H., 63
Algerian National Liberation
Front, 95
Algerian War, 94–95
Ambrose, Stephen E., 316
American Legion, 96
American spirit, loss of, 249–50
American Veterans Committee
(AVC), 95–96, 216
Anderson, Walter Truett, 187, 309
Arguelles, José, 184, 268, 302, 303,
309, 312
Aristotle, 165, 250
Armstrong, Neil, 39, 40
Art, empowerment as (Nietzsche),
230–31, 239
Asoka, 258–59
Atonement, for war, 133–35
Attenborough, Sir Richard, 264
Austin, J. L., 311
"Average vet" fallacy, 29–32
Ayres, B. Drummond, Jr., 301

Barnet, Richard J., 62, 99, 304, 312
Barrett, William, 200, 310
Bartley, W. W., 3d, 308
Bateson, Gregory, 184
Becker, Ernest, 307
Being, 204; awareness of, 201–3;
nature of (Heidegger), 165–67
Berger, Peter L., 316
Bird, Thomas, 316
Blainey, Professor Geoffrey, 221–
23, 311
Blake, William, 188
Blame: of government for Vietnam
War, 106; vs. responsible criti-
cism, 105; self-, 107, 131–32
Blank, Arthur S., Jr., 300
Body count, 101–2
Bonus Expeditionary Force, 94
Boss, Medard, 306
Boulding, Kenneth, 300
Bradley, Omar, 265, 314
Broyles, William, 209, 310
Brzezinski, Zbigniew, 299
Buckley, Christopher, 299
Buddha, 40, 226
Bundy, McGeorge, 99
Bundy, William, 99
Burke, Kenneth, 311
Bushido tradition, in Japan, 259–60

Calley, Lt. William, 150
Calvin, John, 260

Campbell, Joseph, 41, 42, 137, 302, 306
Caputo, Philip, 299
Card, Josefina J., 299, 301
Caring: fear of, 69–70; as healing, 108
Carnegie, Andrew, 63
Carter, Jimmy, 272
Castaneda, Carlos, 255, 256, 312, 313
Channon, LTC James, 269, 271, 314
Chogyam Trungpa, 155, 269, 314
Cincinnatus, 100, 102, 304, 305
Cleaves, A., 306
Cleland, Max, 193–95, 309
Combat, effects of, 57–60; revulsion, 60; suffering, 60
Communication, empowerment through, 233–35
Communism, U.S. fight against, 61–65, 197, 198, 289–90
Confucius, 40
Conscience, troubled, 130–32
Consciousness, cosmic, 184, 188–89, 201–2
"Containing communism," 197, 198, 289–90
Contextual Psychotherapy Institute, 315
Conway, S., 306
Corson, William, 100, 102, 304
Culture: cult of hero-worship in western, 184–85; materialist, 185; Nietzsche's critique of, 203–4; trauma as, 158–59; war as phenomenon of, 154; world, war and, 201
Cummings, E. E., 112, 305

Davidson, William D., 316
Death (and dying): constant threat of, 175; empowerment and, 242–43; fear of, 142–43; as force (Freud), 85; healing and, 215;

Hiroshima survivors' view of, 88; logic of, 83–84; and nothingness, 146
de Broglie, J. V. C., 189
Declaration of Independence, 187, 188
de Gaulle, Charles, 95
"Delayed stress," 67
deRopp, Robert, 184, 251, 312
Determination, healing through, 193
Dewey, John, 189
Disabled American Veterans, 288
Distractedness, as life's plague, 203–4
Distress, 2, 60
Dobson, Terry, 264, 314
Donne, John, 134, 306
Donovan, Major General William J., 63
Douglas, D. C., 306
Dread (Heidegger), 166
Dulles, John Foster, 99
Duncan, Sir John, 305

Ecstasy, war as, 209–10
Eddington, Sir Arthur, 189
Egendorf, Arthur, 299, 300, 301, 302, 306
Eilert, Rick, 191, 309
Einstein, Albert, 188, 189, 311
Eisenhower, Dwight D., 20, 63, 64, 265, 314
Eliot, T. S., 188
Emerson, Ralph Waldo, 188, 312
Empowerment: healing as, 222, 224–26, 230, 233–34, 237–39, 242–44, 251, 252, 316; meaning of, 235–37; as new national policy, 288–94; through psychotherapy, 283–84
Erhard, Werner, & Associates, 308
Erikson, Erik, 34, 35, 36, 87–88, 301, 303
Esalen, 187, 266

est, 195, 308
Ethics, war and (Freud), 86–87
Etzioni, Amitai, 273, 307, 314
Experience, personal, healing and, 120–21

Fall, Bernard, 300
Fallows, James, 272–73, 301, 314
Feel, learning to, by vets, 118–19
Ferenczi, Sandor, 303
Ferguson, Marilyn, 269
Fingarette, Herbert, 305
Fisher, Roger, 316
Foot, Philippa, 311
Ford, Henry, 63
Fornari, Franco, 316
Fox, George, 261
Franklin, Benjamin, 188
Frankl, Viktor, 141, 306
Free Corps Movement, 94
Freemasonry, 188, 253
Freud, Anna, 87
Freud, Sigmund, 35, 48, 115, 116, 139, 178, 215, 217, 302, 310, 311, 317; interpretation of World War I by, 85–86
Friar, Kimon, 310
Fromm, Erich, 153
Fuller, R. Buckminster, 300
Fuller, Robert, 270, 314

Gandhi, Mohandas, 226, 262, 263
Gendlin, Eugene T., 297, 300
Gershon, David, 271
Geyer, G. A., 304
Goethe, Johann Wolfgang von, 116, 207
Göring, Hermann, 94
Grand Army of the Republic, 89
Gran, Guy, 316
Gray, J. Glenn, 45, 76, 109, 177–78, 207, 302, 303, 305, 308, 309
Greenaway, G. W., 306
Grinker, Roy R., 59, 302

Guilt, 124–27; surviving as, 132; "survivor," 127

Harp of Burma, The, 43–44
Harris, Louis, and Associates, Inc., 142, 301, 302, 304, 306
Hawthorne, Nathaniel, 188
Heard, Gerald, 184
Heidegger, Martin, 165–66, 217, 233, 307, 309, 311, 312, 313
Heisenberg, Werner, 189
Hemingway, Ernest, 23, 134, 216, 301, 306
Herbert, Lieutenant Colonel Anthony, 102, 304
Herr, Michael, 57–58, 302
Hershkowitz, Aaron, 143, 306
Hitler, Adolf, 94, 153, 216
Ho Chi Minh, 20, 21
Hoffman, David, 201, 310
Holistic healing, 10–11, 43; vision of, 225, 230, 244–46
Home, problems in returning, 17–44, 106; identity, vets' self-, 35–36; self-questioning, 42; sympathy, 29–32; "troubled vet" image, 26–29; women, 23–24
Homer *(The Odyssey),* 80, 133, 145, 210, 254, 302, 303, 306
Hoover Administration, 63
Horne, A. D., 299
Horror: healing and, 11–12; nature of, 139; as nothingness, 166; "stories," 52
Humanity: meaning of, 4; and war, 13–14
Huxley, Aldous, 183, 184, 300, 307, 311

I (first person singular), meditation and, 164–65
I Ching, 42, 211
Identity: crisis, 88; Erikson's concept of, 87–88; self-, strategies

Identity (*continued*)
  for creating, 158–59; vets and,
  35–36
Indefinable, the (Heidegger), 166
Indochina, oppression in, 36–38
Industrialization, consequences of,
  250
Injury, fear of, 142–43
Insight, flash of, as healing, 10–
  11, 43
Institutions, established, disre-
  spect for, 149
Intimate relationships, 239–41
Intuition, of being (Heidegger),
  165
Isherwood, Christopher, 134

James, William, 185, 189, 215, 216,
  217, 251, 311, 312
Jantsch, Eric, 302, 311
Japanese warriorship (*bushido*),
  259–60
Jeans, Sir James, 189
Jefferson, Thomas, 188
Jesuits, 258
Jesus, 134, 226, 244–45, 250
Johansen, Robert C., 316
Johnson, Lyndon Baines, 196
Jones, Ernest, 303
Jones, Rufus Mott, 313
Joyce, James, 188
Juergensmeyer, Mark, 313
Jung, Carl, 69, 178, 204, 303, 308

Kadushin, Charles, 299, 301, 302
Karnow, Stanley, 300
Kato, Suichi, 260
Kaufmann, Walter, 307, 311, 312
Kazantzakis, Nikos, 145–46, 178,
  210–11, 247, 254, 255, 256, 307,
  308, 310, 312, 313
Kempis, Thomas à, 218, 311
Kennedy, John F., 291
Kennedy, Robert, 40
Kenworthy, E. W., 305

Kerry, John, 304, 306
Killing: atonement for, 132–35; as
  crime against humanity, 135
King, Martin Luther, Jr., 40, 226
Kinnard, Douglas, 102, 305
Kissinger, Henry, 296, 299, 300
Knights Templar, 258
Ku Klux Klan, 94

Language (speaking): empower-
  ment through, 234–35; as heal-
  ing, 52
Laufer, Robert S., 299, 301, 302
Lawrence, D. H., 188
Lee, General Robert E., 310
Legacies of Vietnam, findings of,
  2–4
Leibnitz, Gottfried Wilhelm von,
  183
Leonard, George B., 199, 265, 300,
  309, 314
Liddell Hart, B. H., 103
Life: difficulties with, 131–32;
  force (Freud), 85
Lifton, Robert, 14, 88, 89, 297,
  300, 304
Listening, as healing, 51–52
Litwak, Leo, 266
Love, 135; difficulties with, 131–32
Luther, Martin, 260
Luthuli, Albert, 263

MacArthur, General Douglas, 94,
  265, 292, 314
MacLear, Michael, 300
McNamara, Robert, 99
MacPherson, Myra, 300, 301, 304
Managerial rationality, 99–102
Mao Tse-tung, 294
Mapes, Mike, 289
Marks, John, 271, 314
Marx, Karl, 153
Maslow, Abraham, 189, 309
Meaninglessness, sense of, 141–43
Meditation, as healing, 163–65

"Melancholy" (Freud), 86
Melville, Herman, 188
Meyer, Cord, Jr., 216, 310
Miller, Victor, 314
Miyakawa, Chumin, 313
Moffett, James, 187, 309
Montville, Joseph V., 316
Moon, R. H., 300
Mo Tzu Project, 270
Mourning, 48
Mozart, Wolfgang Amadeus, 188
Muller, Robert, 269, 270, 314
Mumford, Lewis, 64, 303, 307
Murphy, Michael, 309
Mussolini, Benito, 94
Mutilations, of women, in Vietnam war, 98
My Lai, 150
Myths vs. truths, 117, 200

Nagler, Michael H., 262, 314
Napoleon, 153, 222
Nathan, Colonel Reuben, 102–3
National interest, 275, 289
National Institute for Human Empowerment, 289, 292
National Peace Institute, 289
National security apparatus of U.S., problem of, 99–102
National war machine, U.S. as, 62–65
Neoisolationism, 3–4
Neuhaus, Richard John, 316
Ngo Dinh Diem, 20
Nietzsche, Friedrich, 141, 179, 184, 203, 229–31, 255–56, 306, 308, 311
Nihilism, culture as (Nietzsche), 203–4, 230
Nitobe, Inazo, 260, 313
Nixon, Richard, 105, 294
Nonveterans and Vietnam, feelings about, 148–51; accountability for war, 149–50; error of

war, 149; pity for vets, 150; regrets, 149, 150; sorrow, 150
Norden, H., 305
Nothingness, 12, 145–46; facing, 12; sense of (Heidegger), 166–67, 170

Odets, Clifford, 27
Odysseus: Homeric legend of, 17, 23, 26, 47, 48, 80–81, 132, 144, 210; Kazantzakis's modern sequel, 178–79, 210–12, 255
Office of Strategic Services, 63
Operation Outreach, 31
Oppenheimer, Robert, 171, 308

Pain, 139; as therapy, 125–27, 130–32
Paine, Thomas, 95
Palmer, Lieutenant Colonel Dave Richard, 101, 304
Papini, G., 305
Past, role of, in "delayed" response of vets, 67, 68
Pauli, Wolfgang, 89
Peace Corps, 291
Peace, theory of, 222–23
Penn, William, 260, 261, 262
Pentagon Papers, 105
"Perennial philosophy," 183, 184, 187, 189, 225
Perrin, Noel, 313
Philosophes, 188
Pirsig, Robert, 312
Planck, Max, 189
Plato, 250
Podhoretz, Norman, 62, 303
Poe, Edgar Allan, 188
Politics: sovereignty and, 277; Vietnam, as war of, 62
Polner, Murray, 26, 301
Pol Pot, 152
"Post-traumatic stress disorder," 67, 107–8
Postwar responses, 67–73

Power: empowerment vs. domination, healing and, 221–24; war and, 222–24
Presence, sense of, 202–3; and self, 204–5
"Psychic numbing" (Lifton), 88
Psychological well-being, demographics and, 176
Psychotherapy, 221; as empowerment, 238–39, 283–84; communication and, 233–34; healing through, 115, 120

Quakers, 261–62

Rap groups, Vietnam veterans', issues in, 89, 97, 105, 140; disillusionment, 145; killing, 135; learning to feel, 118–19, 125; psychotherapy and, 115–16; self-reflection, 112–13, 117–21; troubled conscience, 130; women's movement and, 130
Remarque, Erich Maria, 24, 303
Retelling war experiences, as healing, 69, 73–74
Richardson, Hugh, 313
Ricoeur, Paul, 306
Rogers, Carl, 51, 302
Roosevelt, Franklin D., 20
Rostow, Eugene, 99
Rostow, Walt, 99
Rothbart, George, 299, 301, 302
Rusk, Dean, 99

Salvation Army, 258
Savage, D., 306
Schiller, J.C.F. von, 188
Schroedinger, Erwin, 189
Schweitzer, Albert, 226
Scrugs, Jan C., 314
Search for Common Ground, 271
Selective Service Act, 64
Self-discipline, healing through, 213, 215

Self-doubt, 131–32
Self-healing, 81, 139
Self-identity. *See* Identity
Self-mastery, healing and, 213–15
Self-protectiveness, by vets, 69
Self-questioning, by vets, 42, 111–13, 126
Self-reflection, pain of, 111–13, 117–21, 126
"Self-surrender" (James), 185
Senate Subcommittee on Veterans' Affairs, 89
Service, as antidote to war, 215–17
Shakespeare, William, 137, 187
Sharp, Dr. Gene, 273–74, 314
Shaw, Robert, 297
Shays, Daniel, 94
Sheehan, Neil, 305
Simmel, Ernst, 303
Sloan, Lee, 299, 301, 302
Smith, Hedrick, 305
Smith, Lieutenant Colonel DeWitt, 101
Snellgrove, David, 313
Socrates, 40
Solidarity, 273
Sovereignty, surrendering, 274–79; aesthetics and, 277–78; economics and, 278; education and, 275–76; eros and, 278–79; ideology and, 276; national character and, 274–75; national interest and, 275; politics and, 277; spirituality and, 276
Spiegel, John P., 59, 302
Spirit, transformation through (Jung), 178–79
Stevens, Wallace, 247, 312
Stimson, Henry L., 63
Straub, Gail, 271
Stress, 11–12; "disorder," 60, 68, 69
Suffering, as combat effect, 59–61
Summers, Colonel Harry, 196–98, 309

Sun Tzu, 103–4, 305
Surviving, guilt and, 126, 132
Survivors, 88; psychology of, 89
Suzuki, Shunrya, 307
Swazo, Norman K., 316
Swerdlow, Joel L., 314
Sympathy, for vets, 29–32
Symptoms, 124, 127, 141; guilt as, 124–27

Talbott, John, 304
Task Force Delta, 270
Therapists, as healers, 139–40
Thinking, meditative (Heidegger), 165
Thoreau, Henry David, 180, 189, 312
Tick, Edward, 299
"Time bombs," vets as, 67–68
Time, healing and, 73, 74
Toffler, Alvin, 300
Tokugawa shoguns, 259
Tolstoy, Leo, 134, 306
Toynbee, Arnold, 256, 313
Transformation, 199–204; as spiritual phenomenon, 178; of trauma, 173–79
Trauma, 11–12, 130, 134; bottoming out and, 169–70; compassion for, 160; as cultural failure, 158–59; dying, awareness of, 143; healing of, 163–65; meaninglessness of life and, 142; nature of, 139; responses to, 159–60; transformation of, 173–79; war and healing and, 160–63
"Troubled vet" image, 26–29
Trungpa, Chogyam, 155, 269, 314
Tulka, Tarthang, 307

Ungar, F., 305, 310
United Nations, 223, 264, 269, 292
Ury, William, 316
Uyeshiba, Moriher, 263

Veterans Administration, 31, 67, 96, 194, 287; healing and, 284–86
Veterans of Foreign Wars, 96
Veterans Ensemble Theatre Company (New York), 316
Veterans' groups, as genuine service organizations, 286–88
Vidal, Gore, 302
Vietnam: casualty statistics, 20–21; France in, 20; reconciliation with, 293–94; Summers' critique of, 196–98; U.S. in, 20–21
Vietnam Era Research Project, 297
Vietnam Veterans Against the War (VVAW), 89, 95, 97, 98
Vietnam Veterans of America (VVA), 96, 270, 287, 306
Vietnam Veterans Leadership Program, 31
Vietnam Veterans Memorial (Washington), 31, 32, 96
von Clausewitz, Karl, 305
Vonnegut, Kurt, 109, 305

Waller, Willard, 15, 26, 75, 93, 301, 303, 304
War: absolution from, 134; biological determinism and, 153; Christianity and, 134; cult of, 134; as cultural phenomenon, 154; "healing from war," 315; love of, as ecstasy, 209–10; modern, causes of, 61–65; moral equivalent to, 215–18; as nothingness, 166; obsoleteness of, through world culture, 201; as power struggle, 222–24; theories of, 222–23; trauma and, 160–61
Warriors (warriorship), transforming, 249–52, 254–66, 268; in American experience, 260–62; Gandhi, 262–63; Japanese history, 259–60; martial arts and, 263–64, 265; "no position," tak-

Warriors (*continued*)
ing, 257–58; spirit of warrior, 251, 252, 254, 257, 271–74; vulnerability, 257; vs. warfare, 252
Washington, George, 188
Watts, Alan, 171, 184, 202, 203, 308, 310
Webb, James, 299
Webster, Nesta H., 313
Wecter, Dixon, 75, 303, 310
Weitzman, Bernard, 307
Westmoreland, General William, 101, 196
Wheeler, John, 300, 314
Whitman, Walt, 188, 189

Wilbur, Ken, 189, 307, 309
Wilhelm, Richard, 302, 310
Wilson, Charles, 64
"Winter Soldier Investigations," 95, 97
Wittgenstein, Ludwig, 233, 311
Woito, Robert S., 313
Wollheim, Richard, 305
Women: homecoming and, 23–24; intimacy and, 130, 131; mutilation of, in Vietnam war, 98

Yankelovich, Daniel, 200, 310
Yeats, W. B., 188